ANTHROPOLOGICAL STUDIES
IN THE EASTERN HIGHLANDS OF NEW GUINEA

James B. Watson, *Editor*

Volume VI: Auyana: Those Who Held onto Home

*Anthropological Studies
in the Eastern Highlands of New Guinea*
James B. Watson, *Editor*

VOLUMES PUBLISHED:

# AUYANA

# Those Who Held onto Home

STERLING ROBBINS

UNIVERSITY OF WASHINGTON PRESS
SEATTLE AND LONDON

This book is published with the assistance of a grant from the National Science Foundation.

Library of Congress Cataloging in Publication Data

Robbins, Sterling.
  Auyana: those who held onto home.
  (Anthopological studies in the eastern highlands of New Guinea; v. 6)
  Bibliography: p.
  Includes index.
  1. Ethnology—Papua New Guinea—Auyana. 2. Auyana (Papua New Guinea)—Social life and customs. 3. Warfare, Primitive—Papua New Guinea—Auyana. I. Title. II. Series.
GN671.N5R58   1981   995'.3   81-2707
ISBN 0-295-95788-3      AACR2

To Anu

# Foreword

The sixth volume to be published in the series "Anthropological Studies in the Eastern Highlands of New Guinea," Dr. Robbins' monograph is the second ethnography. The Auyana he describes are one of four "study peoples" included in the New Guinea Micro-evolution Project. Like the names of the rest, "Auyana" is in the first instance a linguistic designation, identifying one of four to nine languages (the number depending on taxonomic criteria) of the Eastern or Kainantu Family of the East New Guinea Highlands Stock (Wurm 1964; McKaughan 1973). Together with the remaining study peoples, the Auyana form a territorial chain, with Gadsup contiguous to Tairora, and Tairora, Auyana, and Awa all contiguous to each other. None of the four peoples is separated from another by speakers of a language outside of the Eastern Family.

The four study peoples were deliberately chosen for their linguistic affiliation and spatial continuity. Such a coincidence of spacing and language, incidentally, is found widely in the Central Highlands of New Guinea, suggesting a similar ethnogenesis throughout much of the region. Although the Micro-evolution Project has been described elsewhere at some length (Watson 1963), for convenience I will sketch it here. The project is concerned with the genetic, phenotypic, linguistic, and cultural diversification of a putative original community whose modern descendants—the study peoples—are identified by their common linguistic roots. As an original community or cluster grows and divides, its offshoots expanding in space, diversification normally ensues. There can be little doubt that the main vehicle of expansion in the present case was an increasing scatter of small local groups, which could not remain a continuous community or unified network. Lacking an organization or ideology adequate to contain their offshoots in a single ethnopolitical whole—that is, lacking any clear advantage in doing so—these groups are no longer one people or tribe. Nor are the 4,500 or so Auyana such a body, though they constitute but a minority of the scions of the original stock. From one putative stem, then, grew branches. As our researchers have cumulatively verified, subsequent crossings and grafts have often occurred, along with the obvious forks, the major ones marked by separate modern languages.

Broadly speaking, the Micro-evolution Project sought answers to two questions, one descriptive, one explanatory. Descriptively, we sought to learn what significant similarities and differences were to be found among the modern descendants of the founding group. Specifically targeted for study were features of biology and language, as well as culture. These are reported in earlier volumes in this series, as is also the human geography of the study area. Character or personality studies were also originally projected but, except for the findings of the individual ethnographers, this intention was provisionally shelved when a qualified researcher and funds for his support could not be brought together simultaneously within the time-span allotted to the project. A study of the prehistory of the area, however, was added, and was published as the third volume in this series.

The explanatory question required that one identify exogenous circumstances to which differences or similarities among the four study peoples of the project could be related. If in the case of a given feature we could identify no exogenous cause, we would presume we were dealing with an element whose continuity among the study peoples could be ascribed to original endowment or to common development, or to both. Variation, on the other hand, might result from accident or drift. Beyond these familiar categories the purpose of the project was to look minutely at change with respect to relative rates and directions of diversification in different aspects of the language, "race," and culture of the study peoples; to attempt to recognize long-term trends and short-term effects; and to determine as far as possible what development or evolution meant in a given, relatively short span of time for people constituted as were the small, autonomous groups of the study area, living where they lived.

Dr. Robbins' research is central to the Micro-evolution Project. The ethnographic phase of the project, however, deserves special comment. Unlike the linguistic, geographic, biological, or archaeological phases, ethnography was the only phase of the study in which no investigator could assume single-handed responsibility for making area-wide comparisons. Each of the study peoples was dealt with separately and by a different member of the research team—normal practice in ethnography, of course, except for regional surveys. In addition to this distinction, the ethnographers, like others of the research team, were not all in the field together and could not, hence, meet to discuss each other's progress. The allocation of funds precluded that desirable arrangement since the overall program was funded in successive segments, each of which had to be committed and reported on before the next could be applied for. Follow-up studies in the field would obviously be costly at such a distance and, although they would doubtless be valuable, were ruled out on this ground.

In the best of circumstances comparisons in ethnography require great care. The circumstances just described obviously called for a comparative procedure and a scheme, as standardized as possible, from which the four ethnographers could all work, given the separation imposed by the circumstances. After conferring, we decided on the *Outline of Cultural Materials* (Murdock et al. 1950) as a point of common reference, since its codes and categories were published and widely known. We devised a schedule of all *OCM* categories and agreed that it would be used uniformly by each ethnographer. For each category we indicated the level of required documentation, from a hypothetical "exhaustive coverage" to "basic" and "nil." In this way the ethnographers' common obligation to provide the basis for comparison of the four study cultures was defined, using the details we judged to be most probably significant. Each investigator could in addition investigate any aspect of the history or culture of the group with whom he worked, doing so in any depth he thought justified. This arrangement was designed to deal with the well-known comparative gap in ethnography at the same time as providing for the fuller study, in individual cultures, of aspects that seemed noteworthy or questions of particular interest to the ethnographer. Cargo cults, for example, were not slated for intensive comparative consideration—although they might have been. If an ethnographer wished to devote considerable attention to cargo cults in the area of his own work, however, he was free to do so.

What Eggan (1954) has described as the method of controlled comparison is surely approached in the present study. It would have been ideal for each ethnographer to have had beforehand a detailed description of the other study cultures. With such information in hand, the distinctive features of his own discoveries would have been highlighted, intensifying both control and comparison. We made good use, however, of what was previously known of the peoples of the study area. The proof of the procedures adopted in the present case can only be judged, of course, as the remaining ethnographic studies are published.

My own first contact with Auyana people provided a glimpse of how insiders appraise micro-evolutionary outcomes. In 1954 I was living in the Agarabi-speaking village of Ayamoentenu, the rather Latinized "Aiamontina" of government maps. During that time Ayamoentenu was visited by a small party of Auyana traders bringing net bags. Widely traveled villagers who professed to know said the Auyana were renowned for their net bags, but to some of the Ayamoentenu in 1954 Auyana was scarcely a name, and obviously not a people or language they often encountered. In fact, they referred to the traders not as "Auyana"—the government's name, I believe—but as "Pore," a traditional and more inclusive designation given to all the peoples of a large area (including Auyana) that lay far to the south. "Far" in this case meant some twenty miles. The Ayamoentenu were fascinated by the Auyana language, and a buzz of discussion arose at the trading site. Related to their own, Auyana speech both amused the villagers and strangely seemed to embarrass some of them; while its intention was often apparent, the words were not quite right. I am guessing at their embarrassment. Perhaps beguilement would be a better term. Some of the women, in any case, giggled and squirmed and crossed their legs in describing how it was to hear utterances that sounded just as if they should be intelligible.

Something under 2,000 "years" probably separates Auyana from Agarabi, according to a lexico-statistical scale (McKaughan 1973:694-738). It was too little in any case to erase all resemblance, even for untrained ears. Yet twenty miles of intervening territory were all the barrier needed for that long separation—a disparity of time and space that provides homely insight into micro-evolution in Kainantu.

Sterling Robbins immersed himself in Asempa, the Auyana community that became his base. He was welcomed there, becoming fast friends with the residents and much admired by them. Such things are often said of ethnographers, it is true, but in this case I risk the cliché because of a conviction that there was a special dimension to Robbins' rapport with his hosts. To him the Asempa were first of all people struggling with the problems and considerable ironies history had handed them. It was a period of uncertainties for the Auyana, and Robbins' interest in them doubtless found a strong, positive response. They called him Sitori, a phonetic approximation of unpronounceable "Sterling." In Pidgin *sitori* means "account," "tale," "myth," or "history." Dickens himself could devise no more felicitous name for an ethnographer. For the Auyana it was no phonetic coincidence.

What endeared Sitori to his hosts was the man himself. He entered their lives with unusual commitment not only to the large questions that concerned them but also to the risks and hardships with which they daily lived, risks that, had he chosen, he might sometimes have avoided. Their acceptance of him, it seems to me, reflected a respect for his physical competence as well as his interest in their lives and his ethnographic mastery, the surprising grasp of an efficient, trained, and keen observer. The interested friend, who was soon at home in their legends and customary knowledge, was also an outdoorsman and natural athlete. To an extent uncommon among Europeans the Asempa had known, he was uninhibited by physical danger. Crossing on foot a log bridge so high and slippery that even village men would sometimes straddle it, he stood out in a country where visitors not infrequently are carried across streams. In short, he was proficient in the physical ways of the ablest young men as well as progressively wise in the ways of their elders.

There is in Robbins' study, it seems to me, a corresponding empathy for the physical realities and the risks and contingencies of everyday village life. If I am right, it is this that gives pragmatism and concreteness to the study. It complements the generalizations and abstractions that modern comparative ethnography demands. It may be true that another ethnographer, equally assiduous and skilled, might compile Robbins' twenty-five-year record of Asempa warfare, but I do not think anything like that had been attempted before Robbins did it. It has widely been said that war is "endemic" in the Highlands. (Even the borrowed term is comfortable.) No one doubts there are casualties. Treachery is widely alleged and the charge undisputed. But how much more eloquent is Robbins' history of a quarter century of fighting, killing, and betrayal. For an ethnographer in the microcosm of a Kainantu village, it is also a documentary *tour de force*.

An energetic man and a skeptical one, Robbins demands to know, in detail, what warfare meant. In the same vein he insists on terms that bring the reader as close as he can manage to the reality described. Impatient with conventional concepts and definitions whose familiarity is their strongest recommendation, he readily discards those that limply serve description and analysis. As a consequence of this tenacious and skeptical demand, the untidiness of behavior is not allowed to be lost in probing for the large designs of structure. The pragmatics of Asempa life are visible even while pattern and tendency are pondered. Pattern and tendency, we do not forget, are not merely embedded in the provisional and the makeshift but contingent on them.

It was the original intention of the New Guinea project that each study be of interest and significant in its own right. None of the monographs, granted that each is part of a larger plan, was to be only ancillary to it. That intention, the reader will surely agree, is amply fulfilled in this monograph.

JAMES B. WATSON
Seattle

# Preface

This monograph is a revision and expansion of my Ph.D. thesis (Robbins 1970). I lived in the Eastern Highlands of New Guinea in Auyana for two years. My theoretical orientation was and is eclectic with a bias toward Freudian Zenarchy. At the time I was living in the Highlands, I was interested in social movements and in the general problem of how best to describe and/or analyze social realities, especially ones that had been characterized as "loosely structured" (Barnes 1962).

As I attempted to describe some of what I had experienced in Auyana, I found that the most useful approach was to formulate a model from which to begin building a bridge to experience. Members of Auyana used a similar approach in presenting themselves to me. But if in interpreting what they said I have only heard the echoes of my own mind, I hope there is sufficient information in my approach to enable someone to construct an alternative understanding. In any case, I have attempted to present what I believe were some parameters in the constructions of reality in Auyana, and to be explicit about the nature of my evidence and the areas in which I was either confused or had no evidence.

As I lived in Auyana, I became increasingly interested in violence and its place in our lives. This interest led to the final development of this monograph, in which I have attempted to provide some low-level generalizations on, and some evidence about, the relationship between warfare and certain other aspects of life in small sovereignties, especially the ability to improvise social forms to fit altered situations—i.e., "loose structure." All social codes can be used to create with, but some perhaps more than others, and while acts in Auyana flowed from a script, it was rare that there was not some improvisation in the performance.

The title for this monograph is an attempt to represent the relative power position of the people with whom I lived. They were those who remained on the home grounds of a population that had grown from around three hundred people to about four thousand over the last three to four hundred years.

They remained there because, among other things, they were able to prevent others from driving them off. Being skilled and courageous warriors with efficient and strong home support was not the only means by which they were able to stay at home, but it was an important one.

Many members of Auyana were also those who stayed at home in another sense. They were at home with their stomachs and their livers—with their feelings. Having become alienated from my own feelings through a long history culminating in my furiously reading books for several years under the illusion that somehow I would know a lot more about myself and other people when it was over, I found it a mind-altering experience to live with people who were much more emotionally aware than I. I hope the chance for some of them to observe a couple of "wild humanlike" beings up close was equally instructive.

I am deeply indebted to the members of Auyana, who gave me a better understanding of the world, mine and theirs. I am particularly indebted to Anu and Taumwe, who bore my incompetence with good humor and provided me with the knowledge necessary to make this study.

I would also like to thank all those who gave me emotional support and intellectual stimulation during the preparation of this manuscript; Juanita Davis, Tim Howard, Phil Newman, and Beryl Bellman in particular.

Dr. James B. Watson has not only chaired my Ph.D. committee, but as editor of this series he has further endured the reading of many rough drafts and made many helpful suggestions.

# Contents

# Illustrations

# Tables

AUYANA
Those Who Held onto Home

# 1. Definitions and Methodology

In their dealings with me, members of Auyana initially presented many of their transactions in terms of groups comprised of agnates. However, as I observed various transactions and began to learn the genealogical background of those said to be members of particular groups, the discrepancies between their initial presentation and the existing social reality multiplied. Many anthropologists in New Guinea have had the same or similar experiences, and there has been considerable discussion over how best to understand the social systems found there. This discussion began as a questioning of whether the image of segmentary lineages which had been developed in the attempt to describe African societies could be used in describing New Guinea Highlands societies, and has become a reexamination of our basic assumptions about how societies are organized (see Barnes 1962, Lepervanche 1967, Cook 1969, Strathern 1969, Watson 1970, and Wagner 1974 for summaries and analyses).

The ethnographic area involved in this questioning is New Guinea, but the questions raised and the shifts in research emphasis are ones that have been occurring throughout anthropology since World War II and especially during the last ten to fifteen years. One major change that has occurred during the last ten to fifteen years is that some basic confusions in the "normative" (jural) view of social systems which have been oft noted but oft repeated are no longer being overlooked.

One source of confusion in the normative approach has been that the concept of a "norm" (a rule or role) has several components, but exactly which components an author is using may be unclear or not specified at all, and the evidence for any of the stated components may be unclear or not specified. These confusions have probably been perpetuated for several reasons, one of which is the explicit or implicit belief that small-scale social systems are stable, with few behavioral exceptions to what "should" be done—i.e., they are "moral" systems. Not only do actors do what they say they should do, but

3

what they say they should do and what they do are agreed upon and unchanging (Redfield 1953). In the linguistic metaphor for social systems, the
social (cultural) "code" is clear, known to all, agreed upon by all, held by all,
and unchanging. If this belief is accepted and not being tested, then it is not
particularly important to know observed frequencies, nor even necessary to
be clear about whether the rule is something stated by actors or inferred by
the anthropologist. Granted, such clarity gives a desired elegance to the
analysis, but given that the anthropologist has somehow arrived at the for-
mulation of a rule and that "most" of the cases of which he or she is aware
conform to the rule, then the rule becomes the only object of further study.
The study of the cases that do not fit the rule can be put in a separate disci-
pline such as "social change" or "deviance."

Given the lack of data, we will probably never know to what extent the
"normative model" descriptions of social systems are applicable. But one
thing has become clear—they are not applicable for many Highlands New
Guinea population. Exactly what theoretical orientation will be the most
useful is still being explored and this exploration has forced investigators to
be clearer about the different components of their descriptions and the evidence for those components.

Several investigators have pointed out the continued confusion of the
"ideal" and the "real" and the necessity of being clear about this distinction;
that is, between what is said to be or should be, according to the actor or the
anthropologist, and what the anthropologist observes (Langness 1964b). In
addition, the anthropologist's descriptions are based on a certain number of
observations and result in statements of contingencies. While there is always
the possibility that quantification may result simply from attributing magical
power to numbers, I agree with those who have put an increased emphasis
on quantitative statements (Meggitt 1965). In this monograph, I have expressed frequencies in quantitative terms whenever possible and have otherwise attempted to give some parameters to nonquantitative statements of
frequency.

Other investigators have focused on the confusion between the actor's interpretations of events and the anthropologist's interpretations, and on the
necessity of keeping these distinct (Watson 1965a). Further, both actors and
anthropologists operate on several levels of interpretation which are often
intertwined, and suggestions have been made for separating these levels
(Wagner 1967).

As a result of the above and other discussions, I have found it useful to
distinguish the following dimensions in describing social life in Auyana and
to consider the relationship between them to be an empirical question rather
than one that can be answered *a priori*. First, there are actors' statements
about contingencies (e.g.,"men who get wealth together to give to others
help one another in fights"). A second dimension includes actors' linguistic
statements evaluating a contingency. There are statements about how the

actors feel when the contingency holds (e.g., "it makes me feel good when men who get wealth together to give to others help one another in fights"); statements about what the actors do when the contingency holds (e.g., "when men who get wealth together to give to others help one another in fights they don't do anything special with one another"); statements about the effects of the contingency holding (e.g., "when men who get together wealth to give to others help one another in fights it makes them strong"); and statements about what happens when the contingency does not hold (e.g., "if a man gets wealth together with others but doesn't help them in fights they will get angry at him; if I am not one of them I won't get angry at him").

Then there are the anthropologist's observations regarding contingencies and which actors do what when the contingency holds or does not hold. Obviously the anthropologist's observations and the actors' statements are the usual components of concepts like "rule," "role," "norm," "sanction," etc. My reason for not using these terms is that each of them has a bevy of associations and usually several dimensions are lumped within the concept. In their place I will use the notions of pressure and demands (Rommetweit 1955). Pressure is placed on "ego" whenever ego perceives some probability that "alter" will deliver a reward or cost to ego contingent on ego's behavior or attributes (Rommetweit 1955:22). A demand is a direct or indirect statement of such contingencies (i.e., a "threat" or a "promise"). I will leave "reward" and "cost" as undefined terms.

Another assumption in the normative view is that social groups have a clearly defined membership with members not changing "at will" from one group to another. This assumption seems to be particularly strong in the analyses of societies comprised of multifunctional segments. Wagner (1974) has suggested that the anthropologist's participation in jurally constituted groups with clearly defined boundaries has led us to see such groups where they do not exist. Perhaps the bias toward a jural/structural view of social life stems both from our own experiences as members of a bureaucratically organized political economy and from a view of social life as being a self-contained system to be understood without regard to the connections between social systems and the material base of social life, a view that is at least in concordance with an ivory tower existence. Whatever the sources of the bias towards "the law" and either/or segmentation, this bias has not been confirmed in research on Highlands societies. Watson (1970) has demonstrated that, for the Tairora, shifting group membership was a constant feature of life and has suggested that many of the characteristics of Highlands groups which do not fit the image of African segmentary lineages (e.g., shallow genealogies) may be adaptations to coping with shifting membership. In my Ph.D. thesis (Robbins 1970), I demonstrated that shifting membership was a constant feature of Auyana social life and I provided data demonstrating that this was a result of warfare. I suggested that the uses of biological descent and certain aspects of the distribution of wealth and marriages were related to the constant social dislocation resulting from warfare, and I suggested an explanation for the extensive use of wealth to make friends under such conditions. These points are pursued at length in this monograph.

Implicit in Watson's and my analyses is a bias toward viewing social systems as comprised of units whose characteristics (including the "principles" in their ordering) are determined by the tasks they perform. The shift toward viewing social systems as open systems has occurred throughout anthropology. In particular there has been increased interest in materialist (energy) explanations, and New Guinea has been no exception (Rappaport 1968). If social systems are to be considered as open systems and in terms of the tasks they perform, then we need some way to talk about them that, as in the case of norms, separates out the various components thought to be important and makes their interrelatedness an empirical question. I have found the following vocabulary to be useful.

I will use the term "collectivity" to refer to any plurality of actors, no matter how constituted. I will give the term "group" a specific meaning derived from Znaniecki (1945) and Shibutani (1961). A group is defined as a plurality of actors knowingly engaged in a cooperative endeavor to alter the state of something external to themselves. The concept of "cooperative endeavor" is central to the definition but unfortunately somewhat ambiguous. To cooperate implies not simply coordinating with someone but acting so as to *facilitate* the accomplishment of some end. However, it is sometimes difficult to decide when actors are acting in this way. For example, are workers in a factory engaged in a cooperative endeavor? They may see themselves as part of a coordinated process producing something, but are they concerned with mutually facilitating that production? Asking them is not an entirely satisfactory way of resolving the question, yet it is the only one I know of at this point and is the one I have used.

The definition of a group implies nothing about the degree of "standardization" or "institutionalization" of an activity, and anything from a mob looting a store to the United States Senate voting on tax appropriations is a group. However, there is a related distinction which I will use to define a particular kind of group. A "social unit" is defined as a set of actors who repeatedly act as a group and who are identified as a single "entity" by those outside the set. By a set of actors, I do not mean that exactly the same actors must participate each time. Rather, there must be some limitations on who can participate and on how frequently one can not participate and still be allowed to act as a member of the group. The stipulation that the actors are "identified as a single entity" means only that there must be some action specific to them. This may mean the use of a name, it may mean a handshake, or it may mean blood revenge.

The shift from being called a turtle to being killed as a result of something done by another turtle is an important one. By "joint responsibility" I will mean that action may be taken against any of a plurality of actors for certain acts by any of them against outsiders. This means persons may be held jointly responsible even if they never act as a group and even though they may deny they belong to one. I will adopt the term "legal unit" to refer to any plurality of actors who are held jointly responsible by some outsider.

There is one type of social unit for which I will adopt a special term, "sovereignty." A sovereignty is defined as the largest social unit whose members help one another in fights with outsiders and are taken as a legal unit by outsiders. My use of sovereignty differs from that of those who consider a sovereignty the largest group making "binding" public decisions (Easton 1959, Gearing 1962:70). The difficulties with this latter approach are in specifying whether decisions are public or somehow involve an entire public and whether they are binding. In a manner of speaking, I have reversed this approach. I am focusing on the situations in which a plurality is taken as a legal unit and acts as a group. I believe that under these conditions there will be public decision-making. Further, it will be "binding" in that if a member of a social unit commits some act, others in the group may be retaliated against.

Given my definition of a group, one could say that a lot of Auyana social life was carried on in groups; that is, a lot of endeavors were cooperative ones. Members of Auyana also presented themselves as being comprised of social units which performed a variety of tasks. However, I observed that, except for the division of bride wealth, never were all those who were said to be in a social unit involved in a given task, and there was always someone from outside a social unit involved in a task supposedly being performed by the social unit. If you focused on the tasks performed, you might say there were no social units, only groups whose memberships overlapped to a certain degree from one task to another (Wagner 1974). But to conclude that the concept of social units is of no use in describing or explaining Auyana social life would be a mistake.

I suggest that to members of Auyana the conception of themselves as being organized into agnatic social units was a model through which to begin the social game. This conception provided a reference point from which to begin building a community and a point to which one could always return if interaction became too confusing or ineffective. The area between rigidly assigned membership with specific tasks and unmanageable confusion over who was to do what with whom provided the area within which Auyana social life was carried out. Metaphorically, a few agnates provided the core to which other individuals connected themselves in order to become members of a social unit, and social units in turn provided the core to which others outside a social unit attached themselves in the performance of various tasks. In this way, social units provided openings for potential new members without losing their identity as units, especially as legal units. This monograph is a beginning at documenting this metaphor.

The people with whom I lived referred to themselves as Auyana. Maps 1-3 show their location within New Guinea. Map 4 shows the largest collectivities recognized by members of Auyana. The information for this map was collected as part of the LeVine and Campbell questionnaire given to three adult male members of Auyana and as part of the warfare, marriage, and exchange history discussed later.[1] The Auyana classifications were made primarily on the basis of language and general behavioral similarities and, with one exception, the members did not act together for any purpose. Table 1 matches the Auyana terms on Map 4 with the terms used by local Europeans and McKaughan (1973) for these populations.

TABLE 1
MATCHING TERMS

| Auyana | European | McKaughan (1973) |
|--------|----------|------------------|
| Wake | Agarabi | Agarabi |
| Tapu | Gadsup | Gadsup |
| Onkena | Oiyana | Ontenu, Oiyana |
| Akarawe | Kamano | — |
| Uwara' | Tairora | Tairora |
| Tau | Fore | — |
| Tate' | Kanite, Jate | — |
| Anepa' | Awa | Awa |
| Kampare | Awa | Awa |
| Indona | Indona | Auyana |
| Arora | Arora, Kosena | Auyana, Kosena |
| Opoimpina | Auyana | Auyana (Asempa) |
| Kawaina | Kawaina | Auyana |
| Isurupa | Usarufa | Usarufa |

As Table 1 shows, the classifications made by members of Auyana correspond closely to the linguistic classifications made by linguists and anthropologists (Berndt 1962). The principal divergence occurs in the linguistic area called Auyana by McKaughan (1973). For the members of Auyana, the name referred to themselves as a social unit within Opoimpina (see Map 3) and was sometimes used to refer to a subdivision within Opoimpina comprised of several social units. McKaughan uses the name Auyana to refer to the Auyana collectivities of Opoimpina, Kawaina, Indona, and Arora (members of Auyana also included within Arora the area named Kosena by McKaughan). The members of Auyana saw the languages within the linguistic areas McKaughan calls Auyana and Kosena as all being "one talk." Those in the linguistic area McKaughan calls Usarufa were considered a different "talk" which was at first unintelligible to a speaker of Auyana but could be learned rapidly (McKaughan 1973: Map 2).

I have firsthand information on the members of Opoimpina and Kawaina,

[1] This version of the LeVine and Campbell questionnaire is highly similar to the one published in LeVine and Campbell, 1961.

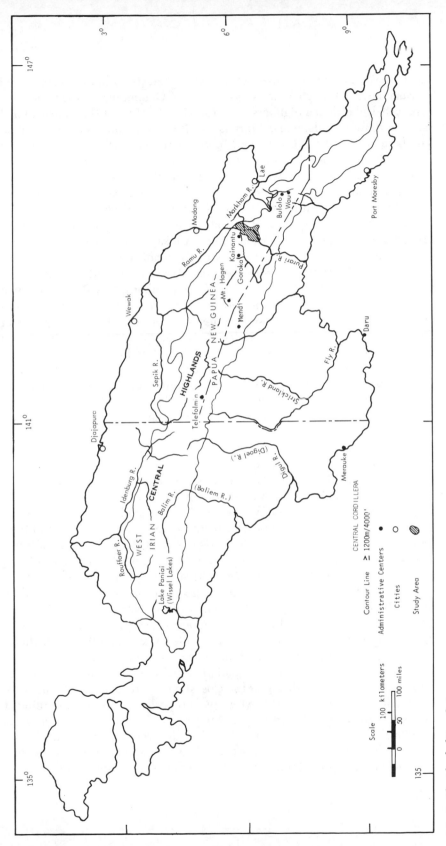

Map 1. The island of New Guinea

but I know about the members of the other dialects within the language of Auyana mostly through hearsay. Members of Opoimpina said that the Isurupa acted like their neighbors, the Tau (Fore). Most of the information I have on those in Indona and Arora is also through members of Opoimpina. The latter said that both Arora and Indona acted partly like Tau (Fore), but mostly like those in Opoimpina. I worked for some time with some of the people in Kawaina. This work revealed that there were several ways in which those in Kawaina differed from those in Opoimpina. Hence, assertions are not to be taken as applying to Kawaina unless so specified.

The members of Auyana said that all those in Opoimpina had "one way" except for those in the subdivision named Anokapa. They claimed that those in Anokapa had been very friendly with their neighbors, the Onkena (Oiyana), who had slightly different customs (McKaughan, 1973, considers Oiyana a dialect of Gadsup). The Auyana claim to uniformity within Opoimpina is supported by the case histories involving members of the Opoimpina and also by what I saw when I went with members of Auyana to other groups in Opoimpina. However, the differences between the members of Opoimpina may very well have been at the level of details, and for many areas of life I never consciously got much beyond the general plan and into details. This applies, of course, to my observations within Auyana. In addition, there are other considerations relevant to the question of the extent to which generalizations can be drawn from the observations I made as reflected in the statements written here.

European power, as seen from the fringes of World War II and in the conquest of neighboring groups, was so overwhelming to the members of Auyana that they decided to do whatever the white men told them, without resistance, which placed them in a position they had never been in before. In fact, prior to the arrival of white men, the possibility of conquest (i.e., indefinite domination) did not exist except perhaps in the parent-child relationship. This analogue formed the basis of one of the initial Auyana interpretations of white men—that they were dead ancestors returned to bring new wealth to their descendants. The notion that, whoever they were, they had come to give everyone new material goods, continues to be fostered by those who have come. In a classic colonial process, Australian government officials support "business" while they suppress "cargo cult" movements— that is, suppress the promises of cargo made by anyone other than themselves or those they approve of and those they work for.

The parent-child metaphor is an individual-to-individual affair and assumes good will. Other than that the closest collective analogue members of Auyana had to their reaction to whites would perhaps have been running at the first sign of trouble with a neighboring sovereignty. This position is imaginable but held to be of such disgrace that very rarely did any group ever fall that low. "They act like we are dogs" is the matter-of-fact way one resisting group leader characterized black-white relationships. A dog, as he

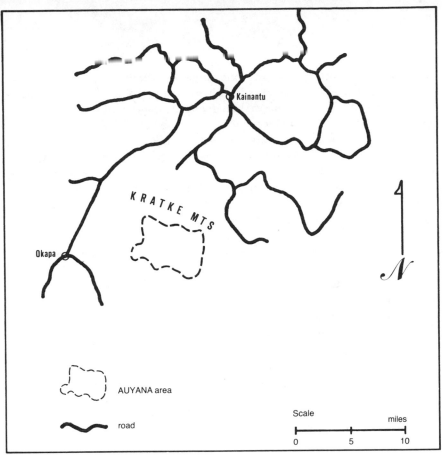

Map 2. Kainantu area

saw it, was an animal kept around for some unclear purpose who oftentimes got very little from its "father" or "mother." Whites, however, were quickly recognized as not being "fathers" or "mothers," no matter how you stretched the terms, which is another way of viewing the indifference of the state to its citizens, especially a state ruled by those whose main interest seems to have been profit.

Although only a worker/citizen in such a state, I came with the privileges and mentality of a member of the occupying forces, and I did not find it necessary to learn the Auyana language in order to live in their territory. In 1962, I worked almost entirely with people who spoke 'tok pisin" (pidgin talk), spoken rarely by whites to one another except jokingly. Most of the members of Auyana did not speak "tok pisin." When I returned in 1965, I tried to learn the Auyana language and by the second half of the second year I could carry on halting conversations. At the time I attributed my inability to become fluent to things like "tone," "reticence," "affixes," and "job pressure." I have now come to see my inability as resulting largely from my racial and empire-building loyalties and prerogatives.

I gathered some information by talking with people during events and listening to conversations. But most of it was derived from informal conversations or through "interviews." Interviewing was channeled, in that I had certain topics I wanted to talk about with someone. Usually I talked with a person whenever I found him or her unengaged and willing to talk. Occasionally, I would make arrangements the day before to meet someone, but frequently something would come up and the person would not be able to meet with me until a different time in the day or some other day. So I spent a fair amount of time walking between hamlets looking for someone to talk to about various matters. At the time I did not realize the extent to which I was attempting to impose my scheme of learning onto the Auyana.

In the best exchange mentality, I solved the problem of reciprocation with those who agreed to talk with me by giving them either tobacco or money. I continued to do this even after I became aware that some would adjust their responses to meet my needs, or what they perceived as my needs. I did this because of some inner compulsion to pay immediately for services (my childhood was fundamentalist Christian and being in debt for anything except, of course, cars was to be avoided by any means necessary). Eventualy I stopped paying for information. But although I became more responsive to individual and community demands, I continued to view my actions as being in return for some favor rather than as part of a mutual endeavor. For I did not know how to consciously convert "them and me" into "us" and was therefore not aware of the extent to which I acted in terms of "them and me."

I tried to check information with at least two people, probably on the basis of some hidden premise that while one imagining is a fantasy, two imaginings are reality. In any case, when I say "It was said that . . . " or "It was presented to me that . . . " it only means that at least a couple of people said that.

Map 5 shows Auyana territory and the hamlets within it during the period of 1962-65. During both visits, I lived in hamlet A, whose elevation was about six thousand feet. Hamlets F, G, and H were on a ridgeline approximately seven thousand feet high. It took about forty-five minutes of hard walking to get from hamlet A to hamlet F. Most of my casual observations and discussion took place in hamlets A, B, and C, particularly A and B. This was modified somewhat by the interaction I had with a few individuals which led me to become a partial member of one of the subgroups within Auyana. Two of these individuals were my interpreters. Another two were a pair of brothers, one of whom had been and was a leader, a "big man." The other brother was in the leadership of the cargo cult movement. I was closest to one of the men who worked as my interpreter. He interpreted a lot more than just what others said. He spent a lot of time telling me the best way for me to go about doing the things I wanted to do and helping me with the mistakes I made. I told him what I could and helped him and his subgroups get together wealth to give to others, and in turn I received part of whatever his subgroup was given. As for the other aspects of events, I was mostly a spectator.

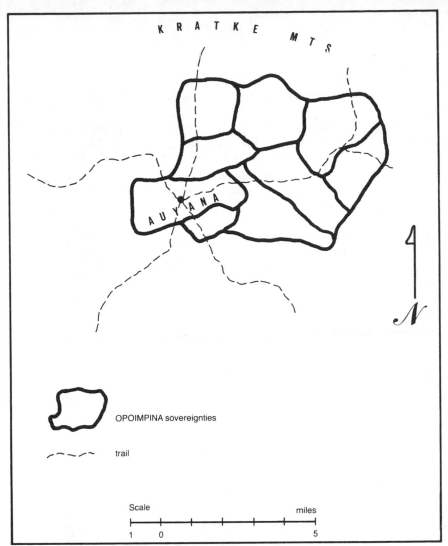

Map 3. Auyana area

All the men I knew well—except for the youngest interpreter, who was a child—had been succeeding in their world before the Australians came and were doing well during the time I lived there. If they added a bias to my already existing biases, it was more likely that of a successful member of Auyana than that of a failure.

One of my interests was to look at a cargo cult. Frequent conversations with the leader and questioning of others about the cult made it difficult for me to avoid being identified as somehow a part of it. Escaping this identification became impossible when the cult leader told others I was the white man who had come to tell them the secrets of cargo. I do not know how much this skewed the information I collected. The cult ideology involved a diffuse rejection of the past. Specifically, it condemned sorcery, fighting, and arguing.

However, I was able to collect considerable data on these topics from both members and nonmembers, and people seemed willing to talk about them, especially fighting.

As most of my analysis is concerned with pre-European times, a summary of the history of Auyana contact with Europeans will be useful. Members of Auyana first heard of Europeans shortly before World War II. The first government patrol came to their area in late 1949 or early 1950. As mentioned earlier, there was no opposition to the Australians. The government emphasized the cessation of fighting, and since the time of the first government patrol there has been only one fight involving members of Auyana in which they killed someone. As a result, I observed nothing comparable to warfare as it would have been practiced prior to the arrival of Europeans. The two fights I observed involving entire social units were fought with rocks and sticks only.

Black Christian evangelists arrived in Auyana about 1957. In 1960, a white Lutheran missionary and his wife came to an adjacent group. One or two mass conversions of members of Auyana and of other groups in Opoimpina occurred shortly after the first Black evangelists arrived. But by 1962 only seven Auyana families had been baptized and were active members. The other Auyana families had either given up their affiliation entirely or said they might later renew it. Although the effect of the mission is difficult to assess, the missionaries and government have apparently been instrumental in bringing about changes other than the cessation of warfare. One of these has been a toning-down, and in some cases abandonment, of male initiations and a major "male renewal" ceremony. Members of Auyana said that both the missionaries and government forbade them to practice either of these ceremonies and so they stopped (or were stopping). The missionaries and members of the government I talked with denied this assertion. Whatever the cause, only one of the two initiations I was able to witness was close to the way it would have been prior to European contact, and I neither saw nor heard of a "male renewal" ceremony taking place.

The other principal change has been in the area of material goods. The cargo movement mentioned earlier began in the 1930s before members of Auyana had even heard of Europeans and has been periodically active since. Members of Auyana were therefore prepared to receive European goods when they first arrived. Steel axes and knives were among the first items people attempted to acquire. It was said that by the time the first government patrol came in 1950, every family either owned or had access to an axe and a knife. By 1962, some young men could not even use a stone adze. In fact, by that time it had become comical to attempt to use one. By 1962, most men wore belted "laplaps," a few wore shorts, and some had shirts. Most women owned dresses but these were worn only on special occasions and then over traditional clothes. Soap, matches, newspaper for cigarettes, stick tobacco, salt, and tin pots were common. There were a few kerosene

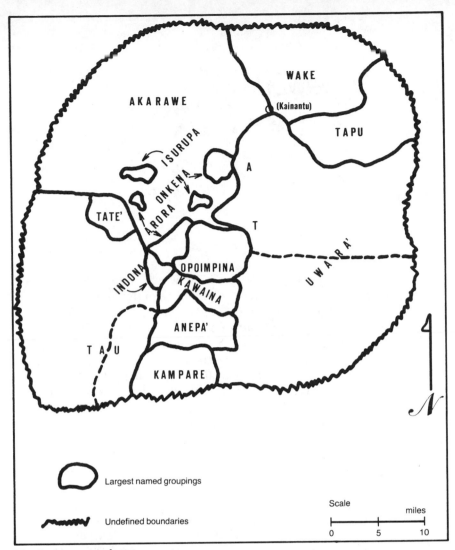

Map 4. Auyana social environment

lamps. People would occasionally walk one to two days to a store to purchase packaged foods (meat and cookies mostly).

Although women had no direct access to money through wage labor, men obtained money in a variety of ways. Some men worked as indentured or volunteer laborers at coastal plantations. Three young men were doing this in 1962 and returned to Auyana in 1964. Some worked for short periods of time on the plantations around Kainantu, but during the period of my field work, no one did this. For a while in the early 1950s, people grew and sold white potatoes to Europeans at Kainantu, but that commodity rather quickly ceased to be a source of income. The government has tried to get the people to plant coffee; however, partly because they would have to walk two to three days to sell it, only five men were raising coffee in 1965.

# 2. A Framework

HUMAN ENVIRONMENT

The wider human environment within which members of Auyana lived prior to the arrival of whites can best be seen through their perceptions of the various collectivities on Map 4.[1] The members of Opoimpina (Auyana, Asempa) were those with whom the members of Auyana carried on most transactions. They are considered in detail in later sections. Kawaina was one of the two Auyana enemies of long standing, having been driven off part of its land by Auyana within the previous fifty years. Little interaction other than fighting took place between Kawaina and Auyana and what little did is dealt with in a later section. Arora (Arora, Kosena, Sefuna) was the second long-standing Auyana enemy. However, unlike Kawaina, some transactions occurred other than fighting. These are discussed later.

Indona was an ally of Auyana. At one time the members of Indona were refugees who lived on Auyana territory for several years. Transactions between them and Auyana included marriages, exchanges of wealth, and visits. These will be discussed later. Isurupa was relatively unknown to Auyana. It was somewhat distant and the language was unintelligible. Members of Auyana went to such places only to trade. However, very little trade was conducted with Isurupa, as members of Auyana said they were afraid they would be killed. Although they knew relatively little about Isurupa, they claimed that it, or a segment of it, had originated from a population that had once lived where Kawaina was in 1962 and had been completely dispersed by warfare. Akarawe (Kamano) was also relatively unknown to members of Auyana. Occasional trade took place with some segments close to Arora, but members of Auyana said they were afraid the members of Akarawe might kill them and therefore did not like to go there to trade. Although the members of Onkena (Oiyana) spoke a different language than Auyana, many of them, through their association with Anokapa, also spoke Auyana, and

[1] The information for this section was derived from a variety of sources but mostly from answers to the LeVine and Campbell questionnaire.

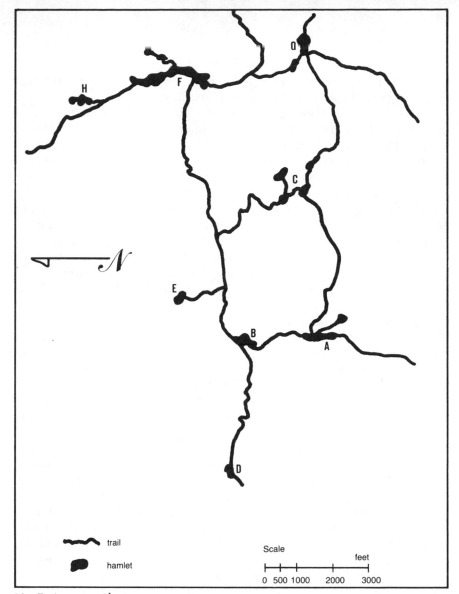

Map 5. Auyana residences

many transactions between them and Auyana occurred. These are discussed later. Wake (Agarabi) was never visited by Auyana, and the members of Auyana knew about them only by hearsay.

Uwara' (Tairora) was divided into two segments: Kari'uwara' (little Uwara') and Ora'uwara' (big Uwara'). Little Uwara' is referred to by Europeans as Southern Tairora and the other division as Northern Tairora. On Map 4, a dotted line separates these subdivisions. A portion of little Uwara' constituted a principal trade avenue for members of Auyana. The latter said they traded for a variety of goods but mostly for

bows and arrows, offering pigs, feathers, and shells in return. No transactions occurred with the remainder of little Uwara'.

There was only sporadic trade with all except two segments of
Ora'uwara'. I will discuss the two more intensive relationships in detail,
because they illustrate several featues of life in and around Auyana. One
of these segments, show as T on Map 4, was called Tondona. Tondona
lay over the Kratke Mountains from Auyana. Members of Auyana had a
story that an Opoimpina boy hunting in the forest strayed toward the
Kratke Mountains separating Tondona from Opoimpina—which means
he "strayed" a good day's walk. A Tondona woman came along and, by
promising him better game "just ahead," lured him further into the
mountains and eventually to her home on the other side. Once there, he
was lost and had to stay. Although she raised him, when he grew up she
forced him to marry her despite his protests against their incest. Their
offspring formed Tondona which was therefore a combination of
Uwara' and Opoimpina. Intermarriage apparently took place between
Tondona and members of the Opoimpina group closest to Tondona, although none occurred between Tondona and members of Auyana.
Those from Auyana used the story of the boy who strayed into the forest, and connections with those in Opoimpina who were married to Tondona, to develop trading partners in Tondona—people who would not
only trade with them but would house and feed them while they were
there. It was said that Auyana mostly gave bows, arrows, feathers, and
salt and received pigs in exchange.

The other Uwara' segment with which there was a special relationship
was called Kaiyona and centered on the village of Abi'era, marked A on
Map 4 (see Watson 1970). This relationship again involved a claim of
common ancestry. However, in this instance, the claimed common ancestry was only between a segment of Auyana and a segment of Kaiyona.
The segment within Auyana claimed they were formed from refugees
driven from a segment of Arora. They said the members of this dis-
placed segment fled to many areas, including Kaiyona and Auyana, and
that they and those living in Kaiyona were the same as members of a
sovereignty. This claim was not converted into group behavior, but was
used in order to develop and maintain a special trading relationship.
This included exchanging several boys from each population so that the
youngsters could learn the language of the other group. As this implies,
Kaiyona was a principal source of trade for this segment of Auyana and
also for other members of Auyana who would accompany them. It was
said that Auyana received primarily pigs and shells from Kaiyona in exchange for bows, arrows, feathers, and salt (as was the case with Tondona). Other than trade and temporary residence of the exchanged
boys, few transactions occurred between members of Auyana and Kai-

yona. They gave war aid to each other several times, but there were no marriages and rarely an exchange of wealth other than trading.

Anepa' (Awa) constituted another major source of trade. It was said that Auyana principally traded pigs and shells and received bows, arrows, and feathers. Some members of Anepa' were refugees at Auyana briefly and vice versa, and a few instances of reciprocal war aid had taken place. There were, however, no intermarriages and only rare transactions of wealth other than trade. Anepa', then, was much like Kaiyona in its relationship to Auyana. Kampare (Southern Awa) was never visited by Auyana, and Auyana knew about them only by hearsay. The same was true for Tate.

Tau (Fore) was divided into two segments indicated by the dotted line on Map 4. The segment labeled K on the map was said to be a major source of feathers, in return for which members of Auyana gave pigs and some shells. In addition, a segment of this population fled to Auyana and remained there for several years. During the segment's stay in Auyana a few marriages were arranged, but after it moved back to its original ground only a single instance of war aid occurred, in addition to trading. Those in the Tau segments labeled O on Map 4 were also a major source of trade for Auyana. The items traded varied, but Auyana was said to receive primarily pigs, shells, and stone adze blades in return for anything except those items. One segment of O also briefly refugeed in Auyana, which resulted in a few marriages. Otherwise, the main transactions with O involved fights resulting from the Auyana alliance with Indona (which bordered on Tau).

From Map 4 it is obvious that the Auyana world was, by American standards, a geographically small one. Although small, Auyana included a large number of subdivisions and languages. However, at least three generalizations can be made: (1) transactions other than trade were infrequent with distant populations; (2) trade was infrequent with close populations; and (3) pigs and shells were usually traded to the south; and bows, arrows, feathers, and salt were traded to the north.

My guess as to why trading was conducted with distant populations and why there was a dichotomous flow of goods is that each phenomenon was a consequence of unequal productivity. The Markham Valley in the north led to the sea and was apparently the major shell trade route in the Eastern Highlands. As for pigs, members of Auyana claimed that groups in the north raised more pigs than those in the south. I do not know whether this claim was valid; however, there was more open grassland in the north and more forest in the south, and if peoples dwelling in grasslands raise more pigs per capita, then the Auyana claim would be correct. Langness (personal communication 1969) thinks that in the BenaBena area, grassland dwellers had more pigs, which gives some support to the Auyana claim. Feathers, bows, and arrows are items more readily obtainable from the forest and, assuming that items were traded from areas of greater production to areas of lesser production, the result would be the dichotomous flow observed in Auyana. If it was also true that the greater the distance, the greater the difference in the relative rates of production, this would partially explain why members of Auyana went to more distant places to trade, although it would not explain why they went no farther than a three-day walk from home.

The converse of trading with distant peoples was that marriages, exchanges of wealth other than trading, and fighting were carried on with those within a day's walk or less. Those close to Auyana also had a great many behavioral similarities to those in Auyana, and it could be argued that it was not so much proximity as similar ways of life that resulted in the many transactions such as marriages which were carried on with these groups. However, there are indications that this was not true. As mentioned earlier, some in Opoimpina intermarried with those in nearby Tondona. Further, those in Kawaina intermarried with Anepa' populations adjacent to them. This does not mean that differences in the way of life were irrelevant; it does indicate that these differences may not have been the primary consideration in delimiting those with whom one traded or had no transactions and those with whom one intermarried, exchanged goods, and fought.

I have discussed some of the internal differentiation of the Auyana world, but no mention has been made of precisely where the world ended for members of Auyana. The wavy lines on Map 4 indicate that the furthermost boundaries of their world were not exact, nor were they given much thought. Auyana members could sometimes see smoke coming from territory they had never visited or heard about and they thought there might be people (or humanlike creatures) there, but for the most part they did not know. To the east along the Uwara' border was an area they referred to as Ana. This was said to be where the sun came from each morning. Inasmuch as the sun arrived over Auyana by the middle of the day, it could not have been over Ana very long. Therefore, those living at Ana had only a short time in which to do their gardening and other work. Beyond this, total ignorance was professed of what the people there were like. To the south beyond Kampare was said to be an area where the people had sharp spiked lower trunks and consequently could not sit down fully but, rather, sat on their tail, as one would sit on a stool. Further, the men always had intercourse with the women from the rear, "like dogs," and the women masturbated by rubbing their buttocks up and down against a tree. They were also fierce cannibals and to go there would mean certain death.

When pressed as to whether anything lay beyond areas such as Ana, members of Auyana said there was only virgin forest (*umi'*). According to some, the sky and ground were like two plates and the trees at the edge of the world held up the sky, preventing it from falling to the ground. Others said the sky and ground were two plates but nothing held them apart, they were just apart. According to others, the ground was like a plate but the sky was simply the sky. When one looked from any point within Auyana, the world was always bounded by forest, as there was no gardening on the upper parts of the higher ridges. Everyone believed that in the areas about which they knew nothing there was only forest—a forest whose extent was unknown.

## SPIRITS, GHOSTS, AND SOULS

To the best of my knowledge, the members of Auyana had no distinction which corresponds to the one we make between "natural" and "supernatural." They referred to the inhabitants of Ana as *apa'wasi*. This term was also used to refer to individuals who went "crazy" or to anyone who was particularly stubborn or foolhardy or refused to listen to others.

For example, when describing fights, men would frequently refer to themselves as "like *apa'wasi*." That is, they would take no mind for their safety, would not listen to the pleadings of others (especially their wives), and would instead plunge headlong into the fight, thereby terrorizing and routing their enemies. When Europeans appeared on the scene, they were referred to as *apa'wasi*. This was partly because they were taken for ghosts, but mostly because they were totally unmanageable and seemed particularly likely to kill others for no apparent reason. In 1962, they were still referred to as *apa'wasi*.

As used by the members of Auyana, the term *apa'wasi* more closely corresponds to wild (vs. tame) or unsocialized (vs. socialized) than it does to supernatural (vs. natural). However, *apa'wasi* did not simply mean "wild," it meant a certain class of wild things. Other wild things were *apa'poi* (pigs that were not being looked after by anyone), *apa'iya* (dogs that were not being looked after by anyone), and so forth. What was a *wasi* then? This term was used both for a class and for a subdivision of that class. When referring to the entire class, it meant "anthropomorph." When used to refer to a subclass of anthropomorph, the distinction was between *wasi* and *apa'wasi*. If *apa'wasi* is translated as "wild anthropomorph," then *wasi* (considered as referring to the subclass) is best translated as "tame anthropomorph." However, the only tame anthropomorphs were what we would call "humans" or "persons." One might argue then that *wasi* is best translated simply as "human." The simplest demonstration of the inadequacy of this translation is that although someone we would label crazy is still called by us a person or human, such a person would not still be called a *wasi* by a member of Auyana—he or she would have become an *apa'wasi*. Read (1954) made essentially the same point when he stated that Highlands populations have no concept of a human essence and no universal morality based on this concept. (Valentine, 1965, makes a similar point for the Lakalai). Nonetheless, I will translate *wasi* as "human" in the remainder of this discussion with the understanding that it is only a convenient gloss.

Although I never directly asked, humans were the only objects I heard of which could move back and forth between being *wasi* (tame anthropomorph) and *apa'wasi* (wild anthropomorph). Other *apa'wasi* could be only *apa'wasi*. There were three types of such wild anthropomorphs: (1) *ore'ore'pamba* (mud beings); (2) *wanta* (ghosts); and (3) *upaema* (spirits).

The name *ore'ore'pamba* had no translation. However, they could also be referred to as *toime* (mud beings), as they lived underground in slightly swampy areas. All *ore'ore'pamba* were males and almost all of them lived alone. They were not identified with any particular individuals or groups. Most of the mud men lived within the forest because swampy areas were usually small and would dry up when the forest was cut for gardening. If the garden areas did not dry up, the mud men would remain there living in the mud even after a garden was made. In 1962, there were six mud men living on Auyana territory, four in the forest and two in gardens. One man told me that one of the garden places had two mud men living in it, as one had moved in with the other recently because his home had been made into a garden and dried up.

As the above implies, mud men did not retaliate when their homes were destroyed by gardening, and there were no preventative actions taken when a mud man's place was being cleared. The main danger from mud men was their ability to make small children sick. It was said that a mud man might steal some of a child's clothing, feces, leftover food—anything close to the child—and bury it in the mud man's home. Alternatively, an adult who was angry at a child, or at the groups the child was a member of, might do the same. Or a child might blunder into or close to a mud man's house. The result of any of these circumstances was to make the child sick, although not deathly so. It was said that children did not often get sick this way. One of the men I was especially close to was a curer, and I think I probably heard from him about most of the cases of illness within Auyana, although not in great detail. Unfortunately, the cases of sick children would have been the ones I would have been most likely to miss. In any case, during the two years I was in Auyana, I heard of only one case of illness due to a mud man. The victim was an eight-year-old boy with a mild but persistent illness. Finally, the illness was diagnosed as resulting from the burial in a mud man's home of a piece of a sweet potato which had fallen to the ground after the boy had been eating it. Whoever buried the sweet potato wished to do the boy harm.

The infrequent adult encounters with mud men were frightening although I could find no cases of an adult having actually been harmed by a mud man. One reason mud men were frightening was that they wandered around only at night. Most members of Auyana were frightened when out in the dark because ghosts and sometimes assassins were out at night and were definitely dangerous. Although there was some disagreement about their appearance, everyone agreed they basically looked like luminescent men, and parts of them were distorted. Everyone also agreed they could suddenly disappear and reappear in a different spot. But they could not transform them-selves into other beings. Some said they had pointed heads; others said they had gigantic heads (as in the case given below). Some believed they were entirely covered with hair; others claimed they had only head hair but it was so long that it sometimes hung to the ground and covered their entire body.

Two of the men in Auyana had each had an encounter with a mud man and I will end this discussion with one of the accounts. The narrator was a newly-married man in his middle twenties.

> One night in the eighth month of the year you were back at your home [1964], I went to hunt marsupials in the middle of the night. I went by myself to Kopimpa and when I got close the mud man came. He came from up above me and at first I thought it might be a marsupial. It kept on coming above me and then I saw it. Nope, I thought, maybe it's a man up there, could it really be a man? Then I saw it had a big head and I got afraid. My soul left me. I thought, here I am all alone and whatever it is, it isn't a human.

> There was this one big mahogany tree and I was on one side and the mud man came up to the other side. I notched an arrow and pretended to aim at some-thing. The mud man thought I was going to shoot a marsupial. I drew the arrow all the way back and then whirled and shot the mud man in the ribs. The mud man ran back up from the direction he had come and I heard the arrow clattering on the bushes and trees as he ran. Then he was gone. I was scared and came back home and went inside and went to bed. In the morning I told everyone I had shot a wild humanlike thing with a big head. Then I got all the men and we went back to the place where I saw him. When we got there we found my tracks but no mud man tracks. I said he was right there and after I shot him he went clattering up that direction and inasmuch as he didn't leave any tracks he must have flown like a bird. Then I went back along the way he had gone and found my arrow. There was no blood on it and it was broken cleanly at a node [arrow shafts are made of cane and usually splinter between nodes]. That's the story.

As the above discussion implies, mud men were not of much importance to members of Auyana and seemed mainly to provide a source of amusing stories. But *wanta* (ghosts) and *upaema* (totems and spirits) were anything but amusing. Before discussing them, I will first consider the Auyana con-cept of "life" and "death." Information on the following topics came primar-ily from two persons, one a curer, the other not, and from answers to the LeVine and Campbell questionnaire.

The Auyana lexicon contained distinctions corresponding to our distinc-tions of plants, animals, and humans, except that humans were not classified as animals and there was no term which could be used to refer to all three categories. All three categories "grew." However, humans and animals had "breath" (*ha*) and "voluntary motion" (*auwa*), whereas plants had neither. This distinction of plants versus humans and animals was maintained in the Auyana terminology for death: for animals and humans, *pu-*; for plants, *ai-*. *Ai-* was translated into pidgin as *i drai* and seems best translated as "dry up."

*Pu-* was translated into pidgin as *in dai* and seems best translated as "ceasing to have voluntary motion." *Pu-* and *in dai* were used to refer to what I would call unconscious, stunned, or knocked out, as well as what I would call dead. The contexts, and in some cases affixes, determined which of these meanings applied. As this discussion implies, stillness and no breath were said to be the main criteria in determining whether someone was dead. When someone was found who was not moving, the first thing you looked at in determining whether the person was breathing was the chest area in general. If the ribs were not going in and out or you could not tell, you then looked at the solar plexus and/or the area where the clavicles connect to the sternum.

Humans were distinguished from animals in that humans were endowed with a *-ma-* (soul), which they acquired around toddling age, which was also when people were said to begin talking, thinking, and dreaming. A person's soul was diffused throughout his or her body but was concentrated along the spine. Partly for this reason and partly for anatomical reasons, the spine was compared to the center pole of the house without which the house could not stand. In the same way, when a person was so ill he or she could hardly move, was knocked out, or had fainted, it was said that the soul was loose from the body and unless it returned the person would die. Death, then, was the result of a person's soul leaving the body and never returning.

A person's soul was not restricted to the body. Everyone also had a "sun soul" (shadow) and a "water soul" (reflection). Reflections in mirrors were also a person's soul, but no one was certain about photographs. One's shadow and reflection were found only with one's body and when the body ceased to exist, the shadow and reflection ceased to exist forever. I was told that shadows and reflections had no particular use or significance and I did not pursue their meaning except for casual questioning.

Another aspect of the soul which, while not found only with the body, ceased to exist at the death of the body, was dreaming. As a person slept, the soul traveled and the dream was what was experienced by the soul as it traveled. Because the person's soul was away from the body while dreaming, the person was in a situation which could become dangerous (but rarely did). For if a person's soul did not return after traveling, the person would be dead. But everyone's soul always returned after dreaming unless a person awakened so suddenly that the soul did not have time to get back and became lost. People should be awakened slowly; otherwise they might end up like a young man who was sleeping under a tree. One of his friends, wanting to surprise him, held a drum up to his ear and hit it very hard. The sleeper sat bolt upright, his eyes bulging open, and fell back dead. This was the only case of anyone being killed by being awakened too suddenly.

A person's soul did not perceive waking reality in dreams, but what was perceived might indicate something about that reality. Children were encouraged to tell their dreams, especially if they were vivid ones, and adults usually told their dreams to someone else to see what the other person could make of them. Although there were standardized dream portents, interpretations of dreams were only tentative and confirmation of an interpretation might not come until years later. The members of Auyana seemed to use dreams as signals of possible events rather than as directives to be followed.

Both men and women could get messages about the future through dreams. For example, during his initiation into manhood, a man had the following dream. In the dream he went at night to a big pool of water in a distant group. There were lots of fires and men all around the pool. As he looked at the pool and the fires, an eel came up in the middle of the pool and kept on rising out of the water until finally it was totally out of the water. It then came over to the dreamer and twisted itself around and around him and covered him with the water from its skin. It then told him to tie a firebrand on its tail and hit its tail. He did, and the eel slithered around and around him and then went back into the water. The men by the water said, "Pay attention to this and don't be afraid of anyone assassinating you by making you sick, for this eel has made you cold." Then he awoke. He discussed the dream with the adult men and eventually the accepted interpretation was that he would have lifetime protection from any attempt to kill him by making him sick. Apart from the statement by the eel, the fire was also interpreted as representing an attempt to kill him by making him sick, and when the eel took the fire into the water, this symbolically stopped attempts of this sort. The interpretation of fire and "hotness" as representing destruction, either of the dreamer (as in the above dream) or of others (as in dreams which gave the power to kill), was common in analyzing dreams and waking reality. There were other dream portents, but I made no analysis of them. I also made no attempt to find out all the kinds of powers that could be conferred in dreams. The following are the ones I did collect: all the person's pigs and children would grow well; all the person's pigs and children would die; the dreamer would kill a lot of people (the dream specified the type of arrow for him to use); the dreamer was told he or she would die if he or she went to a certain place; the dreamer was told he would fall out of a tree in a certain part of the forest if he went there; the dreamer would have many wives; the dreamer was told he or she would get bitten by a poisonous asp if he or she went to a certain grassy area; the dreamer would be a good hunter in general or of specific animals; the dreamer was told certain crops would grow well for her and certain would not; and the dreamer would be able to kill many people by making them sick. It was said that no one ever dreamed of becoming a curer and you only knew you were a curer if you tried it. I was given no reason for this, nor have I been able to link it with anything else.

Dreams giving information about the future could come at any time, although there were certain times when they were more likely and more potent. I never found out what these times were for women other than the time just before they were married. For men, during initiation was one time and during a male renewal ceremony was another. I was also told that the younger the person when the dream occurred, the more powerful it was.

Dreams providing means of avoiding illness or harm were sometimes different from dreams conveying messages about the future in that in the former the dreamer would encounter a form of his or her soul. When the soul in its travels ran across a separate form of itself, it was always a plant or an animal. This form of a person's soul was usually referred to as his or her *-wa'na*. It was said that the term *-wa'na* could be used interchangeably with *-ma-*; that is, they were two words for the same thing. But in the texts I collected and in conversations about the subject, *-wa'na* was usually used to refer to a person's soul when it appeared in a different form than the body *and* the body was still alive. If the body was dead, then the soul and any form it appeared in were referred to as *wanta* (ghost). It was possible to have more than one plant or animal soul. Two members of Auyana had three, several people had two, and everyone else had one.

There were no signs in a dream by which a person could tell whether any plant or animal encountered was his or her soul. Sometimes a person would have a strong hunch, or, if a dream occurred at one of the auspicious times mentioned above, it might be likely to involve the person's soul. In the cases I collected, the interpretation of a dream as involving the dreamer's soul usually occurred *after* some confirming event. In answer to the question, "How do you get a plant or animal soul?" I was told, "When a person is small like P [around six to seven] he or she may have a dream. But then the person forgets it. Eventually, he or she grows up, gets married and has children. Then the children get sick and the parent goes to a curer. The curer asks if the person ever had a dream about such and such an animal or plant. If the answer is yes, then the curer says the person can't eat that plant or animal or the person or the person's children will get sick. This plant or animal is the person's soul." This general process of interpretation is illustrated by the following two cases which occurred while I was in Auyana.

N was a young lady who had her second miscarriage in a row. Two curers were consulted who "saw" that her husband's soul was causing the miscarriages. They asked her husband if he had had a dream about eels and if he had eaten any eel. Several years back he had had a dream about an eel but had not taken it to mean anything, and when he was at the coast as a worker about a year before N's second pregnancy, he had eaten eels. The husband was told never eat eels again, and certain activities were undertaken to drive off his soul.

J was a middle-aged curer. One night he had a dream in which he had to make his way through some wild cucumber vines as he was hunting. He thought there was some significance to the wild cucumbers but did not know what and eventually forgot about it. Several months after that his two-year-old son got a cold which would not quit. At this point J remembered the dream and also that he had cut wild cucumber while making his garden. He concluded that the wild cucumber in the dream had been his soul and that in the future he would have to avoid harming the plant. Nothing special, however, was done to cure his son's cold, and it ended not long after that.

Eating or in any way harming your soul was equivalent to harming yourself. As the above two cases illustrate, a man's self included his children. It also included his wife or wives. If a woman harmed her soul, however, harm would come only to her and her children, not to her husband, her co-wives or her co-wives' children (nor to any members of the sovereignty she came from).

A person might also encounter his or her soul while awake. The following case illustrates this type of encounter.

> One night I went into the forest alone to hunt marsupials. It was in the middle of the night, and there was a slight moon. I was waiting under this tree when I heard some noise and thought a marsupial was coming. Then I saw it and started to shoot it. But as I aimed at it, my soul left me and I became weak and so scared that the sweat ran off me like water. I started home, panting and sweating, and I came to this place and rested, and there I stopped sweating and panting and my soul came back to me. But I couldn't hunt any more marsupials that night and I went home and slept. The next day I told people about it and we decided I had met my animal soul.

One interesting thing about a person's waking encounter with his or her soul is that the person was always weakened and unable to continue acting, whereas encounters in dreams never had this quality. This may have been because in none of the dreams was the person harming the plant or animal that was later identified as the soul, whereas all the waking encounters involved efforts to harm the plant or animal. The fright a person felt then was the fright of one's own death as one was unknowingly about to kill oneself.

The encounters with plant or animal souls discussed thus far were all unsolicited and sometimes even unnoticed for a long time. The next, and final, type of encounter to be considered, that of a curer with his or her plant or animal soul, was just the reverse. It was solicited, sometimes repeatedly when initial attempts failed, and it was definitely noticed when it occurred. As mentioned earlier, serious illness was almost always attributed to circumstances in which a person's soul had become loose from the body. When the soul became permanently loose, a person was dead and the soul became a *wanta* (ghost). A curer, then, was a person who could find a loose soul, return it to its body, and negate the energy that caused the soul to be loose.

When I collected genealogies, I asked for the cause of death of each person. Except for those killed in combat and the "very young" and "very old," what ultimately caused a person's soul to become permanently loose was always said to be soul assassination. Granted, "very young" and "very old" are not precise terms. Nor were they precise the way members of the Auyana used them, and there was sometimes disagreement over how old someone had been when he or she died. Disagreements also developed over whether someone had died only because he or she was old or as a result of soul assassination. Roughly speaking, very young meant around toddler or younger (i.e., prior to the time people were said to acquire a soul). Very old meant that the person had mostly gray hair and sagging skin from atrophying muscles. Socially, it meant the person was pretty much out of the public social arena and he or she had few, if any, elders.

One of the favorite forms of soul assassination was for the assassin to "shoot" (the same verb was used as for shooting an arrow) an ink-like substance into the person which then spread throughout the victim's body as well as knocking the victim's soul loose. To do this, an assassin gathered certain leaves or barks and reduced them to ashes while saying and/or singing secret phrases. The ashes were made into a bundle about the size of a large acorn. The bundle was then placed in the middle of three or four tines made from the black wing bone of a cassowary which were lashed together at one end to form a sort of conical-shaped basket. To shoot a person, the basket was held vertically and each of the tines was pulled back and let snap against the bundle of ashes while the assassin aimed at the person and said what was going to happen to him or her. The snapping shot the ink-like stuff into the person. It was said that the force of the stuff hitting the victim was sometimes so great that he or she might stagger or even fall, although usually the victim had slipped or stumbled for some other reason. Although I never saw an assassination attempt, I did see several of the baskets. The cargo cult leader in Auyana had decided to try to stop soul assassinations by collecting the baskets. One morning he came to my house to show me what he had collected. People with him were extremely nervous and only he and another person would even handle the objects. If a basket happened to get pointed at someone, the person would lie on the ground to avoid any chance of being shot. It was as though someone were handling a loaded gun that might go off unpredictably at any moment.

After shooting someone, an assassin would return to his house and make himself "hot" in order to aid the attempt. This was done by sitting close to the fire, not drinking any liquids and not eating any of several foods, such as sugar cane and certain greens, which had a lot of liquid in them. The procedure followed by the assassin was the same as the one followed at male initiations and at "male renewal" ceremonies in order to make males "hot" and killers. As this implies, soul assassination was performed only by males. Women might be helpers in some forms of soul assassination as described below. Women could also make males, especially unmarried ones or their husbands, sick by taking part of the person's body, such as feces, semen, or sweat, and putting it in a hole in the menstrual hut floor and squatting over it while menstruating. But this was not deadly and was rarely practiced.

In the other form of soul assassination, the assassin would get some item (semen, sweat, and feces were the best) belonging to the person and do to it something similar to what he wished to be done to the victim (i.e., "imitative magic"). If the assassin wanted his victim to die from not being able to breathe, he would put the stolen item into a bamboo tube with certain leaves, and then seal the tube and place it over a fire. As it was cooking, the assassin would say certain things to insure that the victim's breath would be fastened inside him or her just as the steam was fastened inside the bamboo tube. Women could steal some items from their husbands, especially semen, but this rarely happened in the cases I collected.

One characteristic of all the "imitative" forms is that they caused only fairly specific illnesses in contrast to the favorite form, which caused deaths due to accidents *and* illnesses. As mentioned above, the assassin could determine what would happen to the victim by saying certain things as he shot the victim. But such sayings did not specify the mode of death and therefore any accident or illness could result from them. Once the person's soul had been knocked loose, then some normally harmless activity, such as climbing a tree to hunt a marsupial or having a child, would result in death by, for example, falling or hemorrhaging. When a person's soul was loose, he or she became weak and might be killed by processes going on all the time. Therefore, both accidents and illnesses resulted from the favorite form of soul assassination, and it was the only cause of nonfatal accidents, which were said to occur when an assassination attempt had not fully succeeded.

Nonfatal physical injuries could also result from knocking a soul loose but not permanently loose. Such forms of causing harm were like the imitative form of soul assassination. These forms were not referred to by the term *uwa'a* (soul assassination), but the harm resulting from them was referred to by the same term as the harm resulting from soul assassination: *nai*. *Nai*, then, covered what we would call accidents and illness and also some, but not all, of the things we would call bad luck or bad breaks. Generally speaking, *nai* seemed to be restricted to "physical bad breaks." For example, a person could be made unable to talk, or one's knees might become swollen all the time, making it difficult to walk. However, as it was a labor-intensive economy, status was to a large extent dependent on physical well-being and so "physical" bad breaks very quickly became "social" bad breaks.

Means of causing harm to people by attacking their souls varied, then, in their severity and in whether they were imitative or not. They were alike in that they involved the use of leaves and of some words or phrases, and in that the assassin would keep himself "hot" afterwards. Most of the imitative forms also involved heating or burning the item stolen from the victim and thus were analogous to the burning of leaves in the shooting form.

The information that a person's soul was loose obviously might not be apparent to the victim or to those around him just from the appearance and activities of the victim. In these cases, the information might be found out by someone other than the victim—for instance, if the victim's soul showed itself in the form of an animal. I heard only one firsthand account of such an encounter. In this case, a man was hunting in the forest when he saw a marsupial. At first he thought it was just another marsupial and started stalking it. But then the animal began rocking back and forth and the man saw that it held certain leaves (the same ones used to cool a sick person) in one of its paws and was waving them back and forth. As he was watching the action, the marsupial just sort of faded away. The encounter puzzled the man, and he went back and told others. It was decided that someone in his group had a loosened soul through soul assassination and everyone should be especially careful. Eventually, one of the important men became ill, and it was thought that it was his soul the man had seen earlier. Such encounters, it was said, occurred only when the soul of an important man was loose.

I was told that another premonition might occur through encountering the loose soul in the form of the person himself. Such an encounter was recognized when it was discovered that a person could not have been where he or she had definitely been seen earlier. This type of encounter had the same implications as the above encounter with an animal. I received no firsthand accounts of such an encounter. Both it and the encounter with a person's soul in the form of an animal were said to be rare, and when they did occur, there were no preventatives that could be used. Rather, everyone, and especially important men, were extra careful and help came quickly if someone got sick.

Assuming there were no premonitions, as an illness developed a curer might either volunteer his or her services or be asked to come. I know that several considerations were involved in these decisions, but I did not attempt to determine them all nor their interaction with one another. Minimally, a curer would not volunteer or be asked for unless some form of soul harm was suspected. I was told that the main criterion leading to the suspicion that soul harm was involved was that the illness became "big" or lasted a "long time." In addition, the social relationships of the patient and/or his or her affiliates also entered in. In some cases, slight illnesses were immediately suspected of being soul harm because the person had been made ill by soul harm before and there was reason to believe the grudge which led to the earlier attacks had not been forgotten. I was also told that some people were much quicker to assume ill will and soul harm than others.

In general, curers were more likely to volunteer their services and less likely to turn down a request for help if the sick person was socially close or close to someone who was close. Curers were expected to take care of those close to them, whereas for more distant people, the curer was freer to accept or reject the case. The one exception to this generalization was when the sick person was in the curer's family or the family of the curer's children. In that case, while the curer might take part in the curing, outside curers would be called in (or would volunteer). I was told this was because the curer was close to the sick person and sadness might make the curer see unclearly; hence it would not be good if the curer worked on the case alone. In these circumstances, it was necessary to have someone not quite so close come in and work on the case as well.

As mentioned earlier, a curer was a person who could find a loose soul, return it to its owner, and negate the energy of the attempted soul harm. The curer did this by calling up his or her animal soul, which then searched the area for the lost soul and performed the operations necessary to return it and negate the soul harm attempt. Curers, like everyone else, might have more than one plant or animal soul. However, only one soul was used in curing, and this was always an animal soul. For example, the curer I was closest to had a white cockatoo as his soul.

The plants eaten by the curer included the bark of a tree called *pinto*, and curers were referred to as *"pinto* people." *Pinto* smelled somewhat like cinnamon but I never ate any of the bark or had it analyzed. There were no *pinto* trees in Auyana and I was told that almost all of it was procured by trading to the south. I do not know whether it was a hallucinogen or not. Some people who ate it had nothing happen to them, and in this way they found out that they would not be cures. Perhaps, if it was a hallucinogen, it was a mild one. Even if it was not a hallucinogen, it was eaten with about a third of a cup of raw ginger and salt mixed in equal parts while smoking enormous draughts of tobacco and these alone might have caused enough alteration to enable a curer to begin "seeing."

While the plant mixture was necessary, it was not sufficient for a curer to call his or her soul. The curer also had to sing certain songs and whistle, and the more helpers with singing he or she had, the stronger the calling. Curers almost always worked together with at least one other curer for this reason (and also to mutually validate what they saw). All curers worked only with those within their sovereignty and generally preferred to work with curers from their close subunits.

The helpers with singing were persons close to the sick person and, if the sick person was a woman, persons close to her husband. Staging any event which involved more than just immediate neighbors would always take at least a day to get people and things together, and there were almost always contingencies which might result in further delays. The bigger the event, the longer the time necessary between starting and finishing it. But a look by a curer involved at the maximum the number of people who could fit into the patient's house, around ten to fifteen, as this was where the looking was done. As the curers' and helpers' singing called the curers' souls closer, the curers began to shake and whistle. As their souls came to them and they in some sense became their souls, the whistling mostly disappeared and certain songs were used or songs were improvised to indicate what the curers were seeing.

The curer I was closest to said that each curer's soul lived an indefinite distance away but in a specific direction. For example, his soul always came to him from the south. When he first contacted his soul, it always looked to him like a small star in the distance. Gradually it would come closer and finally become visible as a cockatoo. At this point he would begin seeing with the eyes of his soul and fly around looking for the apparatus and/or the person involved in harming the patient's soul. At the same time, the curer remained his normal self and could switch from being a cockatoo to talking to the people singing and back again. However, a curer's control was sometimes shaky and a curer could become "wild" while engaged in looking at an illness. It was said that if a curer became wild, he or she no longer remained in contact with his or her animal soul. There were no cases of a curer becoming a soul animal and never returning to his or her body. Curers did not run the risk of leaving their bodies and dying, but they did run the risk of losing control, especially of their violence toward others. Practically no suicides occurred with Auyana. Only one man had killed himself (by hanging) as far as the present members of Auyana knew. I take it that, in general, male members of Auyana expressed their hostility outwards rather than against themselves.

Apart from the curer becoming wild and causing trouble, the curer's animal soul could be dangerous to anyone who entered or left the patient's house while a curer was engaged in looking. A curer told me about a case of this happening and I will present it here, as it also illustrates how a curer could use his or her soul to steal. The curer told me that all curers could use their souls to steal but seldom did so, because it was necessary to eat plants and sing and hence possible that the curer would be discovered by someone, who would surely become very angry. But he and his closest friend used to do it when they were adolescents. One day when the village was empty they decided to do it and barricaded themselves inside one of the houses. They were well into it when one of the curer's older brothers came by and heard them singing and took away the staves they had put up at the doorway and came into the house. As he stepped into the room, the soul of one of the curers attacked him and he fell to the floor unconscious, blood gushing from his nose and mouth. At first the two curers thought he was dead and they were about to run off before anyone discovered them when the victim started stirring, so they stayed and revived him and he was all right. This was the only instance that the curer telling the story knew of where someone had been attacked by a curer's soul during the curing process, but he had heard of other cases and such an attack was taken as a serious possibility. Closing the door to the patient's house was a crucial point in a curer's taking a look, for from that point on it was strongly advisable for no one to enter or leave.

A person could be ill from several soul assassination attempts at the same time and once the curer's soul had been called, the next step was to locate the assassin(s) and/or their equipment. If the curer's soul found the equipment, it might take it, tie certain tree leaves on it, and drop it into a pool of water to make it cold. Or the curer might tell people that his or her soul said to go to a particular place and they would find the equipment there. If they found it, they would treat it in the same way as the curer's soul treated it. Curers' souls frequently found the assassination equipment. They less frequently found the assassin. It was said that if the assassin was still keeping himself hot, it was easier to find him. If the curer's soul did find an assassin keeping himself hot, the curer could sometimes specify who and where the assassin was, and sometimes members of Auyana went over to a neighboring sovereignty and found an assassin making himself hot in his house and made him go bathe in a pool in order to prevent the assassination attempt. However, I was told of only two such cases and I gather it was not done often, partly because even if there was good reason to suspect an assassin, it was pretty explosive to make such an accusation and even touchier to prove it and get something done.

Another step in a cure was to cool the patient. This was accomplished in two ways. One was for the curer's soul to insert into the patient's blood the same kind of leaves as were tied to the assassination equipment. The other was for the patient to have cold water poured over the sorest parts and/or to drink some cold water out of a bamboo tube which had the same tree leaves stuffed into its mouth so that the water ran through them as the patient drank. There were a number of additional standard procedures to bring about a cure which did not involve the curer's soul. Certain leaves might be rubbed over the patient's body in order to cool it. Stinging nettles might also be rubbed over part of the body in order to make the patient strong. Bleeding was sometimes used, especially if there was blockage or swelling. Bleeding was accomplished by puncturing the skin with a toy arrow and then rubbing salt, ginger, and leaves into the puncture to increase the bleeding and to nullify the energy put into the attempted assassination.

The final standard procedure I will discuss is that in which the curer would suck out of the victim the ink-like substance, as well as any rocks, bones, or other hard objects that might have been put into a person by a soul assassin. The first look at an illness was an all-night affair and often there was no sucking done at that time. Rather, sucking usually took place the next day or night. It could be done without eating special plants, but having at least one other curer and some singing was necessary. The curers used tobacco smoke and leaves in order to gather the stuff put inside the patient into an area which could be covered by their mouths and sucked out. The smoke was used by blowing it near the designated sucking area and directing the stream of smoke toward that area, pushing the stuff along ahead of the smoke. The curer held the special leaves in his hand, rubbing them on the victim's body and pushing the stuff ahead of them, as though scooping sand into a pile.

What the curer saw on taking a look was both a diagnosis and a prognosis. For if the curer could see nothing or saw the assassination equipment but was unable to cool it, this meant the patient would most likely not recover, no matter what else was done to cool or help the patient. There was another form of prognosis independent of curers. If the encounters discussed earlier as premonitions occurred while a person was sick, they might be taken to mean the sick person's soul was lost and would never get back. However, such an encounter might also be taken to mean that although the person's soul was lost, it was attempting to get back and hence the person would recover. In any case, such encounters rarely happened, so prognosis was the task of the curers, and curers could enhance their reputations by correctly predicting death as well as recovery.

A person became a curer by trying it and seeing if anything happened. The power to cure was never revealed in dreams, although I never found out why. The younger a person was when he or she began to cure, the more powerful a curer the person was likely to be. It was possible for women to be curers, although curers were usually men and it was said that men were the most powerful curers. When I was in Auyana, there were six male curers and one female curer. In addition, there were two young male apprentices. The two or three curers who seemed to be generally recognized as the best were men. One of the best curers began curing after he was initiated and before marriage, and the remainder, except for one man, began not long after marriage. The one exception was a man in his late thirties who began curing the year before I arrived. During the time I was there, his position as a curer was somewhat ambiguous. He worked on cases, but as far as I know he never had the major responsibility for a case and if he contradicted the other curers, they would be listened to rather than he.

I will bring out a few more points about curing and end this discussion of it by giving a case history of a cure which occurred while I was there. The patient was a newly married young woman who developed a swollen knee. The swelling persisted for several days and then the other knee became so swollen she could not walk. She and her husband were closely affiliated with a curer, and were living with him and his family. However, he did not want to work on her case and he and the patient's husband asked two other curers (A and B) who were close to them and who often worked together as a team to take a look at her illness. The two curers agreed and arrangements were made for them to take a look on the night following the request. The patient's husband asked a few individuals close to both him and his wife to come help. These people assisted primarily by singing, which helped the curers to see. Some also brought extra vegetables to feed the others who had come, for the patient's husband was expected to feed those who had been invited, especially the ones from farther away. If possible, the patient's husband also provided the special plants eaten by the curers in order to take a look. If not, the curers could usually provide the plants themselves.

I had earlier told curer A that I was interested in going to the next case he went to if possible, and he told me I could come to this one. Around dusk, I went with him to the patient's house where most of the invited people had already assembled and were sitting around smoking and talking. Not long after we got there, curer B arrived. The patient's husband began preparing the plants to be eaten by the curers. By this time it was getting dark and the patient's husband, with occasional help and/or advice from curers A and B, was finishing the preparation of the plants. When it was decided to begin the session, the door to the house was closed and no one was to enter or leave until after the looking was over. The two curers ate some of the plants and then arranged themselves side by side on two mats toward the center of the house but facing the patient and most of the helpers. I was sitting with a few other people somewhat to the side and a little behind curer A. As the two curers were finishing the plant mixture, they began smoking enormous draughts of tobacco from their pipes, sucking it in as deeply as they could, taking several draughts in succession, pausing for a moment and then repeating. As the curers were smoking, the helpers gradually quit talking and arranged themselves in comfortable positions. There were two kerosene lamps in the house and the curers said with a chuckle to put one of them out but leave the other one on so people would not think they were faking. Those present seemed relaxed and the bantering, talking, and general feeling of having a good time was slowly replaced by a calm readiness. Slowly, one of the curers began to sing. The song was a well-known one and the helpers began to sing along with him. After a little singing, there was a pause and the curers smoked some more tobacco. Then the singing began again, this time with more intensity. Soon, the curers and helpers were singing almost continuously, with a few short pauses between songs. After about twenty minutes, curer B began shaking, much as though he were laughing almost uncontrollably while sitting upright. Shortly after this, curer A began shaking too and gradually both began shaking more violently. Their singing became shaky too and their voices changed timbre as they began whistling occasionally. The songs were sometimes ones improvised by one of the curers by repeating a single word or phrase several times followed by a refrain from some well-known song. The songs referred to the curers' souls, where they were coming from, their arrival, and the places being looked at. Both curers were singing and looking up toward the center of the house. After about thirty minutes from the time the door was closed, curer A suddenly turned to me and, while continuing to shake, told me his soul had gone to such and such places and found nothing and now was going to other places. He then began singing. Shortly after this episode, a stone fell onto the mat the two curers were sitting on, and I was told the stone had been shot through the roof by curer B's soul. The curers then began singing a song which indicated they were down at curer K's pig house searching through it. There was more singing and then curer B said to turn up the lamp as the *pinto* bark he had eaten was hot and it was possible that his animal soul, which had a reputation for being hot, might kill someone if it could not see clearly who the person was. Curer B then described the kind of soul assassination that had been attempted and how it was done. After this, several people got up and left. They said later it was because they were afraid curer B's soul might really kill someone, for in the past curer B had gone wild while curing and had attacked people. Being attacked would be dangerous enough, but in this case it would have been particularly dangerous, for curer B was one of the two main warrior/killers in Auyana.

After several people had left, the two curers began singing again with those who remained. While they were singing, curer K, who had gone out of the house with the others, came back in. The two curers stopped singing, and curer B gave a lengthy speech to curer K to the effect that the latter had almost been killed by curer B's soul but that curer B had prevented it and curer K should shake his hand. Curer K did. Curer A turned aside to me and told me his and curer B's souls had gotten certain leaves which they were trying to put under the patient's skin in order to cool her but they could not do it and this meant the sickness would last for a while. More singing followed. Curer B then announced that he did not think they could cure the patient, and she was going to have to get around on her knees like an old person. He said it was because the assassin had put the equipment into curer K's pig house, and being so close it was very powerful. This was followed by more singing. The songs said that the curers' souls were still trying to locate some of the assassin's equipment and put leaves under the patient's skin. After about two hours had passed, the songs indicated the session was coming to an end as the curers' souls returned from their search. The songs indicated the curers had been able to negate some of the assassination energy but not all of it. After two hours and forty minutes, the singing was very sporadic and the two curers were only shaking a little. A lot of people got up, went outside to urinate and stretch, and then came back in. However, after a few more songs, the two curers had quit shaking entirely, and it was decided there was no use looking any further that night.

The next day, the two curers went to the patient and, with a few people helping by singing, sucked out some of the ink-like stuff shot into her by the assassin. After about a week, the two curers again got together with helpers to take a look. This time their souls were able to cool the assassination energy, and they said that the patient would get well soon. The next day the patient's husband killed and cooked a pig and gave large portions to the two curers and distributed the rest to friends. After that, the patient began to recover slowly and the curers were no longer involved.

There was no sure way to prevent soul assassination, although it was said that a person could wear certain barks around the neck and this would help prevent it. A variety of widely known remedies existed which could be used where bodily harm was not due to soul assassination. If cuts or gashes were big, the leaves used to cool soul assassination energy might be placed over the cut and tied on. A mixture of pig grease and ashes was rubbed over burns if they were bad. Swollen joints were bled by shooting them with a toy bow and arrow, the arrow tipped with a small stone flake. It was said that if a person was bitten by a poisonous asp, a sharp object should be jammed into the bite and the flesh lifted up and sliced off until there was no more "black" flesh. Compound fractures were supposed to be reset (there were no anesthetics), and pieces of bamboo lashed on the limb to hold it in place. However, in the one case while I was there where someone broke a bone, the injury was not diagnosed as a break and nothing was done. In this case, a woman had been attacked by a man with a fence post. She afterwards complained of pain in her arms and just sat around her house. Her arms were swollen, but I could not tell whether they were broken or not. A few days later, a government patrol came through and the medical orderly diagnosed one forearm as a compound fracture and the other as a simple fracture and put them both in casts.

People sometimes got pieces of wood jabbed into them while fighting, hunting, or gardening, and in such cases a piece of bamboo was used as a knife to trim the flesh away from around the object, especially where pieces were jagged and they could not be pulled out smoothly. Water was used to wash away the blood so the surgeon could see. Cysts and subcutaneous infections such as cellulitis were lanced with a bamboo knife when they came to a head, and the pus was milked out of them. Following that, leaves were tied over the incision. It was said that an impacted tooth would be removed by filing notches on the tooth so that a cord could be tied around it. It was then pulled out while the gum was cut loose from around it. The only dental work I saw done was to scrape out decayed areas with a hard stick. Headaches were treated by tying a cord tightly around the head like a headband. There were no special diets for treating illness; people ate whatever they felt like eating. Sick people liked to keep warm (except when feverish), and lying in the sun was a favorite way of handling some mild illness.

No matter how strong a person's dream of health and no matter how powerful the curer, eventually everyone died—the soul permanently left the body and became a *wanta* (ghost). A ghost did not immediately leave to travel north to ghostland, which was said to extend northward from Tairora (see map 4). Part of this may have been due to some ambivalence about ghostland. The conceptions of ghostland were vague. Life there was supposed to be pretty much like life in Auyana except that ghostland was sometimes said to be cold, damp, and heavily forested and not a pleasant place to live. And the journey there could be dangerous. For example there was the story of a hermaphroditic person who guarded the path to ghostland and might attack a ghost or make it perform some undesirable sex act. However, people said it was just a story, and they did not know if this person actually existed (see the later discussion of "myths"). Further, after ghosts had gone to ghostland they did not come back except to hurt people who before had been close to them, and this was interpreted to mean, among other things, that the ghost was unhappy about being dead.

Another reason why a ghost did not leave immediately is that it had to be helped to find the road to ghostland by the people close to it (or close to people close to it), who would gather together and cry and sing for a couple of days and nights. As a person became seriously ill and it looked as if the person might die, the people close to the person would come over to see him or her once more before he or she died. If the person died, these people would begin mourning, and as the word of the death got around, others would come over and the mourning would go on continuously for at least a day and a night and usually a couple of days and nights. During the mourning period and sometimes for a few days afterward, the ghost might be encountered by those close to the deceased, although it was said this did not often happen. Such encounters were benevolent although often initially frightening.

One type of encounter occurred only between a ghost and members of the family or families it was from, and the family or families it had created (whether for the purpose of procreation or not). This encounter was said to be similar to the experience of encountering a live person's soul in an animal form, except that the encounter with a ghost in the form of a wild animal resulted in the animal's allowing itself to be killed and eaten, and by this means the ghost showed that it had no ill will. Women were rarely involved in such encounters, most of them occurring between brothers or a man and his son. Such encounters were rare and none of the members of Auyana had had one within the last generation or so.

A person's ghost might also guide the men setting out to revenge his death if the revenge attempt occurred soon after his death. This happened infrequently in the past and not at all during the time I was in Auyana due to the cessation of warfare. In the only firsthand account I have of this type of encounter, the revenge group set out one morning before sunrise in order to surround the enemy men's house and shoot someone as he came out in the morning. As the raiders left their hamlet, they heard clacking noises and rustling. At first they were unsure what the sounds were, and they thought it might be someone following them or someone in their group trying to join them. Eventually it was agreed that the sounds consistently came from slightly ahead of them and sounded like arrows banging together, and it was decided that the dead man's ghost was leading them in the dark. They decided to follow the ghost, as ghosts can see in the dark. The ghost took them to the enemy hamlet without being caught, and they were able to shoot and kill a man and flee home without injury.

Other encounters with ghosts during the mourning period or shortly thereafter occurred as part of the attempt to revenge the death. Revenge is discussed later. It is only necessary to mention here that revenge was sweetest when the killer was killed. But anyone in the killer's sovereignty would do, although the closer the victim was to the killer, the better. So, in order to revenge a death it was best to know the killer and necessary to know at least the sovereignty to which the killer belonged. Curers were one source of this information, but as they had been unsuccessful in curing the corpse, either they were unable to locate the assassin's equipment and had no idea who the assassin was or they knew some of the assassination attempts but did not know all of them, or even though they claimed they knew who was responsible, they were wrong.

Occasionally, a ghost would communicate through one of the women close to the dead person and name the sovereignty or the killer. This happened three times in the ten to fifteen year period just before the Australian conquest (1934-49). All three occurred near the end of the mourning. The women suddenly began shaking all over, much like curers when looking at an illness. In one case, the woman also danced around. Their eyes rolled back and at first people thought the women were being attacked by ghosts, but when they held the women and asked them what was happening the women said that the dead person had appeared to them and told them who the killer was. Shortly after telling this, they stopped shaking in each case, although they remained a little disoriented for a while.

Whenever a ghost spoke through a woman, its message was believed and acted on almost immediately. However, as mentioned above, ghosts rarely spoke this way. A killer's identity could be revealed in another way, which was also sporadic but immediately acted on when it occurred. When the killer or those in the killer's group came to look at the dead person and mourn, the corpse would move or urinate or defecate or make some noise as the killer approached, and especially as the killer touched the corpse while mourning. This did not occur in Auyana during the time I was there but it did occur in a neighboring sovereignty and resulted in a bow-and-arrow fight in which one person was killed. It was said that in the past, the killer would often not come to the mourning for fear of being revealed. So if a suspected person or group did not show up at the mourning, this was taken as pretty strong, although not certain, evidence that the suspect was guilty.

The killer might reveal himself, although this also did not happen often. If no revenge had been taken by the time the person was buried, the soul assassin might sneak to the grave at night and get some "liquid" from the dead person (graves were holes in the ground partially filled with leaves and grass, with planks put over the top). By performing certain secret operations on the liquid, the killer could then prevent anyone from discovering his identity. That is, he would render ineffective the main methods of finding him out, which are discussed below. To prevent this from happening, people sometimes kept watch at the grave for a few nights after the person was buried, hoping to catch the assassin.

Three ways were regularly used to double-check curers or make certain who the killer was. All were done secretly. The favorite method was to steal some sweet potato from the gardens of suspected sovereignties and/or killers. An equal portion was taken from each suspect's garden and a little of the dead person's hair was put with the portion, which was then wrapped in some leaves and cooked in an earth oven. The hair was added so that the ghost of the dead person would come and "hold" the bundle of the killer, thereby preventing the sweet potato from cooking. Another method was to wait until at some point in the mourning most everybody was asleep—usually late on the second night. The people close to the dead person took a long bamboo pole, stuck it up through the roof of the house the dead person was in, and tied a seed rattle on the end sticking outside the house. The other end was held near the dead person's head. Then the people close to the dead person held the pole down near the dead person and began calling off the name of suspected groups or people. When the killer's name was called, the dead person's ghost would grab the end sticking outside the house and shake it violently. It was said that sometimes people holding the pole were almost knocked down from the shaking. Although this technique was sometimes used by itself, it was usually used to double-check the method of cooking sweet potato, described above.

Another method was used only for double-checking and not often then. In this one, the people close to the dead person would arrange to meet at some place where they would not be detected by others, and cook an earth oven during the mourning. As mentioned earlier, after an earth oven was filled and covered, water was poured into it; when this water percolated down to the hot stones, it sometimes made popping sounds. The double-checking procedure called for some of the dead person's hair to be tied across the mouth of a bamboo tube full of water so that as the water was poured out it ran over the hair. The tube of water was held by the people close to the dead person, and they would call the name of the suspected killer and then pour some water. When the name of the killer was called, the ghost would cause the water to explode loudly as it hit the stones.

Once a ghost went to ghostland, it usually stayed there. It only returned to cause someone trouble in one of two ways. One was to attack a person's soul or body and try to kill the person; the other was to "shoot" little sticks, stones, or bones into the person. The latter caused the target area to become painful and/or swollen up. The cases I saw while there and the ones I heard described to me involved things like swollen knees, stiff shoulders, and stiff backs. It took a curer to remove objects that had been shot into someone by a ghost, but a single curer could do it using only tobacco and sucking. These remedies were applied on occasions when the curer was going to be around anyway rather than arranging a special time, as in taking a look at an illness.

Ghost attacks upon a person's soul or body were more serious. For example, I was standing outside my house one afternoon as some Auyana neighbors were returning from a distribution, and suddenly one of the older men became weak and short of breath and collapsed. His eyes rolled up, he grew pale, and finally he fainted. One of the Auyana curers was standing there and immediately diagnosed it as a ghost attack on the man's soul. He said later that he could smell the dead man's ghost. He immediately had someone get some ginger and chewed it up and spat it over the person, putting some in the man's mouth, for ghosts could not stand the smell of ginger and would leave. Shortly after this, the victim began to come around and soon regained consciousness. He was still extremely weak and did not recover for a long time. His slow recovery was not due to the ghost attack, however, but was later diagnosed as resulting from his soul having been shot by an assassin as he was returning from the distribution.

When a ghost attacked a person's soul, it grabbed the soul and tried to take it away to ghostland. This usually caused sudden collapse and/or unconsciousness, as in the above case. A ghost might also attack a person's body directly. I was sitting one evening in my house when I heard the middle-aged woman next door begin hollering, "Get away! Aiiiiiieeeeee get away!" There was a lot of banging and thrashing around in her house. This went on for a few minutes and then the curer who lived a few houses away hurried over and spat some ginger on her and, with others, held her near the fire. Eventually she became her usual self again. Once she became normal, the episode was finished and she was all right. In every other case of ghost attack on a person's body, the person seemed to recover rapidly and the attack did not have any lasting effects. Unlike when a ghost attacked the soul, a person whose body was being attacked usually remained conscious and sometimes fought back against the ghost.

One day I was sitting with a group of men discussing ghosts, and I asked them to describe all the ghost attacks they knew of on the present members of Auyana. It was said, and the cases I collected confirmed this, that ghosts attacked only those with whom they had lived and cooperated. Apparently, in Auyana your enemies killed you while they were alive and your friends killed you after they were dead. Eight of the present members of Auyana had been attacked by a ghost. One of them had been attacked four times, two of them had been attacked twice, and the remaining five had been attacked only once. One attack was by a co-wife, two were by dead husbands, and the rest were by members of the person's subpooling unit (see Chapter 2).

Each individual soul was, in a sense, an individual manifestation of the collective soul of its sovereignty. Each sovereignty had a specific plant or animal, called a *upaema*. The *upaema* was said to be the soul of every member of the sovereignty and I will translate the term as "collective soul." When a member of Auyana died, the individual soul joined or merged back into the collective soul before separating again and going on to ghostland. Interestingly enough, births did not involve a similar process in reverse— that is, an individual soul being separated from the collective soul to emerge as an individual human being.

The merging of a dead person's soul with the collective soul might be evidenced by some unusual action on the part of the collective soul. If the collective soul were in the form of an animal, it normally kept itself hidden. When the dead person's soul merged with it, the animal might then show itself to someone in the dead person's sovereignty. For example, the Auyana collective soul was a tree python which lived underground inside a tunnel that opened near a couple of large boulders located more or less in the center of the original Auyana territory. If someone in Auyana died, the python might come up out of its hole, at least far enough to be seen. If the collective soul were in the form of a plant, then as the dead person's soul merged with it, a limb might break off or it might sway strongly as if blown by a strong wind. Such unusual actions by the collective soul were interpreted as the dead person showing himself or herself to friends for one last time. The collective soul might also show itself if the person was very sick, and this would be taken as a premonition that the sick person was dying, a premonition almost identical to that of an encounter with an individual's soul in the form of some animal.

It was said that in the past the Auyana python used to show itself more, because in the past there were *really* important men. The only case of the python showing itself in the last two generations involved an important man in his early thirties who was sick. The man who saw the python, "K," was in his late fifties or early sixties in 1962, and he had seen the python when he was in his late twenties or early thirties. The sick man was the same age as K and a close friend as well as being in the same subpooling unit. According to K:

> I was sitting behind the sick man holding him and I went to sleep. I dreamed he came and talked to me and told me he had gone inside the python's hole and he would make the python come out and I could go and see him. When I awoke, I told the sick person and he said to go take a look. So, I took his wife with me so others wouldn't say I was lying and went to the python's home. As I got close to the hole, the python came out and held itself upright. It was as big as a pole used to climb up on to tend bananas [about eight feet tall and four inches in diameter] and was the color of your book [blue]. It waved its head back and forth and ran its tongue in and out. The sick man's wife was frightened, but I wasn't and I told her not to be, as it was the *upaema* of Auyana and we had come to see it. The python was pleased with me and wagged its tail back and forth. Then it turned around and went back in the hole. I had made friends with it by putting some of the leaves used to cool soul assassinations on it and saying, "Before, everybody used to talk about you, but I had never seen you. Now I have seen you." This was so it would be pleased with me and not give me bad dreams. After the python went back into the hole, we went back to the sick man. As I was telling the sick man the story, he died.

The fear of seeing the python was the fear of confronting something immensely powerful, even if it was supposedly on your side and your friend. The python was "hot" and just as a fire destroys a piece of wood, so might the python destroy a person. For the collective soul was not only hot but was the source of the killing power of the men of the sovereignty, and the one or two best warriors were referred to as the community's *upaema*.

As mentioned above, the Auyana python's dwelling opened out into the tame world through a hole. It was said that a member of Auyana could kill those in other sovereignties by taking the debris from the area immediately around the opening and placing it on the trails and in the house of an enemy sovereignty. This would cause many to get sick and die. While no one knew of any cases of this having been done during their lifetime, they had heard of such cases and there was always the possibility it might be done again. From this and the seriousness with which I was told about it, I gathered that this destructive power of the collective soul was taken literally by the members of Auyana. In any case, the use of the collective soul's destructive power was risky and could kill the person using it. The person who went to collect the debris had to be an initiated male, be a "true" member of Auyana, know certain songs and sing them exactly correctly, and take pig fat and certain leaves for cooling. He also had to have no fear. The one condition which could be relaxed was that of being a member of Auyana. It was said that a man who could approach the collective soul could teach his real sister's son to do the same. But she had to be married into a friendly neighboring sovereignty and had to be really friendly with her brother. This happened infrequently, and I heard of only one case in Auyana over the last generation.

An individual soul assassin ran much the same risk as someone approaching a collective soul. A person had to be very cautious when first learning to assassinate souls or the energy might double back and kill him. One man explained that he did not mess around with soul assassination, because it once had almost killed him. He had been young and had gone on a trading party. While in another place which presumably had hot equipment, he traded for one of the basketlike devices to shoot a person's soul. On the way back home he somewhat jokingly thought he would try it and shot a tree. Nothing happened to the tree and he must have done something wrong because shortly after he got home he got sick and when the curers took a look they asked him if he had been messing around with soul assassination, and when he said yes they told him that he had only made himself sick doing it.

After a man had put the debris from the collective soul on the trail and returned home, it was necessary for him and those in his hamlet to cook and eat some pig together and to drink water out of a bamboo tube with certain leaves stuffed in its mouth in order to cool off the collective soul's destructive energy towards them. This was just the reverse of the procedure of an individual soul assassin, who made himself hot in order to further the working of the destructive energy he had initiated. The collective soul was also dangerous independent of the human use of it. If a nonmember of Auyana was to go close (how close was negotiable) to the area where the python lived, he or she would become seriously ill, and if the person were so unfortunate as to see the snake, he or she might even die unless members of Auyana performed a special ritual. Accordingly, everyone knew where the collective souls of nearby sovereignties were located and avoided these areas, especially those in enemy sovereignties. People had less knowledge about the collective souls of more distant sovereignties, partly because this knowledge was not necessary, as it was extremely unlikely they would ever be walking around alone in these sovereignties' territories.

The members of a sovereignty were physically identified with their collective soul. Each collective soul had a story concerning its activities "before now," before Auyana had a history (i.e., a myth, *mani'e*). In the myth about the Auyana tree python, the python at one point fell into a fire and was burned. Members of Auyana said that they frequently did the same thing and pointed to this as evidence of their identity with the python. Members of other sovereignties were said to have similar relationships to their collective souls, but I never checked this. Another aspect of the identification between a collective soul and the members of a sovereignty was that there were no food demands, unlike in the case of a plant or animal manifestation of an individual's soul. For example, members of Auyana said they were free to eat pythons if they ever caught one. Nor was any special behavior of any sort demanded with reference to pythons in general. While individuals had demands made on them with respect to *classes* of living plants or animals through their *individual* souls, classes of individuals (i.e., sovereignties) had demands made on them with respect to a *specific* plant or animal through their *collective* soul.

The Auyana relationship to its *upaema* was very similar to that of the Lakalai of New Britain to certain animals (Valentine 1965). However, unlike the Lakalai, the Auyana collective soul could also be referred to by a term meaning roughly "ancestor." As will be discussed when considering groups, the claim to have a certain collective soul was transmitted by social and biological parenthood through males. Despite this and the reference to the collective soul as an "ancestor," the members of Auyana said they were not children of males who were children of males who were descended from the collective soul. Nor were they children of anyone who was a child of the *upaema*. In the strictest sense then, members of Auyana would not claim they were biological descendents of the collective soul. Nor were they created by their collective soul as some of their neighbors claimed to be created by certain deities (Berndt 1962). Yet they in some sense "came from" their collective soul. The vagueness of this sense also existed in the Auyana conceptualization of the origin of the various sovereignties speaking the same language.

So far I have been talking about collective souls as though each sovereignty had only one. However, this was not true. Based on a survey of the members of Opoimpina regarding their collective souls, I came to the following conclusions concerning the location and number of collective souls for each sovereignty. Sovereignties such as Auyana, whose members did not know when the sovereignty was established (that is, the sovereignty had been established for a long time), had one collective soul located somewhere on their territory. If a sovereignty split into two or more sovereignties, one of the new sovereignties would have the original collective soul on its territory. The other sovereignty or sovereignties would for a period of time continue to claim the original collective soul as their collective soul even though it was not on their new territory. At some point, they would claim a new collective soul as well, and for some period of time would have two collective souls. Eventually, as memory of the founding of the sovereignty was lost, the original collective soul would no longer be claimed, and members would claim the collective soul on their territory as their only collective soul. The same process occurred if a sovereignty did not split, but for some reason moved to a new territory: at first, the members would claim only the original collective soul; eventually, they would claim both it and a new one; and finally, they would claim only the new collective soul. If having the same collective soul meant a common origin, then it is interesting that in the myth about the Auyana python, the python was killed by his wife near the end of the story, and his mother put him in a net bag and took him with her as she went looking to find someone to marry. First, she went to Uwara' (Tairora) and was told, "No, your skin is wrinkled and you smell. You're too old." Then she went to Tawaina in Anepa' (Awa) and was told the same thing. Finally, she went to Eyakia in Anepa' (Awa), where an old man agreed to marry her and she hung up the net bag in which she carried the python. The net bag was supposedly still there in 1962. All these areas are ones speaking languages related to Auyana and all were important trade avenues for members of Auyana.

Many personages appeared in the myths, but collective souls were the only ones with a place to live, which is why they were the only ones to continue living until the present. The other myth figures were said to have existed "before" but to be alive no longer. This implies to me that having a territory was a necessary condition for continued existence, especially for the continued existence of groups (Berndt 1962). Collective souls and groups appeared to remain immortal as long as they could hold onto their territory. Members of Auyana said that unless they were strong they would be driven from their territory by enemies and then would eventually no longer exist as a sovereignty. When a group died, its collective soul did not go to ghostland, nor were there any collective souls in ghostland.

The collective soul was also related to a sovereignty's territorial boundaries. In the myth of the Auyana python, the python traveled to other sovereignties to attend all-night dances and the Auyana boundaries were delineated by the points at which it rested or did something as it returned and by some of the trails it took. However, the boundary laid out in the myth did not include all the territory that members of Auyana were claiming in 1962. Initially, the members of Auyana claimed to have been given the extra land "free" or claimed they were only using it temporarily. I eventually found out that part of the land not included in the myth had been won through intensive fighting which resulted in one of the traditional Auyana enemies' moving farther away from Auyana and no longer using a section of land. Another part was acquired through gradual encroachment into the adjacent forest of a friendly group which, it was said, was becoming less friendly as a result of this encroachment and other controversies with those in Auyana.

In addition to the present use of territory which lay outside mythological boundaries, the boundaries themselves were not in fact as precise as the myth would imply. The boundaries stated in the myth were trails or a series of spots where something had been done by one of the myth actors connected by an imaginary line. The contemporary boundaries were zones of varying widths, the width seeming to be inversely related to competing claims for the use of the land, especially its use for gardening. In the mythological presentation, then, each sovereignty had a territory bounded by a clearly marked zone no wider than a path. In the contemporary scene, each sovereignty had a territory with a clearly agreed upon focus, but with a boundary of varying width surrounding it. In this sense, each sovereignty's territory was being continually negotiated. The consequent expansion and contraction of territory did not seem to negate a group's claim to still be living on their mythological territory, as long as they maintained control of the focal area.

The last personages in the Auyana world to be discussed here were also referred to as *upaema*. Although they bore the same name as a collective soul, they were said to be different. A collective soul was not an *apa'wasi* (wild thing) whereas these *upaema* were. I translated their name as meaning "spirits" and although that does not seem to be quite right, I will adopt it. These spirits were an old man and a middle-aged woman with a child who lived in separate places close to one another in a locale said to be the general area from which all those in A, K, and R on Map 6 came, although it was denied that they had all ever been one sovereignty. Within the three collectivities, the woman and old man "appeared" at dances and male initiations, which centered around, and were controlled by, males. I was told by men when I asked whether the old man and woman belonged to any sovereignty that they belonged to all the *men* in every sovereignty in A, K, and R. The woman and old man could not be seen; rather they were heard. The woman sounded like a pair of flutes each blown alternately; her child sounded like a squealing rat. The old man's sound resembled a bull-roarer. It was said that the old woman made her sound because the men were holding her and doing things with her, not good things either. Her child was crying because it was hungry and could not nurse. The old man just made his sound. If an uninitiated male or a female were to encounter either of the spirits, he or she would die. All of the spirits appeared at male initiations, but only the woman appeared at dances.

In summary, I would like to consider some of the distinctions between the wide anthropomorphs (mud men, ghosts, and spirits) and the collective

souls, which were not wild and not anthropomorphs. The wild anthropomorphs were mobile within and between sovereignties, whereas the collective souls were not. The Auyana python might come up out of its hole, but it
never left that spot. The wild anthropomorphs had no power to confer on
members of a sovereignty in their struggle against other sovereignties, nor
did the wild anthropomorphs independently act on behalf of a sovereignty
against other sovereignties, whereas collective souls conferred power. While
a ghost obviously had to be from a sovereignty, it would not in any way represent that sovereignty against outsiders, even when leading a raiding party
to revenge its (the ghost's) creation. Such assistance was a personal affair for
the ghost and it did not help on other raiding parties. Further, the ghost did
not even attack anyone in the enemy sovereignty. I mentioned earlier that a
distinguishing feature of wild things was that they did not "listen," that is,
they were not responsive to demands of others. Considering the above discussion, I would suggest that in particular they did not recognize territorial
boundaries nor demands for mutual defense and aid, whereas collective
souls did. Wild things only caused trouble for those living near them, and
this was true of humans as well when they became "wild."

MAKING A LIVING

I will begin this section with a discussion of diet in Auyana, then consider
the production of food, and then the use of other items in the material environment. The "material environment" was not an Auyana division but is one
I am using here for convenience. Members of Auyana had no category that
corresponded closely with the anthropological usage of "material" in the
sense of *materiel* rather than material/immaterial. They did make the latter
distinction, although without the occupational boundaries associated with its
usage here.

I made an estimate of diet by keeping rough track of the food eaten by five
families for 240 days of the first year I was in Auyana. Family 1 was that of an
important man's eldest wife. Sometimes, a ten-to-twelve-year-old girl ate
with her and sometimes her husband ate with her. She was in her late twenties. Family 2 was comprised of a middle-aged man of some importance, his
wife, a six-year-old son, a twelve-year-old daughter, and an eighteen-year-
old daughter. The oldest daughter did not eat at home regularly. Family 3
included a middle-aged man of little importance who had moved into Auyana from a foreign group, his wife, who was from Auyana, and their two
boys, one about seven and the other two. Family 4 was made up of an older,
very important man, his wife, and their ten-year-old daughter. Family 5 included a very important middle-aged man, his wife, and two boys, one about
twelve and the other about six.

Each day in the late afternoon or evening as family members returned
home and food was brought up from the gardens, usually by the wives, I

went to each family and by counting and guessing based on my experience of weighing vegetables to buy, I made estimates of the amount of food brought in. I asked about how the food was used and whether any other food had been eaten elsewhere during the day. My main purpose in this endeavor was to get a reasonable idea of the consumption of animal protein. As it turned out, this was fairly easy. Unless stolen, pigs were eaten after having been distributed at a public gathering, and by asking around I was able to go to most of the distributions attended by any of the families. Even if I could not go, the pig was almost always brought home and eaten there, so I saw almost all the pig eaten by members of these families. Other than pigs, dogs were eaten, but only two were killed while I was there. Chicken was sometimes eaten by a family at home, but this was such a special occasion that it would be known. Food provided through hunting was also something that would be quickly mentioned. A hunter returning home with an animal hung on the end of a long pole would sometimes parade through the hamlets, carrying the pole casually over one shoulder so that the game swung around. One young man swaggered so grossly that people laughed at him and mocked him behind his back because of his insistence that everyone notice whenever he did anything "great." In any case, all sources of animal protein, including bugs, were special enough that I think I was able to record all the times when the five families got animal protein, if not the exact quantities. Table 2 presents these data. When it says, for example, "2/rats," this means there were two times they ate some rats, not two rats eaten.

I have divided vegetables into those eaten almost every day, those eaten occasionally, and those not eaten often, either because they were seasonal or just not preferred. Two vegetables were eaten regularly: sweet potato and greens. Beans and a short succulent cane (*pitpit*) were eaten fairly regularly. Table 3 provides estimates of the average daily amounts of these four vegetables eaten by each family. A family that ate an average of one-half pound of beans a day probably ate a pound or pound and a half of beans every two or three days. The same is true of cane stalks.

Corn was also eaten fairly often, about once a week on the average, and the families ranged from averaging about one ear to three ears per day. Corn was a crop introduced by Europeans about ten years earlier, although members of Auyana had only begun planting a lot of it within the last three to four years. Bananas and cucumbers were eaten maybe once every couple of weeks, one family's banana consumption averaging from a pound and a half to ten pounds every two weeks, and cucumbers averaging from about a pound to five pounds every two weeks. A variety of other plants were eaten only occasionally. Yams and taro, for instance, were eaten almost exclusively at special occasions, such as marriages or dances—anytime guests were invited. Sugar cane was the same, except that it was eaten even less often than yams or taro. Bean tubers (*as bin*) and pandanus nuts were seasonal, and several pounds of the former and a few pounds of the latter were eaten in

TABLE 2
PROTEIN CONSUMPTION

|  | Number of Times per Type of Protein | Total Quantities |
|---|---|---|
| Family 1 | 11/pig meat | 30-40 lbs. |
|  | 3/pig innards | ca. 5 lbs. |
| Family 2 | 16/pig meat | 55-65 lbs. |
|  | 2/pig innards | ca. 3 lbs. |
|  | 2/marsupials | 16 lbs. |
|  | 2/rats | 7 lbs. |
|  | 1/canned fish | 2 lbs. |
|  | 1/grasshoppers | couple of handfuls |
|  | 2/frogs | about 10 each time |
| Family 3 | 15/pig meat | 40-45 lbs. |
|  | 3/pig innards | ca. 5 lbs. |
|  | 1/marsupial | ca. 8 lbs. |
|  | 2/canned fish | 3 lbs. |
| Family 4 | 14/pig meat | 50-55 lbs. |
|  | 3/pig innards | ca. 5 lbs. |
|  | 2/rats | ca. 10 lbs. |
|  | 2/canned fish | 4 lbs. |
| Family 5 | 17/pig meat | 50-60 lbs. |
|  | 1/pig innards | ca. 1 lb. |
|  | 5/canned fish | ca. 20 lbs. |
|  | 3/chicken | ca. 10 lbs. |
|  | 1/wild bird | ca. 1-2 lbs. |
|  | 1/marsupial | ca. 5 lbs. |

TABLE 3
VEGETABLE CONSUMPTION

|  | Sweet potato (Lbs.) | Greens (Lbs.) | Beans (Lbs.) | Cane Stalks (Number) |
|---|---|---|---|---|
| Family 1 | 20 | 1.1 | .5 | 6.4 |
| Family 2 | 16.5 | .5 | .5 | 4.4 |
| Family 3 | 13.7 | .8 | .4 | 3.6 |
| Family 4 | 18.3 | 2.1 | .3 | 6.0 |
| Family 5 | 17.4 | .8 | .3 | 3.4 |

season. Peas, cabbage, bamboo, tomato, peanuts, squash, scallions, and tapioca were just not eaten much.

Food was prepared in several ways. If it was cooked inside a house, it would be cooked at the central hearth. Anything which had a tough skin on it such as tubers or corn, might be stuck in the ashes. Insects and some nuts were roasted on sticks over the flame. Greens, sometimes mixed with sweet potatoes, yams, taro, peanuts, or onions might be stuffed into a bamboo tube and roasted at the edge of the fire. Sometimes sweet potatoes (and the rare chicken) were boiled in a pot or tin can. Prior to European contact, members of Auyana traded to the north for clay pots with pointed bottoms which could be stuck into the ashes. However, these were seldom used, just as boiling was not a common practice during the time I was there. If food was cooked outside the house, it might be cooked by several families gathering around a firepit and employing the same techniques as were used inside a house. Or the food might be cooked in an earth oven. If a gathering of people involved more than just a couple of friendly families eating together, an earth oven was always prepared. Oftentimes, when a pig was being cooked in an earth oven, it would be boned and laid over the vegetables. As it cooked, the fat would run over the vegetables, cooking and flavoring them. Sweet potatoes were especially delicious cooked this way, and, in general, eating from an earth oven at a public gathering seemed to make the food more delicious and the company friendlier.

Hollowed logs were also occasionally used as containers in an earth oven. They were stood upright on the hot stones (or hot stones were dropped into them) and the food was placed on top of grass, banana leaves, etc., which were laid over the stones. More grass was then stuffed in the top of the log, followed by a layer of dirt to seal it, and water was poured into it. In the past, bamboo knives were used for cutting, a cassowary bone for gouging, a spiny stem for grinding the tubers into paste (this was rarely done except for bananas), and hands for everything else in the preparation and consumption of food. Women were responsible for most food preparation. Men prepared the stones for the earth ovens and helped cover and open them. Men also sometimes cooked for themselves at home or at special gatherings restricted to men. Women did the rest.

Food played a part in many situations in Auyana other than just eating at home. Compared to my experience in white lower-middle-class America, there were many more occasions in Auyana in which people ate together. Especially notable were the many occasions when a group got together, invited other people over, fed them, and gave them something to take back with them. An earth oven almost always indicated that this was happening, although occasionally it meant that some neighbors were just eating together. I tried to record all the instances of earth ovens in Auyana in 1962 after about the first month I was there. I recorded a total of ninety-three occasions when an earth oven was made (some of the occasions had two or three earth ovens at once). Fourteen of these were neighbors getting together to eat, and seventy-nine of them were the sort described above. I did not try to find out all the times members of Auyana went outside Auyana and were fed and given gifts, but I heard about twenty-seven such occasions.

An earth oven was itself a display of food. The size and number of earth ovens being prepared immediately gave information about quantity; and when they were opened and distributed, the quality and variety of food was easily seen. The more special the guests, the greater the concern with quantity, quality, and variety (especially in the sense of desirable but seldom-eaten food). These three attributes were said to be important when preparing food for any guest, and the definition of a guest as more or less special was at least partly made through the amount of energy the host put into preparing the guest's food. Special foods were ones that were desired but in scarce supply—yams, taro, sugar cane, bananas, bean tubers, and especially pig or any animal protein. In addition, these foods also had particular symbolic signficance in certain contexts. Sweet potatoes, greens, and cane stalks were eaten in almost all contexts and hence had no particular importance except generally signaling that people had gathered together. However, all the foods, except for sweet potatoes, had mythological origins, regardless of whether they were special foods or not.

The first type of food production I will consider is gardening. Vegetables were grown in fenced gardens planted on fairly steep slopes. Individual gardens were planted next to one another with one large fence surrounding a large number of them. By individual garden I mean a continuous plot of land whose use was controlled by a single person, if unmarried, or by a husband and his wife or wives. If a man had more than one wife and his wives were using a continuous plot of land, the plot could be referred to as *imbola kisau* (one garden), although it would be subdivided, with each wife using a separate section. However, each wife's section could also be referred to as her *kisau*. The area gardened within a single fence was also referred to as a *kisau* in the sense that it could be referred to as "our" *kisau*, "this" *kisau*, "such and such hamlet's" *kisau*. I never heard such a plot referred to as "one" *kisau*, although I never asked whether it could be referred to that way so I do not know for sure. I will use the phrase "collective garden" to refer to a plot of land within a single fence being used by a number of families, although as the definition of an individual garden implies, families only rarely and with certain crops planted plots of land together, jointly harvesting and dividing the products.

Each plot of land was cleared—using fire, stone adzes, dibble sticks, and bamboo knives—planted, left fallow, cleared again, and so on until the plot was covered with grass. At that point, the land would eventually be abandoned because it was thought to be relatively worthless. Through burning, a grass climax was maintained (Robbins 1962). Most families had at least one garden made from cleared virgin forest. Because of this and the ease in getting raw materials from the forest, hamlets were usually located near the edge of the virgin forest with an expanse of grassland comprising the remainder of the landscape. Hamlets were comprised of one or two men's houses with individual houses for their wives strung along a ridge sloping away from the men's houses. Prior to the arrival of the Australians, there were, at any one time, only three or four such hamlets in Auyana. The eight shown on Map 5 are post-contact phenomena.

The region was generally favorable to horticulture. The slopes were not steep enough for erosion or slippage to constitute a major problem. Every garden had a drainage ditch around it in order to prevent runoff from the slope above from eroding the garden. However, drainage ditches within a garden were used only to facilitate drainage, not to control erosion. Similarly, contouring was never used. The temperature was normally in the seventies to eighties, fahrenheit, during the day and in the fifties at night. It sometimes got cooler, but frost never occurred. Rainfall during the two years I was there amounted to eighty to ninety inches per year. Although there was a wet and a dry season, these were not markedly distinct. Periods of rain occurred during what was considered the dry season and, similarly, there were periods of no rain at all during the wet season. The records of the government agricultural station at Aiyura (near Kainantu) show that during any single year, the amount of rain during what is presumably the dry season may be as great as the amount falling in another year during what is presumably the wet season. Members of Auyana said they had never had widespread loss of crops due to a drought or especially heavy rainfall.

If a garden was to be made from land with only grass or small shrubs on it, the first step was to set the vegetation on fire. If the plot was away from houses and gardens so that the fire did not have to be controlled but could be allowed to burn itself out, usually along the crest of a ridge unless there had been an extremely long dry spell, the firing could be done anytime after the area had become hot and dry enough to burn. Otherwise, the firing would have to be done when things were dry enough to burn but not so dry that the fire could not be controlled by clearing away some of the vegetation and, if necessary, beating at it with leafy branches. While I was there, on two occasions fires on plots near a hamlet got close enough to the houses to cause a general mobilization of anyone around to beat out the fire. I took it this was not unusual.

If a garden was to be made from primary or secondary forest, the first step was to cut out the undergrowth and then the forest. As mentioned earlier, by 1962 everyone owned or had access to steel axes and machetes and no one used a stone adze. In the gardens I saw cleared with steel tools, all the undergrowth was chopped out, with roots left unless they could be pulled out by hand. Trees up to approximately eight inches in diameter were chopped down. Trees larger than that, and especially trees of extra hard wood such as mahogany and ironwood, were treated in various ways. The basic choice was whether to chop them down or leave them standing. If it was decided that it was unnecessary or just too much work to chop them down, they would be girdled and enough of their branches chopped off to let sunlight through. Some of the felled trees were split into staves and used to make a fence around the garden. Before white contact, trees were split by using an extra-large adze to get a crack started and then jamming two sharpened poles into the crack and prying them in opposite directions. After the log had been split into staves, the staves were cut to the desired length. Ones to be used as vertical uprights were sharpened at both ends.

The most common fence consisted of a pair of pointed vertical staves jammed into the ground about five to six feet from each other with the members of each pair about three to four inches apart. Horizontal staves were then laid down and the vertical staves were lashed together, usually in the middle and at the top. Fences were about three to four feet high. Another type of fence which was less sturdy but could be made much faster was constructed by simply jamming pointed staves into the ground adjacent to one another and then lashing a vine around the top to hold them together. However, this type of fence would not keep out determined pigs and was seldom used. All fences had stiles at places where trails crossed them or where a person entered the garden. One type of stile was comprised of one or more flat-topped poles jammed into the ground to make crude steps. This was not used much, as pigs could also use the steps. The most frequent stile was a Y-shaped branch which was leaned against the fence, and sometimes simply a straight branch was used.

When making a collective garden, each man was responsible for the section of the fence bordering his garden. As this implies, there were rarely plots which did not border on a fence, and men rarely failed to make their section and keep it repaired, even though making fences was hard work and to be avoided if possible. For example, fences were not built along the edges of any sharp drop-offs and oftentimes not along streams running along the lower part of an area. In the latter case, instead of a stave fence, logs were piled on top of one another braced by stumps or whatever was available. But making a fence was usually necessary and usually well done, the fences lasting for the life of a garden without requiring much repair.

Men did all the clearing of trees and fence-building and almost all the clearing of undergrowth. Adolescent unmarried males sometimes helped a married man, especially by climbing trees and topping off branches, as this was particularly hard and dangerous work. A son would usually help his father, especially if asked to, and sometimes an adolescent would help his older brother. Adolescents might also get together in work teams, as described below. Unmarried adolescent males practically never made gardens for themselves. For example, in 1962, only two small gardens belonged to adolescent males. Young married men usually had no help in clearing the forest or building fences. Rather, like adolescents, they gave help to older men, sometimes as part of work teams. Two or three young married men and sometimes a rare adolescent might get together and help an older man with whom they were closely affiliated, either at his request or on their own. Such help was said to vary a lot, with some men getting practically no help this way and others getting it regularly. There was no demand for any specific goods or services in return for this kind of help.

Another work team consisted of a man's "in-laws"—usually the members of his wife's natal subpooling unit—who would come to his place and help him for a day or, sometimes, a couple of days. Both older and younger men came, with the younger men doing most of the work and the older men visiting with their in-laws and others they knew. A man might make a request for help or his in-laws might volunteer to help. In either case, the help had to be agreed on beforehand and arranged for a given time, because such help established an obligation for specific goods in return. The host was expected to feed his guest-helpers, whose wives usually came with them, if they were friends of the host or his wife, and helped the host's wife to prepare the food. If possible, the host would kill a pig and give it to the helpers when they finished helping him. Sometimes, the host might have a lot of some special vegetables and would give these instead of pig to the helpers.

Another kind of work team was generated when a man made it known that he needed help from those "close" to him. He might make this known by word of mouth and/or standing at the edge of his hamlet some morning or evening and hollering that he was going to make a garden and would be pleased if those close to him would help him. This kind of request was not made often. During the two years I was there, almost every man cleared some virgin forest. A public request for help was made by only five men. Those who responded to the request were mostly younger married men and adolescents, and the bulk of their aid consisted of climbing trees and trimming branches. The five men who requested this aid were all important men in the community and all received aid.

In a garden made from grass or an area covered with shrubs which could be burnt, the fence was made after the area had been burnt. Following the completion of the fence, the area could be prepared and planted a section at a time. This was true also of gardens made from forest. However, in this case, the fence was usually finished before even the clearing had been completed. For example, in one collective garden made out of forest some sections inside the fence had been planted for several years and had no trees left on them, whereas others were still covered with primary forest. As one part of a plot was cleared and the branches and debris were piled, a man would start clearing another part, returning to the earlier cleared section to burn the piles when they had dried. After the burning, a man's wife, helped usually by her daughters, came to dig out the surface roots and clear off any remaining litter. Fires were sometimes started in big stumps or trees in order to speed their removal. Depending on what was to be planted and how much, a man might help his wife with the roots or he might go on clearing and piling.

When a forest was initially cleared, no attempt was made to remove all the roots. Rather, the ones which could be gotten by pulling or chopping were taken out and the rest left to rot. This meant that tubers were not usually planted initially in a garden made from forest. It was said, and a rough survey I made of all the gardens in 1962 confirmed it, that greens, succulent cane, beans, corn, and sugar cane were planted in a garden made from forest, and as the roots rotted and the soil was worked enough, sweet potatoes or other tubers were planted. The one exception to this was taro, which might be planted right away in a damp area because such areas might dry out as the forest was fully cleared and opened to the sun.

Greens and succulent cane were said to grow best when the soil was moist and they were not exposed to the full sun all day. Hence, as a plot of land was used and became fully exposed to the sun, fewer and fewer greens and succulent cane was planted. After several years of use, it was said that not only greens and succulents grew less well, but almost everything except bananas, yams, and sweet potatoes began growing less well. Because not many yams were grown (and when they were, they were usually grown in a separate plot mixed with beans), eventually most plots were planted almost entirely in sweet potatoes with some bananas.

Considering only the variables mentioned so far, the optimum condition for gardening would be to have one or more plots recently made out of forest and one or more plots either made from a grass-covered area or which had been in use for several years. In the garden survey mentioned earlier, I ended up documenting complete records for fifty-one of the married men in Auyana. Of these fifty-one, thirty-seven had at least one plot made recently enough from forest that it was still classified as a "forest garden" (*umi 'kisau*). Five other men had plots made originally out of forest but used long enough that they were in between being a forest garden and just a garden. Of those forty-two men who either had a forest garden or a transitional garden, thirty had just one such plot. Eight of them had two such plots, three of them had three such plots, and one of them had four forest gardens. Another consideration in gardening was availability of the plot. People generally preferred to have at least one plot close to their home so on rainy days or days when they did not feel like it, they would not have to go far to get food. People also liked to have bananas as close to the hamlet as possible, and would grow them next to the house in order to ward off fruit bats and theft. Tobacco was also grown close to the hamlets or next to the house for convenience and to avoid theft.

Another set of considerations had to do with soil conditions. In the discussion of forest gardens, I mentioned that the moisture content of the soil was taken into account. "Moisture content" is only an inexact gloss. The term used was one which was translated into pidgin as "grease" and was the term also used to refer to the oils in oily skin and to the oil gotten from animal fat. Members of Auyana said that oil in the soil was a result of decomposed leaves and the dampness in the forest, which was why soil with a grass climax had less oil. At the same time, a number of plots made from grass climax were growing beautifully and when I asked why, I was told it was because that land had oil. I was told that you could not always tell whether a plot of land had oil until after you had tried planting something there. This was why people would sometimes plant small trial plots just to see how things would grow.

Soil was also classified into three categories based at least partly on color. The Auyana color lexicon had three terms: white, black, and red. Two of the soils were referred to by the terms for white and black. The other soil was not referred to by the term for red, but it was always translated into pidgin as "red ground," and the soils I saw labeled this way were varying shades of red. At the same time these types of soil were not just color-coded but were differentiated in other ways as well. White soil was said to have a lot of small stones in it, and I found this to be true in the garden survey. Black soil and red soil were said to have fewer stones. However, red soil was usually *ak-ari'e*, which seemed to correspond to our concept of clay; and the red soil in Auyana would turn into straight gumbo clay if it was rained on for a while without adequate drainage (as happened around houses). Black soil was said to have a lot of oil, but no stones; it was not clayey and was considered the best soil. A lot of this soil was said to be in Fore and Tairora, but not much in Auyana and the neighboring area. I do not know about the area close to Auyana except that superficially it appeared to be made up of much the same soil as Auyana, mostly white soil and red soil with just a few patches of black soil.

The choice of a garden plot also depended on the availability of land. Initially, I was told that if land had never been gardened or had been gardened and left fallow for a long time then anyone in Auyana could use it. As it turned out, those living closest to such land had the first claim, especially on virgin forest. If land had been gardened and not left fallow a long time, the land belonged to the previous user's son. If his children were from different wives, then each son could claim the part his mother gardened. When making the garden survey, I recorded the history of use of the plot as told by the present user. This history did not always coincide with other accounts, but I did not attempt to collect information necessary to say anything definitive about the discrepancies. What data I have I will present here and suggest some of the variables I think were operating. My impression is that most discrepancies were the kind where the present user was claiming his father (or his father's father) had cleared the land and first planted it, and someone else was claiming that his father first cleared it and the present user's father only used it after it had been cleared. Because a man did not always use his father's land, such competing claims were sometimes generated.

I recorded 191 individual gardens within Auyana. Of these, 74 were from either virgin forest or land that had not been gardened in a long time or land adjacent to a house (the latter was treated like the other two as far as claims to garden it). Gardens made from land which had been previously gardened by someone else numbered 117. Of these, 90 were made without the user consulting anyone. Rather, the user let it be known he was going to garden a certain area and then if he met no resistence he went ahead with it. Occasionally, someone went ahead with it even if he was criticized for doing so. Of these 90 cases, in 43 of them the land had been transmitted from father to son or the original user had been close to the present user's father and had helped sponsor the present user. In the remaining 47 cases there were no agnatic claims at all to the land. The claims that were made varied a lot and for many of them I have only superficial data. Some claims were made when a man used land cleared by his wife's father or brother. Others were made through his mother's father or brother, or by just claiming to be close to the original user or his sons. Some claimants would even say they only planned to use the land for a little bit and then were going to relinquish it to whoever had agnatic claims.

Of the nonagnatic claims, only those made through a wife or a mother were ever said to have the possibility of being passed on to the user's sons. This possibility existed only if the person who could claim the land agnatically felt friendly toward the users because he was related to them through a woman (Strathern 1969). However, I found no cases in which it was said that the present user's father had gotten the land originally through a female. I believe this means that if a man made a claim through his wife or mother and then continued using that land for the rest of his life until his son took it over and no one else ever used it during that time, then his son either would not know or would "forget" that the land had been gotten by his father through a female. Of course, it could simply mean that claims made through females were not passed on to a man's sons but reverted to agnatic ownership. I do not have the data to resolve this question for, as mentioned earlier, my histories came from the present users and were not checked with others. Inasmuch as different people's accounts conflicted in some instances and the initial information I received was frequently different from the data I later collected, especially where the division of valuable resources was involved, there is good reason to believe that the information provided by current land users was only suggestive of the actual state of affairs.

Returning to the question of the consideration entering into where and how to garden, several things were obviously taken into account. I never worked intensely enough with anyone to find out how a person went about making choices. I do know that there were only three men who had only one plot of land, and one important middle-aged man had twelve plots. Having a lot of plots did not necessarily mean having a lot of land, but it did mean having different kinds of land in different areas, and this might have been important in trying to maximize the production of different crops. Once the land was cleared and burned, a man's wife, and sometimes his unmarried daughters, would remove whatever live material and debris they could and turn over the soil with a digging stick. Ditches were dug around the outer edge of a gardened area within a single fence in order to take care of runoff from above. Initially, cultivation was somewhat superficial. As the garden was used for awhile and sections were recultivated and replanted, the soil was broken up finer and finer. Recultivation and replanting were done in sections as various crops matured and were harvested. There was no crop rotation except as it occurred incidental to changing the crops desired at a given time.

Mulching, raised beds, and seed beds for transplanting were not used, although the germinating part of a plant might be temporarily stuck in water or moist soil for a couple of days if it could not be planted immediately. I do not know the Auyana concepts of companion planting beyond the fact that various crops were intermixed with one another and crops were planted so as to be touching when mature. Yams and beans were often planted together. Greens, beans, corn, and succulent cane were sometimes planted in solid patches of a single crop and sometimes intermixed. Sweet potato was always planted alone. Various flowers were sometimes planted throughout the garden and certain of these were said to make the plants grow better. Others were used for dyeing and in other activities, and some were planted just because they made the garden look good.

As mentioned in the earlier discussion of dreams, it might be revealed that a person would be a good gardener in general or of certain crops. It was also possible to learn secret things to say or sing to plants which would make them grow well. The words went inside the plants and made them grow rapidly and strongly. Both males and females knew these words and the information was passed on to friends and to those who wanted to learn. While talking to plants might help them grow, its effects were modest and plenty of people who had beautiful gardens did not know how to talk to their plants.

Insects and animals sometimes damaged gardens. A couple of types of larvae got into beans especially, and sometimes rats or marsupials ate crops. Insects were controlled by piling up and burning any living vegetable material from clearing or weeding, and rats or marsupials would be hunted or trapped if they caused much of a problem. But pigs were another order of menace. In one night, a couple of pigs could devastate the entire area a person had cultivated. More often, a pig would get into a garden and do some damage, and then the problem became how to keep it from getting in again. Domestic pigs were allowed to run loose, and if the owner of the pig that had done the damage could be identified, he would be asked to move the pig to another area. He might also catch the pig and gouge out an eye, sever a hock tendon, or stick a piece of sharpened wood into its nose. The idea was that these techniques would disrupt the pig's habits, and it was hoped that by the time the pig recovered it would have forgotten how to get into the garden.

If a pig continued to get in a garden, and putting a higher fence where it regularly crawled over failed to stop it, then the garden owner would consider killing it. Pigs could be killed by shooting them, which was the method preferred by men who were good with bows, or sharpened stakes could be put into the ground at the point where the pig came over the fence and as it jumped down it would impale itself. Even if this did not kill the pig it would discourage it. However, killing a domestic pig was a risky affair no matter how justified the owner of the garden felt he was. Pigs were an extremely valuable commodity and the owner of a pig might insist that the animal had not been given enough of a chance before it was killed. So, minimally, the garden owner had to catch the pig in his garden in order to kill it without antagonizing the owner.

Once a pig had been killed, the most conciliatory course of action was for the owner of the pig to say that the owner of the garden could have the pig, as it had destroyed his garden. The owner of the garden could then ease the anger even more by killing one of his own pigs and giving it to the owner of the pig, saying that they were friends and he wanted to give the owner of the pig one in return. If the garden owner did not want to ease the anger especially, he could simply say "thank you" when given the pig by its owner, and give him nothing in return. If the owner of the garden was somewhat angry, he would take the dead pig without waiting to hear from its owner and would give one of his pigs to the dead pig's owner. If the owner of the garden was very angry, he would simply take the dead pig and give its owner nothing. And if he was so mad that he really wanted to put the owner of the pig in a spot, he would kill it and then give it to its owner and refuse to take it if the owner should offer it to him. This left the owner of the pig in the position of having to kill another of his pigs and give it to the owner of the garden in order to make peace. To really rub it in, the owner of the garden was usually overly cordial when he gave the dead pig to its owner, saying that he did not want to offend the pig owner and the pig had not really done much damage.

Once a fence had been made and the land cleared, men varied in the amount of time they spent in the garden. Sugar cane and bananas were taken care of exclusively by men. Sugar cane grew to seven or eight feet tall and was tied to stakes to keep the stalks off the ground. As a stalk of bananas developed, it was wrapped with bark to keep fruit bats from eating the bananas before they had ripened. In addition, men planted and tended a few trees. Black palm might be planted near a dwelling area to be used for bows and arrowheads. In 1962, there were six such trees owned by three men. People said that in the past more trees had been planted, as there was more need for bows and arrows. But black palm also grew wild. Breadfruit and pepper tree were sometimes planted, but usually enough of them could be found in the secondary growth on an abandoned garden. Casuaraina might be planted around dwellings as a sort of marker of having been in the same area for a long time—e.g., "My father planted this tree when I was a baby." Of the eight hamlets in Auyana, five had at least one and usually a couple of casuaraina which had been planted there before. Pine was also planted for much the same reasons as casuaraina but occasionally also to use its bark in house walls. Nut bearing pandanus was occasionally planted both around dwellings and in gardens. All these trees were planted in clumps and, when seedlings, were taken care of by males. The son or sons of the planter had control of the use of the trees, even if the land on which they were planted was being used by someone else.

Taking care of sugar cane and bananas and tending trees took very little time, and if a man's wife were a good worker, he did not need to go into the gardens at all (except for sex). To the best of my knowledge, a couple of men spent no time at all working in their gardens except for clearing and making fences. However, most men spent some time and some spent a lot of time. But spending a lot of time in the gardens was a somewhat ambivalent endeavor for men. For a man to be a hard worker was great, but for him to be a "garden man" might be an insult.

A garden man could be someone who spent all his time in the gardens with women, especially when there was fighting. After fighting, male initiations, male renewal ceremonies, interaction with mud men or collective souls, or making salt out of leaves gathered from wild plants, a man could not go into the gardens for three to four days, especially gardens where there were yams, taro, or *as bin*, because he would be too "hot" and might damage them. A woman had to stay out of the garden for a few days after menstruation and after childbirth, periods when she was considered "hot" and dangerous.

Most sexual intercourse was carried on in and around gardens. Intercourse between a man and his wife in their garden was said to help things grow, but any other intercourse hindered plant growth. I twice heard of adulterous sexual intercouse being blamed for someone's garden doing poorly. Sexual activities that ran the risk of making someone angry (any intercourse except between a woman and her husband) were troublemaking for gardens as well as for people. I never asked what would happen if a person died in his or her garden but it was said that if a person was buried in his or her garden (or in the case of a child, in his or her parent's garden) it made the food grow well. This was because the dead person was pleased to be buried there rather than in the wilds, and this pleasure helped the garden do well.

In general, then, gardening was a fairly relaxed endeavor with little chance of serious failure, although production could vary. I kept no records of the amount of time it took men to clear plots of forested land. Nor did I keep records of the amount of time women spent in the gardens. However, both men and women when working at gardening usually sat around the hamlet until mid-morning and came back in mid-afternoon. Every three to four days they would take a couple of days off from clearing forest or tending the gardens. I never saw anyone working sunup to sundown except for a couple of days at a time for some special occasion. The work pace in the gardens was usually relaxed with rest when necessary and sometimes a short nap.

There was no "normal" use and fallow cycle for a plot of land. When I collected the histories of the gardens in Auyana in 1962, the reasons given for leaving a plot of land usually had little to do with production. Rather, a person might move to another hamlet or a whole hamlet might move. Warfare was often given as a reason for these moves, and warfare was also given as a reason for a man or woman no longer going to a certain section to garden because it was too close to the enemy and possible ambush. In fact, people said that in the past men spent a lot of time acting as guards for women working in the gardens. Whether on account of warfare, internal fighting, sickness, wanting to be close to a certain person, just moving, or whatever, a plot of land was often left before its productivity was exhausted. For fourteen gardens, I studied closely the history of their use and matched this with a detailed history of Auyana warfare and movements. I also asked several times about how long land could be used, how long it took it to become productive again, how fast it wore out after being fallow, etc., using children as the time markers. From this information, I have made up the following schema which I think gives a rough idea of the productivity of the land in Auyana. First, as mentioned earlier, most Auyana soil was said to be and appeared to me to be about the same. So I will start with a virgin forest somewhere on Auyana land. After clearing, it could be planted continuously for somewhere around eight to thirteen years (there were a couple of cases which went sixteen to twenty years). As the land was abandoned, pigs were allowed to forage on it and they pretty much turned over everything. Eventually, a cane cover was established and some young pepper trees and breadfruit trees began to show. At this point, which seemed to be around five to seven years after the land had been abandoned, it could be replanted again and would give a decent yield for maybe four to six years. It could be fallowed again, this time letting the pepper trees and other growth become a bit more mature before clearing it and planting again. It would then produce for maybe three years. Next it was usually left fallow for a long time—until there were at least young trees of the climax forest and maybe longer, perhaps on the order of thirty to forty years, at which point it was back to full productivity. If a plot from virgin forest was planted for around eight to thirteen years, it took about fifteen years for it to be restored to full productivity.

Domestic animals were spatially and, to some extent, behaviorally a part of the human community in Auyana, and some people looked after their pigs better than they did their children. Prior to the arrival of whites, dogs and pigs were the only domestic animals except for a rare young cassowary which was captured and raised in a pen. Chickens were introduced by whites and a couple of Seventh Day Adventist converts had goats. There was also one wild cat in the Auyana area which had escaped from the Lutheran mission about a three-hour walk away. Some people said they wanted a cat in order to keep down the rats around the house, but no one was successful in raising one during the time I was there.

Before describing the techniques of taking care of animals, I will first consider the numbers of each type of animal in Auyana, starting with pigs. I made a census of the domestic animals in Auyana in 1962. However, the census was not based on actually looking at the pigs; rather, I just asked people what pigs they owned or were raising. By "owned" I mean they determined when the pig was to be killed and for what purpose. As this implies, a person might be raising a pig for someone else. This created the possibility of duplication when taking the census, but I attempted to double-check the information I was given, so I think my figures are fairly accurate. I have excluded the nine married males and their families who were Seventh Day Adventist converts in the statement about pig ownership. I have classified pigs into four categories using the distinctions of male/female and young/full-grown. By full-grown I mean a female who can reproduce and a male of the same age. There were a total of 466 pigs in Auyana: 39 full-grown males, 127 full-grown females, 140 young males, and 160 young females.

In Auyana in 1962, no unmarried person owned or took care of any pigs. This was more or less normal, as only occasionally would a young unmarried male (never a female) own a pig. One man over forty and one under forty had previously been married but had no wife during the time I was there. The one under forty had pigs, the one over forty did not. There were six women who had been married but in 1962 had no husband. Four of these were old and were living with their sons or daughters. All of them were taking care of at least one pig, although whoever they were living with could decide how to dispose of the pig. Two of the women were middle-aged or younger and were living by themselves with occasional help from men, either as friends or as suitors interested in marrying them. They both had pigs they were raising, but again the pigs were being raised for some man to dispose of. Six of the married men did not own any pigs. One of them was an old man living with his wife, another was a young man who had just ceased being a Seventh Day Adventist, and the rest were newly married men. Of the remainder of the married men, only one, the cargo cult leader, did not own a full-grown female pig during the time I was there.

There were twenty-nine dogs in Auyana, thirteen males and sixteen females. These dogs were owned by seventeen families. Five of the dogs were considered useful in hunting, the rest sometimes helped in hunting but mostly were just watchdogs. There were seventy-nine chickens, thirty-one male and forty-eight female. Of the seventy-nine, twenty-seven were owned by the Seventh Day Adventist families, and only one of these families did not have any chickens, whereas twenty non-Adventist families had no chickens. There were eight goats, all owned by Adventist families: one full-grown male, two full-grown females, three young males, and two young females. As these figures would indicate, the domestic animal of most concern to members of Auyana was the pig. However, dogs were desired more than the figures would indicate. When a good bitch had puppies, they were spoken for long before she whelped, and any puppies were immediately spoken for after they were born. The males I talked to all said they wanted to own a dog, especially one that was strong, could hunt, and was a good watchdog. Hence, I assume the low numbers of dogs resulted from fertility and mortality rates, not from lack of desirability. Chickens pretty much took care of themselves and were apparently learning to escape hawks well enough to be on the increase. Goats were not in much demand, even among the Adventists. Their meat was not particularly good, they got into everything, and they were extremely expensive to purchase.

As would be expected from the discussion so far, pigs received the greatest amount of care, dogs the next greatest, and chickens none. The one exceptional chicken was a huge cock which followed one man around much like a dog. Eventually, the man began to treat it like a dog and would occasionally throw food to it. On the other hand, most of the chicken's feathers were pulled out a couple of days before a large dance at Auyana. It was a little weak for awhile but eventually recovered and resumed being a dog.

As with so many things in Auyana, the care of pigs varied from person to person. But there were limits. No person cared for a pig unless he or she was going to get some kind of return from it, the greatest return being the ability to determine when and for whom the pig would be killed. If a man had a wife, the pig was cared for primarily by her. A man might occasionally feed his pigs, but no man regularly fed them; this was his wife's (or some woman's) task. Men said that women provided food for the pigs just as they provided food for men and children, except that women did not nurse baby pigs. But if a man had co-wives, each wife had her pigs to look after and if she was unable to, her husband rather than a co-wife would take care of her pigs. In general, older men took better care of pigs than younger men. In summary, the nuclear family was the pig-raising unit with the wife doing most of the work with some help from any adolescent daughters she had and occasional help from her husband. The amount of help her husband gave her usually increased as she got older.

The care of pigs included feeding them, delousing them, and providing a shelter for them, especially when they were young. Before whites arrived, women's houses were divided into two sections, and in the section towards the door, the pigs slept and were fed. The Australians have forbidden people to keep pigs in their houses, and have encouraged men to move out of the men's houses and live with their wives. Men refuse to live with pigs, and so the government policy has resulted in pigs' being entirely fenced out of the hamlets or, at most, coming into the hamlets to be fed (except for some old couples who in 1962 continued to keep their pigs in their houses). Some men have also built small houses out near the edge of an old garden which their pigs can sleep in. The only exceptions to the rule that pigs were not kept in the houses were young pigs and pregnant sows on the verge of having their young. A young pig was trained to follow and come by tying a rope around its foreleg and dragging it along while calling it, until it got used to coming when called and came to expect to be fed occasionally.

Pigs were fed leftover food and sweet potatoes. They were usually fed in the evening when people were cooking their own food. They might also be fed in the morning, although rarely were they fed at both times unless they were pregnant sows or young. Usually only the smaller sweet potatoes were fed to pigs, but if a woman's gardens were bountiful, she might feed the pigs the bigger, more choice sweet potatoes. Of the five families for which I kept dietary records, one family fed their pigs every day, another fed them about four days out of five, three fed them about every day, and one fed them about twice a week. The more often the pigs were fed, the more they were fed at each feeding. The family who fed their pigs only once or twice a week averaged about 0.8 pounds of sweet potato per feeding; the family who fed their pigs every day averaged about 1.9 pounds of sweet potato per feeding; and the other families were in between these two figures.

A pound or two of sweet potatoes a day would not keep a pig going for very long, and the purpose of feeding was to keep the pigs domesticated and to check them out to make sure they were all okay. For pigs foraged around in the forest and in old abandoned gardens during the day and were sometimes bitten by snakes and sometimes stolen and sometimes just disappeared. Not only would feeding them every day give the owner a chance to check them, it would help to keep the pigs from roaming far away and getting into trouble.

A pig might also be marked by taking notches or sections out of its ears and/or cutting off varying lengths of its tail. These were not brands in the sense that an owner had certain notches which were used on all his pigs and no one else used. But they were like brands in that they did identify the pig as belonging to someone and therefore not a wild pig. This would at least stop the people in the owner's sovereignty (unless they lived at the other end of the sovereignty territory from him and away from any of his friends) from shooting the pig as a wild pig and bringing it to a hamlet to eat. If they wanted to kill it, they would have to do it in secret—that is, steal the pig. Unless you and the owner were already enemies, to shoot a pig and bring it back to your place to eat was not theft—it was a mistake. While it would make the owner angry, his anger could be cooled somewhat by giving him the dead pig or by keeping his pig and allowing him to have an equivalent-sized live pig of yours. You might even offer to keep raising the pig you had given him until he was ready to have it killed. But, it was said, mistakes make enemies, and having notches on the pig's ears helped people to avoid making mistakes. Having notches also helped in following a pig that had been shot by its owner but not killed, and had gotten away. Notches were also supposed to keep the pig somewhat scared of its owner so it would not ever bite or attack him.

Getting bitten or attacked could be a real problem with pigs, especially if they were males, and so the males were castrated. Initially, I was told that all males were castrated when they were around four to seven months old, and sows were impregnated solely by wild boars. Later, I learned that sometimes a male pig might not be castrated if it was a particularly good one in order to allow it to breed. As mentioned earlier, there were thirty-nine full-grown boars in Auyana in 1962. I saw one of them scatter a hunting party one day. Five men went in five directions and over the fence before the pig's owners could get it back under control.

Delousing was one of several ways to help pigs grow well. Another was to sprinkle ashes along the pig's spine, and a third was to feed them various chewed up barks and powdered stones, sprinkled over sweet potatoes. These techniques were known by both men and women but not by all men and women. The information was gotten in the same way as information on how to grow healthier plants, that is, through friendship and desire to learn. I heard of pigs being fed barks and stones twice during the time I was there. Another way to help pigs grow was to feed them fermented, mashed wild banana skins mixed with the leaves and bark of a certain tree. The type of tree was known only by some men. This mixture was usually fed only to pregnant sows. I saw it done once while I was there.

Pigs were killed by shooting them with an arrow or bashing in their skulls. To kill a pig with a single shot of a bamboo-tipped arrow was hard. But bashing in its skull was no fun. In fact, killing pigs in general was no fun for the owners. Women said they became fond of the pigs they raised, sometimes calling them "my child," and women never killed pigs. On the other hand, they did not mutilate themselves or go into any kind of mourning after the pig had been killed. Rather, they usually simply were not around when the pig was killed. Although men were said to be less attached to their pigs, a man very rarely killed his own pigs. Usually a friend did it for him. One man had cut off part of an earlobe in mourning for a good sow he had to kill.

Pups were trained to eat sweet potato by beating a dried dead rat on some mashed potato and putting the dog's nose close to it. Otherwise, dogs scrounged for what they could get and for many dogs this was not much. No one commented much on starving dogs or seemed particularly concerned. Nothing special could be done to make dogs grow better. However, men would frequently sit and deflea the nearest dog just for the fun of chasing down the flea and killing it.

Dogs with some bent for it were used in hunting. A clacker of small pig shoulder bones was tied around the dog's neck, and it was let run loose to see if it could scare up a cassowary or pig, or maybe tree a marsupial. In the latter case, the animal was likely to seek refuge in a hole in the tree and the hunter would have to climb the tree and reach in the hole and pull it out, providing he did not get bitten too badly or lose his hold on the tree. Vines were tied into a circle around a tree and a man could put both feet in the loop and use it to help him climb. Although the most effective method of hunting, climbing trees was risky business and sometimes men fell out of them. Running after cassowaries or wild pigs could also be dangerous, especially to the feet. Partly as a result of the danger, men chasing game on foot hunted in pairs or groups.

The less dangerous methods of hunting were either to hunt marsupials in the moonlight or to set traps. Setting traps was an individual affair and a man would usually go out by himself, sometimes with a hunting partner. Hunting marsupials by moonlight frequently involved several men who would sit underneath branches where marsupials regularly traveled and try to shoot them as they were silhouetted against the sky. Several types of spring snare traps were also used, as well as deadfalls. Snare traps varied in size from ones large enough to catch a rat to ones designed to catch a cassowary. There was also a fish trap with a bent pole as a trigger release which pulled shut a door on a tube made from bark and bamboo. Not many men knew how to make the fish trap. Knowledge about the other traps was widespread but only a few men were good at making them. Trapping could be accomplished only during wet times as the loops and cord would become too stiff to slide if they dried out. Finally, rats (or anything else) were hunted by waiting along the edge of a grass area being burned to make a garden, or by having a bunch of kids go out and beat around in the cane and grass, and shooting the rats as they ran out. These methods seemed to be much more effective in getting rats than was trapping them.

My impression on effectiveness are not based on much data, because hunting took up little time in Auyana, as the data on diet would suggest. Still, members of Auyana talked about themselves as being people who lived in the forest and hunted, as opposed to people, like *uwara'* (Tairora), who lived in the grass and seldom hunted. Animals and insects in Auyana were separated into elaborate classifications, and marsupials were required as gifts at marriage and birth. My feeling was that hunting had been more important to them in the past but they had come to have the know-how and the paraphernalia without the interest. Hunting and other activities having to do with the forest were carried on only by men. An occasional woman would climb trees and catch marsupials, but that was the extent of female participation.

Apart from hunting, one of the uses of the forest was to get the wild pandanus leaves and the leaf from another tree to make salt. The leaves were burned, the ashes leached, and the water evaporated over a fire. Lime was also made from the ash of a certain tree bark and a thorny bush. These were burned and the ashes collected and made into a paste which was then wrapped in banana leaves and put into a fire. The flames converted the paste into blocks of lime, which were crumbled into powder and carried in gourds to be eaten with betel nut.

The forest was also of particular symbolic importance at the men's renewal ceremony. A large variety of leaves could be eaten, and leaves and bark could be used for food seasoning. However, in daily life these were not used much. During the men's renewal ceremony, some of the knowledgeable men would go into the forest and collect leaves, and the men would cook them and eat them in order to make themselves strong and beautiful. I took down a list of at least twenty-seven leaves that were used this way.

The forest was also a source of many of the materials used in making tools, houses, and clothes. Adze handles were made out of certain trees whose wood was strong and resilient. Stone adze blades were acquired by trading with groups to the west and north. Members of Auyana sharpened blades by pecking and grinding. At least four kinds of stone adzes existed: a typical regular-sized one; a regular-sized one with the blade rotated about forty-five degrees so it could be used to reach out and chop limbs; an extra large one for splitting logs; and an extra small one for carving out wooden bowls and drums (although the hourglass-shaped drums and circular bowls were hollowed mostly by fire). Bows were made out of black palm wood, as were arrowheads. The arrow shafts were made from cane and the bow string was a strip of bamboo. Arrow shafts were not notched at the end, nor were they fletched. They were made more or less straight by holding them over heat and bending them by hand. The sap from a tree was used to glue the arrowheads into a haft woven from a cane, which was set and glued onto the shaft. Net bags were sometimes used for quivers.

Other than adze blades, there was little working of stone in Auyana. Flakes were used for small arrows and also for scraping, but they were usually not retouched. Pig tusks and other bones were also sharpened to an edge and used for scraping wood, such as a bow. Sharp bone was used for puncturing or for lifting up a weave to slip a strip under when making woven objects.

House walls were built in much the same way as fences except that instead of horizontal staves, a layer of pine bark was put around the outside and inside (or the inside row of staves might be put adjacent to one another) and grass stuffed between to create insulation. The roof was made from grass thatch and was conical with a center pole.

Men's houses were divided into compartments as if by the spokes of a wheel around the central pole and hearth. When the house was completed, the first fire was started secretly by having some man hand the fire down through the roof rather than bring it in the door, and in this way the fire would just appear as far as women and kids were concerned. Or so the men said. Certain leaves were also hung on the center pole to make it strong and secret songs were sung for the same purpose. The center pole of the men's house was compared to several things—a man's penis when he had an erection, the spinal cord, and the best-known warrior/organizer in a group. It was the central force without which everything else would collapse. Women did not go inside the men's house except when helping the men to chase out the ghost of a slain enemy. Otherwise they kept their distance even though there were no clearly delineated male and female areas. The situation seemed to be much like that with territorial boundaries. There were central zones with zones of varying and sometimes negotiable width around them. Just as women did not come too close to the men's house, so the men did not go too close to the menstrual/birth house, usually located somewhere slightly off the ridge where the other houses were located. Men's houses were usually located on the highest area, with women's houses slightly below them and the menstrual/birth house lower than any of the others. In this way, none of the menstrual blood or the remains of birth could ever wash down into the men's house and weaken the men.

Houses lasted about five years or so before the termites started really weakening them. A husband did the work on his wife's house, with his wife getting the grass when the house was ready to thatch. Help in building a woman's house was given in much the same way as in clearing the forest to garden. Men also built the menstrual/birth hut, and they worked as a team to build the men's house. If a hamlet was to be built in a spot where there had never been houses before, a small ceremony was performed to make the place a good one to live in. Other than this and the first fire in a new men's house, there were no ceremonies connected with house-building.

Men's clothes consisted of strips of bark hung down in front and back to cover their penis and buttocks. Women's clothes consisted of strips of bark hung much the same way for unmarried women as for men, with married women's skirts going all the way around their waist like knee-length skirts. Women sometimes also wore bat wing bones or pieces of bright cane stuck in the fleshy parts of their nose for ornament. Men wore headbands of cowrie shell topped with a ruff of cassowary feathers. They said that in the distant past they also wore green beetles on the headband. Men would sometimes stick bat wing bones, or cane in their nose and in addition might put a pair of pig's tusks or a rod of polished white stone through the nose septum. Men braided strips of bark cloth into their hair so that it hung down over their back, and they wore a net bag hung from their neck down their back so that it covered their buttocks. Men also carried a net bag hung from their shoulders in which they put lime gourds, packets of special leaves, and odds and ends. Similarly, women hung a net bag from their forehead down their back like a tumpline. Women also had knit skull caps which they might wear, and some people occasionally donned bark cloth capes.

Net bags were fabricated out of a sisal-like cord made from the inner bark of a certain tree strung on a bone needle. Cord was also made from the inner bark of the mulberry tree, which could be used to make bark cloth. Both these cords were quite strong, and net bags were beautifully useful things, sometimes lasting several years. But use was so hard that women were usually either making the cord out of bark or making the bags out of the cord whenever they were sitting around with little to do. In the past, men used to do much the same with arrowheads as it took a while to carve one out of fire-cured black palm and arrows were being continually lost or broken. Cord and strips of bright yellow and black cane were also used to make wrist coverings and armlets. These were woven by men, although I only saw two men weaving them while I was there.

Dyes were gotten from flowers planted in the gardens and from the bark of a couple of trees found in the forest. The most used dye was a red-brown one. Net bags were usually made out of plain and red cord forming step-like patterns, and men sometimes dyed the strips on their clothes in alternating bands of red. After a little bit of use, the patterns could no longer be seen and the bags and clothes became a uniform dark brown and, eventually, black. This was taken as a sign that their user had been around a while and must have a certain amount of experience and knowledge.

# 3. Auyana Social Units

In this chapter, I will consider what was entailed in being a member of some of the groups in Auyana. I will do this by describing the attributes of the social units as they were *initially* presented to me by members of Auyana. Common ancestry will be the last attribute considered, and Chapter 4 will be devoted to analysis of its relationship to the other attributes. Appendix 1 gives the demography of Auyana in 1962.

My description of the initial presentation of social unit attributes is restricted to what people *said* to me about social units when I first made inquiries. The main reason for beginning the analysis of Auyana social unit attributes in this way is that this provides an overall schematic view of them. Such a view provides a point of reference which makes it easier to conduct a detailed analysis of certain of these attributes. There are two secondary considerations which led me to choose this particular heuristic device. One is an interest in the relationship between verbal presentations of self and other behaviors. The other is an interest in why people initially present themselves to strangers in a certain way. However, these questions will be only incidentally, rather than systematically, pursued in this study. In the first place, the number of respondents on which my descriptions of initial verbal presentations are based is small. For most attributes, I have only the initial verbal presentations of two or three people. Secondly, there are various reasons why the initial verbal presentation of an attribute may have been made. A statement may have been made because it described what usually took place. It may also have been made in order to convey an ideal. Or it may have been made because the actor was attempting to convince a stranger that he possessed certain characteristics in order to be able to carry out some transaction with the stranger—even though the actor may not have wished to be what he was trying to persuade the stranger he was. Also, an actor may have presented himself and others in a certain way because to do otherwise would be to publicly accuse someone. For example, if attempting to assassinate another's soul meant that one no longer intended to cooperate with the person and would instead harm the person if possible, then publicly stating to a stranger that those in one's group might attempt to assassinate one another's souls might imply that one suspected someone in his group of having done this (or might be intending to do it himself). This would not necessarily mean the actor took the absence of soul assassination to be an ideal; it may only have meant he wished to avoid conflict with others in his group. Finally, a statement may have been made which the actor knew to be an oversimplification of a situation, but since he did not know why a stranger was interested, he would be unable to know what was relevant and may have considered it a waste of effort to go into detail. I will not demonstrate which of these or other reasons may have obtained in any given case. For a few attributes, I will *suggest* what may have existed behind the initial presentation, but for most attributes I will only state whether alternatives to the attribute as initially presented were allowed.

The position of married women and children as members of a social unit was ambiguous. I will, therefore, first present the attributes of social units as though they pertained only to initiated males, and then discuss the sense in which wives and children were members of a social unit. The relationship between the following classifications of social units and classifications made by others (e.g., Hogbin and Wedgewood 1953) will be discussed at the end of this chapter.

SOVEREIGNTY ATTRIBUTES

The attributes will be numbered to facilitate later discussion.

*The attribute of having one name was sovereignty attribute number one.* The initial presentation turned out to be only roughly correct. A denial of having the same name was a denial of having the other sovereignty attributes, but to claim the same name was possible and acceptable (i.e., did not make others angry or threaten one's position in a social unit) without claiming the other sovereignty attributes.

*Sovereignty attribute number two was that all the Auyana had one* upaema. The main allowed alternative was for an individual to claim as his collective soul (*upaema*) the collective soul belonging to a sovereignty of which he was not otherwise acting as a member. This happened in the case of men whose biological father was from another sovereignty. They might also say that they belonged to Auyana and to the other sovereignty. However, they varied considerably in whether they maintained any transactions with members of their biological father's sovereignty. The frequency of such transactions are discussed in the next chapter.

*Sovereignty attribute number three was that they all had one forest and one ground.* The dotted lines on Map 4 roughly delineate this territory. As discussed earlier, these lines should be taken as zones rather than as precise boundaries, for members of Auyana did not initially present them as precise boundaries, nor were they. The forest initially described as "their" forest was circumscribed by the boundaries of the dotted line. As initially presented, any part of this forest could be used for any purpose by any member of Auyana. Members of sovereignties adjacent to and friendly with Auyana were allowed to hunt in the Auyana forest, but they could not use it for any other purpose. The allowed alternatives to this attribute involved people in one sovereignty being able to use the forest belonging to another sovereignty for certain raw materials and hunting—but not for gardening. These alternatives will be discussed later.

Land that had been used for gardening was initially presented as being divided into that which had not been used for gardens in so long that any individual was free to use it and that which had been more recently used for gardens and could be used only by certain individuals. The main allowed alternative was that access to this latter type of land was not as restricted as initially presented. Initially, I was told that a man used the land used by his father, and women had no claim to land, nor were any claims to land made through women. Although it was possible and acceptable to grant special access to forest and used land without destroying a sovereignty or expelling any members, it was not possible for a person to be denied access to forest and used land and still remain a member.

*Sovereignty attribute number four was that they were all those who lived at one place.* The phrase used was that they were *imbolanau'*. *Imbola* meant "one." *Nau'* was generally used to refer to a cluster or row of houses. From Map 5 it is obvious that they did not live in a single cluster of houses in 1962, nor had they in the past. However, in a broader sense, they were living at "one place," the place within their territory, which is what I think was meant when referring to the sovereignty as being *imbolanau'*.

Their claim of being *imbolanau'* was true to the extent that coresidence was necessary for full membership. That is, a person could not move from a sovereignty and retain full membership in it (for a more detailed discussion, see Chapter 4). On the other hand, moving to a place did not necessarily mean that the person would become a member there. A person who moved might become, to some extent, someone without a country. Generally, membership was gradually lost and gained following a move and members of Auyana disagreed among themselves on the extent to which those who moved into Auyana became members.

*Sovereignty attribute number five was that when they got into a fight with one another, they did not shoot to kill.* Members of Auyana distinguished between stick fights (*nanda time*) and arrow fights (*paroi time*). They readily admitted that those within the sovereignty sometimes fought with arrows, but they initially claimed that when this happened they did not shoot to kill. The validity of this claim will be examined in Chapter 5.

*Sovereignty attribute number six was that if they fought against each
other, when they finished they would meet, prepare an earth oven, and
share cooked pig and vegetables.* They "gave their hands" to one another and
became friends again. "Giving hands" after a fight was not presented as
being restricted to those with a sovereignty. Two sovereignties which had
fought might "give hands" after the fight also. However, those within Auyana were presented as *always* "giving hands" following a fight. Contrary to
this claim, those within a sovereignty did not always "give hands" after a
fight, but the failure to do so was always taken as a sign of lingering hostility
and an unwillingness to forget the fight or the incident that precipitated it.

*Sovereignty attribute number seven was that they did not attempt soul
assassination or harm on one another.* As discussed earlier, members of Auyana labeled three types of activity *nai,* which I am calling soul assassination
or harm here. The first type involved a woman collecting anything intimately
associated with her husband, such as clothing, and placing it in the
menstrual hut. When the male members of Auyana claimed that they did not
attempt to harm one another's souls, they were not referring to this type of
harm.

One of the other two types of soul harm resulted in various sorts of infirmi-
ties, such as swollen joints, but not death. The other type resulted in death if
it was effective. Members of Auyana initially claimed that they did not practice either soul assassination or harm on one another, and it was some time
before I found that both were actually practiced. The manner in which I
discovered the existence of these practices reveals a great deal about their
attitude towards them. I stumbled across the working of soul harm when a
man living close to me was attempting to cure his swollen knee. He and
others asserted that soul harm was practiced within Auyana, although they
would not name specific cases. However, there was considerable disagreement on its frequency. The fact that some would say it occurred a lot indicated to me that this activity did not usually result in the severance of sovereignty membership.

Soul assassination was a different matter, a discovery I made while discussing with several men the subject of fights within Auyana. According to them,
two men were killed in a fight between members of Auyana about forty-five
years ago. The deceased belonged to the same subdivision as the men to
whom I was talking. Members of this subdivision initially fled and later returned. However, the men said that the fight had not been forgotten, and
they attributed the deaths of two of their children to soul assassinations by
members of the subdivision who had previously killed their two comembers.
When I asked why the other subdivision would continue to kill members of
their group, the men said they did not know. A reasonable assumption is that
the original homicides had been part of a series of deaths on both sides attributed to soul assassination. However, I was never able to collect any evidence that this was so. Men in the "killer" subdivision denied that any of

their children or wives had been killed by soul assassination carried out by the other subdivision—although they did say that those in the other subdivision had a reputation for being powerful soul assassins. Either soul assassination with the intent to kill a sovereignty comember was rare or such accusations were not confided to anyone except a full member, which I, of course, was not. My guess is that suspicions of soul assassination were rare and that if they became frequent or involved important people the sovereignty would split. The case cited above does not contradict this theory, as the people supposedly killed by soul assassination were children, and the death of a child was always taken less seriously than that of an adult.

The major thrust of attributes five through seven was not that members of Auyana were peaceful with one another; rather, it was that they trusted other members not to kill them. Thus, even the *intent* to kill (i.e., attempting soul assassination) was considered sufficient cause to prevent men from being members of the same sovereignty. The emphasis on the avoidance of homicide—as opposed to the practice of peace—came out in other ways. Members of Auyana not only admitted they fought, they also did not present themselves as not wronging one another, although they claimed they wronged each other less than they wronged those outside the sovereignty. Similarly, they claimed to be generally helpful to one another, but did not present this as an invariant feature of their life.

*Sovereignty attribute number eight was that they did not give "wealth" to one another for revenging the death of one of their members*. All items given to others except for garden produce were called *onta* ("wealth"). Prior to the arrival of Europeans, the main items of wealth were pigs, bows, arrows, feathers, and shells. It was said that these were given to whoever revenged the death of a person if the revenger was from another sovereignty, but that nothing was given if the revenger was from the same sovereignty. In fact, if the revenger was from the same sovereignty but from a different pooling unit (discussed below), he would be given some pig, but no other items of wealth.

*Sovereignty attribute number nine was that following a fight between those in Auyana and those in another sovereignty, Auyana members would hold a feast*. This is not to be confused with "giving hands" after a fight (see sovereignty attribute number six). Rather, this was a victory celebration and members of Auyana presented themselves as being those who jointly held one. Members of other sovereignties who were engaged in the fighting might either hold a feast of their own or be invited as guests, but they did not jointly hold one with those in Auyana. Contrary to the initial presentation, it was not true that *all* those in Auyana held a victory celebration; different subdivisions sometimes held their own. However, this was not taken as a serious matter by members. There apparently was no threat to membership within the sovereignty as long as a victory feast was jointly held most of the time. I suppose the reason they did not initially use the qualifier "most" was because they assumed it would not be meaningful to me.

The above attributes were presented as not being used to distinguish subgroups within the sovereignty from one another. However, attributes ten through fourteen were said to be used at lower levels as well.

*Sovereignty attribute number ten was that they collectively sent wealth, or at least pigs, to those outside the sovereignty who helped them in fights against other sovereignties.* All the members of the sovereignty were presented as contributing to the wealth which was given. I will refer to the collection of wealth or other objects as "pooling." Giving wealth for war aid, then, was the only activity for which members of Auyana said they comprised a pooling group. All other poolings were presented as being performed by subgroups within the sovereignty.

*Sovereignty attribute number eleven was that they were one akum (imbola akum) or one anda (imbola anda).* Akum also meant a person's body, and *anda* meant vines, ropes, strings, or rows of objects. Members of Auyana said that *akum,* when referring to a person's body, was the same word as was used to refer to a social unit, and similarly for *anda*. However, I can see no common dimension shared by both the social and nonsocial objects and will instead assume that each term was multivocal.

The characteristic of being one *akum* or *anda* was also used to distinguish lower levels within a sovereignty. However, there was one distinct feature of its use at the sovereignty level: one could conjoin the sovereignty name with *anda* and refer to it as such and such an *anda* (e.g., *auyana/n/anda*), but one could not conjoin it with a person's name and refer to it as so and so's *anda*. At lower levels, the latter was possible. That is, sovereignties were not distinguished from one another by their identification with a single person, but subdivisions of a sovereignty were.

The remaining attributes of a sovereignty involved the matter of who prosecuted whom for an offense. By "offense" I mean anything which made someone angry. The Auyana phrase for this was *arumbakai,* which literally meant that the person's innards got hot. By my definition, what was an offense to one might not be an offense to another. I am concerned here with only those offenses to which there was said to be collective response. Not surprisingly, the activities involved in these offenses were said to make anyone angry.

The one thing members of Auyana could *not* do when they became angry was to present their complaint to a person or body of persons who regularly adjudicated disputes (i.e., a court). They were, then, left with four alternatives: (1) they could make a demand for compensation; (2) they could cease giving rewards or deny promised rewards; (3) they could attack someone; or (4) they could attack or attempt to destroy nonhuman objects. I will refer to these activities as the prosecution of an offense.

*Sovereignty attribute number twelve was that members of Auyana demanded and received help from other members in prosecuting any of the following offenses committed against them by someone from outside Auyana.*

1. Members of Auyana indicated that they would confront any people attempting to use their forest for any purpose except hunting and, if necessary, would attack and drive them away. I could elicit no cases of such an offense and therefore have no idea whether they actually did this.

2. If anyone attempted to use their gardened land, they claimed they would carry out the same prosecution as when someone used their forest for something other than hunting. I was able to find only one case of such an offense. The infraction occurred in the post-contact period and the result of the dispute was a stick fight between "most" of the members of Auyana and "most" of those in another sovereignty.

3. I was initially told that the person who caught anyone robbing or burning a member's house would attack the offender(s) and that others would come to help him. If the offender was not caught in the act, it was extremely unlikely that he would ever be identified with any certainty unless he himself made the disclosure. However, such disclosures occurred only when two sovereignties were fighting and taunting each other. In this context, the offense simply became another reason to be angry at those in the other sovereignty. But assuming that the offender did not reveal himself, members of Auyana said their only recourse was for a few men to slip over to the sovereignty from which it was thought the offenders came, and rob and set fire to their houses. This meant that prosecution was carried on by only a few individuals, although it was directed against any or all those in another sovereignty. Thus, all the members of a sovereignty became a legal unit in such cases, even though only some of them might actually be prosecuting and committing offenses. It was said that individuals who desired to carry out such secret retaliation would consult with some, but by no means all, of those in their sovereignty before they did so. But people did not always consult with others in such situations and consulted with few when they did. So there was the constant possibility that a person's house might be robbed or burned even though he or she had done nothing and might not know any previous offenses had occurred.

4. It was initially presented that anyone caught stealing a member's pig was treated the same way as someone caught robbing or burning a member's house. If the thief was not caught in the act, prosecution would be undertaken by individuals or small groups, as in the case of burglary and arson.

5. If anyone was caught attempting to assassinate or harm the soul of a member, it was said that whoever spotted the offender would attack him, and others would come to assist. I recorded two cases of persons who took soul assassins by surprise; in both cases the alleged soul assassins fled before they could be identified or attacked.

6. If anyone attacked a member from hiding, it was initially presented that whoever was nearby would attack the offender and others would come to help him. Physical attacks by outsiders could occur in other contexts without anyone else in the sovereignty becoming involved (see the later discussion of

the "escalation clause"). Attacks from hiding occurred only as part of a raid to kill someone. Hence, it could be argued that it was not the physical attack which was being responded to as much as the fact that the attack was part of an attempt to kill a member. If so, this attribute could be subsumed under point eight below.

7. If it was discovered that an outsider had had sexual intercourse with the wife of any member, then, as initially presented, the husband would go to the other sovereignty and attempt to shoot, but not kill, the adulterer. It was claimed that all those in the husband's sovereignty would go with him, and if anyone other than the adulterer fired at or otherwise attacked the husband, they would attack that person. This prosecution could be carried out either in the open or as a surprise attack. If it was the latter, then it was tantamount to a declaration of war and all-out fighting would be the inevitable result. Even if the prosecution was executed publicly, with a body of men going to the other sovereignty during the day after sending word that they were coming, it was said that this act, also, was likely to result in all-out fighting. This is discussed in point nine below.

8. If an outsider killed a member of Auyana by physical attack or soul assassination, it was initially presented that those in Auyana would attack and attempt to kill someone in the sovereignty of the killer. There were several exceptions to this presentation; namely, deaths attributed to soul assassination were rarely prosecuted by anything other than soul assassination, and raids to kill someone did not always involve all the members of the sovereignty. Neither of these exceptions necessarily resulted in anger on the part of anyone in the sovereignty, since they were accepted practices under certain conditions.

9. The last situation in which all the members of the sovereignty were presented as involved in prosecution was the one which I have been referring to as the "escalation clause." Stated in their terms, whenever a member of the sovereignty was involved in a dispute with someone outside the sovereignty which erupted into a "big" fight, others in the sovereignty would go to his aid.

Three criteria were presented as those used to determine whether a fight had become big. First, if there was reason to believe that those on the other side were attempting to kill the members of Auyana involved in the fight, the situation became equivalent to condition eight (murder). I do not know which variables were used to assess the intention to kill, other than the previous state of hostilities between the two sovereignties.

Another criterion used to determine whether a fight had become big was whether the members of Auyana were being beaten. This did not have to mean they were being killed or were likely to be killed (although obviously the distinction between this and the assessment that the others were intending to kill them was vague); it meant simply that they were getting the worst of the fight. In such a case, the members of Auyana claimed that other members of the next largest subdivision within Auyana to which the people being beaten belonged would go to their aid. That is, fights were presented as being escalated by successive involvement of the next largest subdivisions.

The last criterion used to determine whether a fight had become big was that the members of Auyana were outnumbered. If so, equivalent numbers from Auyana would enter the fight. Inasmuch as members ordinarily responded on the basis of their membership in subdivisions, whenever the next highest level appeared on the other side the equivalent next highest level from Auyana would respond.

Such a system not only had the potential of converting a minor scrap into a major confrontation, it also contained the mechanisms for preventing one. Because actors implicitly demanded that only the next largest subdivisions come to their aid and not the entire sovereignty, it was possible for those not immediately involved to attempt to stop the fight before they themselves became involved. Even if members were not particularly interested in adjudicating or settling a dispute, they may have been interested in assuring that the dispute did not erupt into deadly violence and would, therefore, have been willing to intervene.

The sovereignty's characteristics as a prosecuting group should be further clarified before considering the sovereignty as a legal unit. First, there was no situation in which most of the members of a sovereignty demanded of one another that they all withhold rewards from an offender. Also, there was no situation in which they demanded of one another that they go together to demand compensation from others. Both of these actions were done at lower levels. When subunits were prosecuting offenses, the entire sovereignty became involved only if fights erupted and became "big." Secondly, when I say that they *pressured* each other for cooperation in prosecution, I mean they became angry if others did not cooperate. They claimed that this did not result in fights or demands for compensation or attacks on property. Instead, there might only be the withholding of rewards by those who were angry. I have found no cases in which a lack of cooperation was the stated event precipitating a fight between members of a sovereignty. However, the failure to cooperate was undoubtedly remembered and, along with other unsettled "grudges," probably contributed to a reservoir of hostility which might have caused a minor altercation to develop suddenly into a serious fight involving many people. A third characteristic of prosecution by sovereignties was that cooperation in prosecution did not have to be given every time in order to avoid hostility or resentment. However, I do not know the extent to which one could be derelict in giving cooperation.

*Sovereignty attribute number thirteen was that regardless of whether they always went to help one another in prosecuting the above offenses, none of them would ever help those in another sovereignty in a fight against those in Auyana.* Although it was not true that this was never done, it was true that those who did it were unable to remain as members of Auyana. It seems, then, that the minimal criterion for membership in a sovereignty was not invariant aid in fights, but a refusal to help those on the other side. This seems to be another aspect of the Auyana stress on the avoidance of the intent to kill one another.

*Sovereignty attribute number fourteen was that the members of Auyana were a legal unit (i.e., any of them might be retaliated against) when one of their members killed someone in another sovereignty.* The main allowed alternative to this presentation was that certain individuals might not be considered as a part of the legal unit under certain conditions. This is discussed further in the section below on women as members of sovereignties and in the chapter on warfare.

In addition to homicide, the members of a sovereignty formed a quasi-legal unit whenever one of their members stole a pig or robbed or burned a house in another sovereignty. For, as discussed earlier, the offended person might steal any pig or rob or burn the house of anyone in the sovereignty to which the presumed offenders belonged. In a lesser sense, the sovereignty might be a legal unit if one of its members became engaged in an altercation with an outsider. It was said that the outsider might go home mad and later attempt to steal pigs, rob or burn houses, or at least inflict soul harm on any of those in Auyana. It was, of course, impossible to tell whether this was the motive behind any given theft or arson. However, the belief that offenses of this kind might be committed meant that members of a sovereignty were forced to become somewhat concerned about what went on any time there was an altercation with those in a different sovereignty. Homicide was a case where they *knew* they would be treated as a legal unit. In other cases, variables such as the state of existing hostilities between the sovereignties, the severity of the altercation, or rumors about plans for retaliation would all enter into a person's assessment of how an altercation might affect him.

Auyana was a sovereignty, which means that Auyana was not only a legal unit but was the largest legal unit whose members repeatedly acted as a group. Members of Auyana not only presented themselves as being the largest legal unit, they also said that they were the only ones who would regularly help one another in fights with outsiders. That is, they said that those in other sovereignties might or might not come to their aid. In their presentation, reliability and regularity of action as a group coincided with being a legal unit. In fact, Auyana was not the largest plurality acting repeatedly as a group, although it was the largest legal unit so acting.

Members of Auyana presented their sovereignty as having one other characteristic: common patri-ancestry. However, I will consider this after I have presented the subdivisions within Auyana. For common patri-ancestry was used at all levels, and its exact role can be more easily discussed once the other characteristics of the different levels have been presented.

First let us consider the place of women and children as members of a sovereignty. Auyana was neither exogamous nor endogamous; as will be discussed later, it was possible for a sovereignty to be exogamous, but none were endogamous. Members of Auyana initially claimed that women moved to live with their husbands and that a male lived at the same place as his father. I will refer to the sovereignty in which a woman was raised as her "natal" sovereignty. The question, then, is whether she remained a member of this sovereignty or became a member of her husband's sovereignty after she married. The answer is that she was a member of both. I will briefly consider the sovereignty attributes as they pertain to women in order to demonstrate this.

Sovereignty attribute number one (one name): women were presented as being able to claim both the name of their husband's sovereignty and the name of their natal sovereignty. I have very little evidence on the contexts in which women actually did this, although being from the same sovereignty was used by women to build friendship between one another if they had not known each other well before they were connected by marriage to the same place or to maintain friendships established before marriage.

Sovereignty attribute number two (one *upaema*): women were presented as being able to claim only the *upaema* of their natal sovereignty. I conducted a survey in which I asked every married male and female in Auyana which *upaema* was theirs. Without exception, women always claimed the *upaema* of their natal sovereignty. I also asked two of them whether they could also claim the *upaema* of their husband, and they denied they could.

Sovereignty attribute number three (one forest and one territory): women were presented as not being able to use the forest and territory of their natal sovereignty once they had married and moved to live with their husband. Instead, it was said that they acquired their husband's forest and ground. The only allowed alternative to this initial presentation was when a woman married within her natal sovereignty.

Sovereignty attribute number four (live at one place): as mentioned above, women were presented as living with their husband at his sovereignty.

Sovereignty attribute number five (did not shoot to kill one another in fights): this attribute was inapplicable to women. Women were presented as not ever becoming involved in fights except with other women or with their husband and children. Further, women were said to never use bows and arrows in fights and were not considered potential killers. As far as I know, both statements were true. Women might taunt men from the sidelines, but once an initiated male from outside her family became involved in a fight, a woman dropped out.

Sovereignty attribute number six (gave hands after a fight): wives were presented as helping to prepare the earth ovens and sharing the food with others in their *husband's* sovereignty, but it was said that it was the men who were "giving hands," not the women. Therefore, women were only auxiliary participants.

Sovereignty attribute number seven (did not attempt to harm one another's souls): this attribute was not applicable to women. As discussed earlier, a woman could not harm the soul of anyone except her husband, and this was not deadly.

Sovereignty attribute number eight (did not give wealth for revenging a death): this attribute was inapplicable to women, as they could not be given such wealth because they never revenged a death.

Sovereignty attribute number nine (held a victory feast after a fight with outsiders): as in attribute number six, wives helped prepare such feasts and shared food at the feasts. However, unlike their role in "giving hands," women were said to take part in a victory celebration. Men said that not only were they pleased over the outcome of the fight, but their wives were also pleased.

Sovereignty attribute number ten (pooled wealth to give to those who helped them in fights): as initially presented by men, women did not allocate wealth outside the family; only the husband could do this. This was partially true, and I will discuss it further in the following section on the subdivisions within Auyana.

Sovereignty attribute number eleven (one *akum* or one *anda*): men presented women as being able to claim they were one *akum* or *anda* with those in their natal sovereignty and also with those in their husband's sovereignty. They said that prior to marriage a woman was one *akum* or *anda* with her father's sovereignty and she would continue to claim this after she was married. After marriage, she came "inside" her husband's sovereignty and could then say she was one *akum* or *anda* there also. I did not ask any women about this.

Sovereignty attribute number twelve (acted as a group to prosecute certain offenses): obviously this was not applicable to women, but three further points should be made. First, men said that when they got into a fight with those in another sovereignty, their wives would help them by fighting with their mouths. The wives, children, and old men gathered where they were reasonably safe from the fight but could see it and were within shouting distance. From there, they shouted insults at the other side, encouraged their husbands and the other men of their husband's sovereignty, and warned them if they anticipated a surprise attack or saw someone in imminent danger.

Secondly, women did not steal pigs, rob or burn houses, or carry out secret retaliatory moves against offenders. Men claimed that their wives tried to convince them not to do this either, as it would result in a fight. In this sense, women were presented as *violating* sovereignty attribute number twelve. I do not know how much of the men's claims were attempts to make themselves seem fierce and brave and the women cowardly, and how much was true. I do know, however, that some women were said to always urge men to retaliate in cases where the men were reluctant. Thus, my guess would be that there was a considerable variation in women's timidity.

Third, while a woman could not assassinate souls, she could collect a person's sweat, clothing, and other such items and give them to a soul assassin. Men claimed that a woman would not do this to someone within her husband's sovereignty, nor to someone in her natal sovereignty. In this sense, women were members of both sovereignties and were included under sovereignty attribute number thirteen (not helping an outsider against a member of the sovereignty).

Sovereignty attribute number fourteen (a legal unit for homicide, and, in a lesser sense, for any altercation): here, women were unequivocally presented as members of their husband's sovereignty. Wives were revenge targets for homicides committed by people in their husband's sovereignty but not for those committed by their natal sovereignty. I found no cases in which a woman was attacked as a result of a homicide committed by someone in her natal sovereignty or any other sovereignty other than her husband's.

Although women were not often killed in revenge for homicides committed by those in their husband's sovereignty, this does not mean, of course, that they were not bonafide members of their husband's legal unit; it simply means that they were not preferred targets. There are two indications that this was true. First, men said it was men who killed and therefore it was men one attempted to kill in revenge. Second, it was said that those in a woman's natal sovereignty would grant her exemption from her husband's legal unit. That is, they would not attempt to kill her when they were retaliating against her husband's sovereignty. As first presented to me, this was discussed as though it simply was not done. But eventually I collected three cases which negated this claim. The three involved women who returned to their natal sovereignty when their natal sovereignty was fighting with the sovereignty of their husband. I will discuss one case which involved the sovereignties of Indona, Auyana, and a Tau (Fore) sovereignty bordering on Indona (see Map 5).

Indona had been driven from its territory by Tau sovereignties and was residing on Auyana territory. However, there were several intermarriages of Indona with Tau sovereignties. Following some deaths attributed to sorcery, one of the Tau sovereignties raided Indona and killed a man. Indona then attacked the Tau sovereignty several times but did not kill anyone. Several days after the last attack, a woman from Indona who was married to a man in the Tau sovereignty got into a fight with her husband and returned to Indona with her youngest daughter of about four or five. An Indona man in a different subgroup of Indona from the woman's and whose brother had been killed by the Tau sovereignty berated the woman for being married to an enemy. In his excitement and anger he grabbed a post and began striking the woman's daughter. The woman grabbed a post and attempted to beat off the man. As men started toward the combatants, one of the woman's blows struck the man on the head and knocked him down. Several men who were presumably affiliated with the man grabbed their bows, shouting that the woman had married into an enemy place and was now attacking them and that they were going to kill her. They began firing at her and were joined by several other men (including two from Auyana who were visiting Indona) and eventually killed her. It was said that nothing more came of this. Her brothers were quoted as saying that she was married to an enemy place and should have stayed there so it was her own fault that she was killed. When I asked my two Auyana informants if they would be angry if this happened to their sister when she visited them, they said they would. However, they claimed that they would take no retaliation against those who killed her and that she should not have visited them when they were fighting with her husband's sovereignty.

This indicates that a woman could become identified with her husband's sovereignty to the extent that even those in her natal sovereignty might kill her. If so, the low casualty rate of women must have been because they were not preferred targets.

Children (i.e., unmarried daughters and uninitiated sons) were not full members of their father's sovereignty only because they were not adults. Children were presented as having the same name and the same *upaema*, living at the same place, being one *akum* (*anda*), and as part of the same legal unit as their father. The other attributes were not applicable to them because children did not participate in the cooperative endeavors defining those in a sovereignty. Consequently, I will not discuss children's membership in social units except as they were the focus of adult activities.

## POOLING UNIT ATTRIBUTES

Auyana was presented as being divided into two groups, which I will refer to as pooling units. Pooling unit members, of course, had all the attributes of sovereignty members. But, as mentioned earlier, only some of these attributes (numbers eleven through fourteen) were presented as distinguishing pooling group members from sovereignty members. Sovereignty attributes numbers one and two were initially presented as not being relevant at the pooling unit level. As will be discussed later, this was not true of either attribute. Sovereignty attributes numbers three and four did not distinguish pooling units although it was true that hamlets were usually comprised primarily of the members of a single pooling unit, and as a consequence the members of a pooling unit tended to have their gardens clustered in the same area. Sovereignty attributes numbers five through nine were of a slightly different order. Except for number five, they did not distinguish pooling units but they were more intense in pooling units. For example, pooling unit members *never* performed soul assassinations on one another. This intensification held true at each successive lower level also.

Sovereignty attribute number five was rather interesting as there was a distinctive attribute of the pooling unit relating to killing. This attribute was that they fought with sticks but not with arrows. It was admitted that those within a pooling unit did sometimes fight with arrows, although it was simultaneously stated that this was not serious fighting. Hence, I interpret the initial presentation as a way of emphasizing the absence of murderous hostility within a pooling unit rather than as a literal statement of a necessary requirement for continued membership in the same pooling unit. If this interpretation is correct, then the presentation that *sovereignty members fought with arrows but with no intent to kill whereas pooling unit members fought only with sticks* was a way of saying that pooling unit members were even less likely to kill one another than were those belonging to the same sovereignty but to different pooling units.

I will refer to the above attribute as pooling unit attribute number one and will next consider the other attributes applicable *only* at the pooling unit level. As in the presentation of sovereignty attributes, these are to be taken as applying only to initiated males.

*Pooling unit attribute number two was that their sons and daughters did not marry each other.* Although children were also prevented from marrying others outside their pooling unit, these prohibitions were determined by individual relationships, and hence the pooling unit was the largest exogamous social unit. There were two exceptions in Auyana to attribute number two. In both cases, the husband remained a member of his original pooling unit for all except one class of activities pertaining to wealth-giving. Then, he was only a partial member.

*Pooling unit attribute number three was that they used each other's daughters as exchanges for wives for their sons.* The main exception to this claim was that exchange marriages did not occur all the time, although when they did daughters from within the pooling unit were used. In fact, the exceptions were so frequent that it is perhaps more accurate to say that members felt it would be best if there were always exchanges of women but that this was not necessary in order for there to be marriages.

*Pooling unit attribute number four was that when a man's wife had a miscarriage, all the men gathered to perform a ceremony for the husband, followed by the consumption of a pig.* Both the ceremony and the consumption were restricted to men. The ceremony involved taking the husband to a stream where an older man would cut the husband's glans penis in half lengthwise. The rationale for this was that it prevented the husband from getting pregnant and dying. They argued that while it was possible for a woman to miscarry as a result of some overexertion like carrying a heavy load, this was extremely unlikely. Rather, most miscarriages were due to the husband having intercourse with his wife while she was pregnant. Men did not bother to protest their innocence as it would have been ignored. The danger of having intercourse with a pregnant woman was that the "blood-water" (see the later discussion of ancestry) comprising the fetus would enter the husband's stomach through his penis. He would then become pregnant and since he had no birth canal, would die. By cutting and bleeding his penis, this fetal blood-water was drained out of him and he was safe.

While the husband was being cut, other married men would voluntarily jab or shoot (with toy bows) small pieces of chipped stone into their glans penis in order to make it bleed and drain out any contaminating vaginal blood they might have unwittingly acquired. Following the ceremony, the men returned to an earth oven prepared earlier, opened it, and divided a pig acquired from someone outside the pooling unit.

I did not attempt to record many cases of this ceremony and therefore do not know the frequency of allowed alternatives. At the two I attended, some male participants were close affiliates, but not members, of the subject's pooling unit.

As mentioned earlier, the above four attributes were not used at any other level. The remaining attributes were used at lower levels or (for the last three) at both the sovereignty level and lower levels.

*Pooling unit attribute number five was that if a man died, his widow would remarry someone in his pooling unit—but not his brother.* In fact, the frequency of leviratic marriages was rather low, although no one seemed to get particularly upset about it. If the widow was young and she remarried someone outside the pooling unit, those in the pooling unit would demand wealth from her new husband. If she remarried someone inside the pooling unit, there was no transfer of wealth.

After finding out that women remarried men in different groups, I asked what happened to their children and was told that unless they were nursing, someone in the father's pooling unit would raise them. Thus, the initial presentation of attribute five might have been a way of saying that the pooling unit attempted to retain whatever any one of its members acquired. This attempt, however, turned out to be as unsuccessful for children as it was for women (see the analysis at the end of this chapter).

*Pooling unit attribute number six was that when one of their members was killed by someone outside the sovereignty (and, according to the initial presentation, a person could be killed only by someone from outside the sovereignty) and someone from outside the sovereignty revenged the victim's death, those in the dead person's pooling unit pooled wealth and gave it to the revenger.* The same comments apply here as to sovereignty attribute number eight. In addition, when they specified that the pooling unit pooled wealth, they did not present it as though only those in the pooling unit contributed. Rather, they said that those in the pooling unit did it and others helped them. That is, those in the pooling unit were the ones held responsible for presenting the wealth to the avenger, but they could get help from anyone who was willing. Further, those in the pooling unit were said to be the ones who had to initiate the pooling or it would not be done, and it was they who contributed the bulk of the wealth. To the best of my knowledge, both of these claims were true. However, the question of the responsibility of the entire pooling unit will be dealt with later when the pooling unit is considered as a legal unit.

*Pooling unit attribute number seven was that they pooled wealth (or at least a pig and food) and gave it to those outside their pooling unit, but never to one another, at certain life-crisis events involving an adult male member of the pooling unit or his wife or his children.*

*Pooling unit attribute number eight was that they were given wealth at certain life-crisis events which involved women married to male members, and/or their children.*

In order to discuss pooling unit attributes seven and eight, it is first necessay to consider more closely the concept of "wealth." Members of Auyana distinguished between *tomba* and *onta*. *Tomba* can be roughly translated as all food except animals. Animals and all valued inanimate items were *onta*. *Onta* could also be used to refer to the subclass of "all valued inanimate items." I will gloss *tomba* as "food"; *onta*, when referring to the entire class, as "wealth"; and *onta*, when referring to the subclass, as "valued things."

I will first consider which items could be exchanged for items in another class (Bohannon 1955). Food could be exchanged for food and for labor, and sometimes it could be exchanged for a portion of pig, if the food was a special crop and there was a lot of it. Food was never exchanged for valued things. At the same time, food accompanied almost every form of exchange. The one time food was not a necessary part of the exchange was when there was what I have been calling a trade. The Auyana term was *meye*, which could be more exactly glossed as "getting together for the explicit purpose of exchanging at the same time some items of wealth." Usually this meant exchanging a live pig for shells, feathers, adzes, salt, shields, bows and arrows. Occasionally, it meant that raw materials for the above items were exchanged, especially wood for bows and arrows. Sometimes it meant that feathers were being exchanged for shells or some other valued thing. Wealth was also pooled together with cooked pig and given to those in another group as a "gift"—that is, there was no specification about exactly what, if anything, was to be given in return, and there was often no specification about when anything was to be given in return.

As stated in pooling unit attribute number six, three things were meant when it was said that a pooling unit "pooled": (1) the members were held responsible, (2) they initiated and organized the pooling, and (3) they contributed the bulk of the wealth. In addition, members of Auyana said they pressured one another to contribute to any given pooling. It was claimed that if someone did not help pool, unless he was ill or had no wealth others in his pooling unit would be angry. However, this was an internal affair. Those outside the pooling unit did not care who within it helped as long as wealth was given by the pooling unit. Another characteristic of pooling was that the wealth items were literally gathered together in one spot and then distributed. If one wanted to determine how much had been pooled, all that was necessary was to count the items collected in that spot.

As previously mentioned, men presented women as not being engaged in pooling wealth. Specifically, men claimed that women did not actually take the wealth and place it in the collection, and further claimed that the decision as to whether wealth was to be contributed was always made by the husband. It would seem that this was a statement of what the men *wished* were true. They readily stated that women did put wealth in the collection area—but only because their husbands had told them to do so. Thus, it presumably meant nothing if one saw a woman walk up and put something down. In fact, the woman may have done so without consulting her husband. Further, wives by no means always let their husbands decide on the allocation of wealth outside the family. However, I have only an impression of the frequency of such decision-making. For, unless someone knew a woman well, it was not easy to find out whether she had consulted her husband before making a donation. Each time I asked a woman, she said that it was all right with her husband. I did not ask the husbands, because this would have been viewed partly as prying and partly as causing trouble.

Much the same was true when I attempted to find out to what extent wives influenced the allocation of wealth outside the family. It was said that there was much variation. Some wives were reputed to control their husbands completely, and some wives were reputed to have no influence on their husbands. The three wives of Auwi exemplified the latter. Auwi was a "hot man" and a killer, and it was said that his wives never interfered with him for fear he would shoot them. Whether this was true or not I do not know, but I was unable to collect any cases in which Auwi had fought with his wives (although there were several times that he had beaten them).

At the opposite extreme was Pu'a, a quiet, tongue-tied, shy young man in his middle twenties in 1962. Pu'a had somehow been matched with a flirtatious, loud-mouthed, assertive woman. As their house was close to mine, I heard many arguments between them and the tongue lashings she gave him. The ultimate degradation arose when he decided to donate a pig which she did not want killed. Knowing she would attack him in order to prevent him from killing it, he told some men in his pooling unit that he wanted to donate the pig and for them to kill it. They cheerfully did so the morning of the pooling. Pu'a's wife did not interfere and did nothing except avoid him until he came home that evening after the distribution had been completed. As he entered the house, she screamed at him for having killed the pig and hurled vicious insults. He only shouted back at her occasionally. By this time, we all were intently listening in order not to miss any part of the show. Suddenly there was a howl and Pu'a staggered out of the door with his wife flailing at him with a firebrand. Just as he got outside, she smashed him on top of the head, knocking him to his knees. She took one brief look at him, whirled around, and stalked back into the house. He knelt a few seconds, appearing dazed, and then got up and staggered back into the house. Nothing further was heard. I did not need to be told that Pu'a had little to say about how "his" wealth was allocated. However, other men did comment on this state of affairs. Pu'a was sometimes described as a "bug," a "nothing," and when his name came up in conversations about male-female relationships, other men would laugh and mock him. Males, then, exerted pressure on other males not to allow their wives to control the allocation of goods, but to the best of my knowledge, there was no pressure exerted on a man not to let his wife *in any way* influence the allocation of goods.

When wealth was given to pooling units it was taken from the general collection and divided into several piles. One of these piles was then said to belong to the pooling unit. Not all the members of the pooling unit necessarily went to receive the wealth. The division of the wealth among the members of the pooling unit was performed at their own place, so it was only necessary for as many to go as would be needed to carry the wealth back. Someone also had to go who could make demands on the givers if the amount were too small. In addition, others might want to visit friends where the distribution was being made, and hence the number who appeared at any given event varied considerably. At the distributions I observed, the members of a pooling unit did not usually sit together. In fact, the only time they sat together was when the distributions involved pooling units from sovereignties with which members of Auyana were not on good terms. For the remainder, the only reasonably consistent spatial division at an Auyana distribution was that of the men and the women.

There were several life-crisis events at which pooling units were involved as givers and/or receivers. Marriage is the first one I will consider. There were terms for specific methods by which a man and a woman could become husband and wife, but no terms which referred to all the methods. My use of the term "marriage" in this discussion is simply for convenience. They did make a distinction similar to the one we make when we say that someone is "divorced." A man or woman who had once had a spouse but did not at that time have one or who was past the age where people usually had a spouse but did not have one was said to be *keto'*. However, I could elicit no term which referred to the opposite condition (i.e., having a spouse). I interpreted this to mean that people beyond a certain age were assumed to have spouses unless otherwise specified. Hence, while there was no term equivalent to ours of "married," there was a similar concept.

The type of marriage which most heavily involved pooling units was when neither the man nor the woman had been previously married. For a male, his first marriage occurred between the age of sixteen and his early twenties, usually to a girl who had not been married before. Ages were hard to estimate, and it could have been that some men were married younger than sixteen. However, there were no cases in Auyana where a man went beyond his early twenties without becoming married. A few cases of bachelorhood

existed in other sovereignties, but the phenomenon was rare. Of the forty-
nine married men in Auyana in 1962, four (8 percent) initially married
women who had been married previously. In three of these cases, the
woman's husband had died. The other case was a young girl who had run
away from her husband in another sovereignty.

It is not clear at what age a girl first married. The upper limit was somewhere in late adolescence. The lower age limit was more vague. In 1962 I
did a survey of all the married couples in Auyana and one of the questions I
asked the women was whether they had been married before they had menstruated. Twenty-seven of the sixty-one, or 44 percent, said they had been
married before they menstruated. The men told me that Auyana, unlike
other groups, did not marry off its daughters until after they had menstruated. It was governmental policy to discourage prepubescent marriages, and
I at first attributed their assertion as a desire to appear to be obedient citizens. But after I had been there a while and came to know several men who
did not seem to care at all whether I thought they obeyed the government, I
was still told that this was the case. Consequently, I was surprised at the
results of the survey. When I asked two men about the results, they said it
was true that there would sometimes be no ceremony or distribution of
wealth at a girl's first menstruation because they had no wealth at the time,
but they insisted the girls were not married until after having menstruated.
This raises the possibility that the women who told me they had been married before they menstruated were actually ones for whom nothing had been
done when they first menstruated, and they did not want to admit this. For,
in the period from 1962 to 1965, the twelve Auyana marriages of previously
unmarried girls involved girls well past menstruation. However, this may
say little about what happened prior to the arrival of the government with its
policy of discouraging "child brides." I have no further evidence to settle this
discrepancy.

Girls also usually first married a man who had not been married before. Of
the sixty-one married women in Auyana, six (10 percent) initially married a
man who had another wife. The remaining 90 percent married men who had
not been married. The number of women married polygynously in 1962 was
twelve (i.e., forty-nine men were married and sixty-one women). Six of these
were by first marriages of the women and six by remarriages. Of the latter
six, five were widowed by their husbands and one had left her husband.

There were three methods by which a previously unmarried girl could
marry a previously unmarried boy. First, the girl might not desire to marry
the man chosen by those in her pooling unit and would run away to a man in
another sovereignty (she would never run to a man in the sovereignty of the
intended husband). Running away was said to be infrequent; of the sixty-one
married women in Auyana in 1962, only two (3 percent) were first married
this way. When it did happen, a pooling unit in the new husband's sover-

eignty would act as her natal group, and she was treated after the marriage as if was she were a natal member of that pooling unit.

Second, there were trial marriages in which the girl was sent to the man she was intended to marry, and if she stayed, full marriage cermonies were performed. Of the sixty-one married women in Auyana in 1962, five (8 percent) were first married in trial marriages. Of these, in four cases the bride's and groom's sovereignties were not on good terms and did not trust each other to complete the events necessary to constitute a full marriage. There was also doubt in each case over whether her natal group would encourage her to remain with her husband and, if they did, whether she would remain even then.

The remaining form of marriage, a full marriage, I will first consider from the perspective of the groom and his pooling unit. Men initially said that although others in a boy's pooling unit had the primary control over where and who he would marry, a boy could at least veto any marriage and had some influence in the choice of his wife. This turned out not to be true. One of the questions I asked males was whether they knew their wife before they were married and whether they had wanted to marry her. While several said that they at least knew who she was, only two (4 percent) said they had carried on any courtship with her before marriage. The rest said that others in their pooling unit had selected her.

Once a decision, not necessarily unanimous, was made about a girl, negotiations were begun with members of the prospective bride's pooling unit. If the negotiations were successful (i.e., nobody actively opposed the union), the next step was the sending of *paiemba*, which I will translate as the "binder." The binder usually consisted of cooked marsupials and vegetables prepared by the groom's pooling unit and given to those in the bride's pooling unit. Occasionally, a pig or a cassowary would be sent. The elapsed time between completing negotiations and sending the binder varied from several days to several months. Following their sending the binder, the next step was for the groom's pooling unit to pool and send *are onta* ("married woman" or "bride" wealth). It was said that the bride wealth had to at least contain one pig, and all 138 bride wealths for which I collected information had at least one pig. Bride wealth also had to contain some valued items, but the amount varied considerably. In addition, estimates of the quantity of valued items given as part of any particular bride wealth varied equally as much. Hence, I am able to make only a guess about an average bride wealth prior to the arrival of Europeans: there were twenty to fifty feet of small cowries sewn onto strips of rope; five to twelve large cowries on strings; six to ten feet of clam shells on strings; two to four cubic feet of unprocessed bark cloth; twenty to thirty bow strings; fifteen to twenty bows with strings; five to ten pieces of palm wood roughly shaped into bows; and forty to seventy arrows (see Brown 1959 for comparative data on the Chimbu in the Western Highlands).

After the bride's pooling unit received and divided among themselves the binder, they waited for the bride wealth to be sent. Either on the same day as the bride wealth was sent or thereafter, they performed a ceremony for the girl and sent her to her new husband. I collected no cases in which this ceremony was performed and the girl sent before the bride wealth was sent. Members of Auyana said that it was better for the bride wealth and the girl to be sent on the same day, as that way there was no chance either side could renege. Unfortunately, I collected data only on whether the girl was sent before the bride wealth and therefore have only the marriages in 1962-65 to indicate the frequency with which the girl and bride wealth were sent the same day or the girl was sent afterwards. Of these, one was a trial marriage which was still undecided and so no bride wealth had been sent. In three (27 percent) of the remaining eleven cases the girl and the bride wealth were sent the same day. Eight (73 percent) involved the bride wealth being sent first. In other words, they were able to do what they said was preferable only about a third of the time.

The sending of the girl can be referred to by a term which was also used to refer to one special part of the sending—*are watoi to'wai*. *Are watoi* was the name for the skirts married women wore and *to'wai* meant to wrap around. I will refer to this as "changing clothes." The first step in changing clothes was to keep the girl and two or three of her girlfriends in her mother's house for two or three days. This was not intended to be an ordeal for the girl, but a way to make her more beautiful and to prepare her for marriage. She and her companions were fed special foods such as greens, yam, taro, sugar cane, and other foods which were normally only a small part of the diet, had pig grease rubbed on them periodically, and were given instructions by the married women on how to treat their husbands. As part of this, the women performed skits to illustrate certain aspects of married life. Initiated males were barred from the house during these times and the women were secretive about what took place. However, in 1965 I was allowed to watch some of the skits, ostensibly because I behaved decently towards women—I did not beat, mock, insult, or order about my wife or other women. The skits were mostly parodies of the demands men made on women.

On the morning when the girl's seclusion ended, she was brought outside and placed on a pandanus mat. For two or three hours, women tried skirts on her, adjusted them, tried them on again, and adjusted them until the skirts which were to be sent with her were thought to fit. During this time, pig grease was periodically rubbed on her by her mother and other women married to the men in her pooling unit. Meanwhile, the men of her pooling unit killed pigs to be cooked in earth ovens. While the pigs cooked, the men collected various valued items which, together with some pig, were sent with the girl when she went to her husband. The valued items and pig were called *kopari'*, which I will call "dowry." After the earth ovens were opened, the pig and vegetables were divided into several piles. I was initially told that these shares were given to various people but that one always went to the natal pooling unit of the bride's mother. This is discussed in Chapter 6. A portion of the pig was set aside, cut into pieces, and stuffed into a net bag to be taken by the bride to her husband's hamlet. The girl was then prepared to leave. If her husband's hamlet was in her own sovereignty or in an immediately adjacent one, all the skirts which had been given to her were put on her, the bag full of pig was hung from her head and she was given several sugar cane shoots to carry. Others in her pooling unit carried the remainder of the dowry. The bride's party and anyone else who wanted to tag along then set out for her husband's hamlet. The trip usually took a while as the girl was so laden she could hardly walk. Upon her arrival, she was again placed on a mat and the married women of her husband's pooling unit removed the skirts from her. She was thus physically and symbolically transferred. Those in her party were given some cooked vegetables prepared by those in the groom's pooling unit and, except for her father and mother, soon returned home. Her father and mother stayed for several days to help her settle in and then they returned home.

It was said that for a trial marriage, the girl was secluded in her mother's house for a couple of days, the skits were performed, and she took several married women's skirts, but nothing else was sent with her. If she stayed, more skirts and the dowry were sent, and pig was distributed to her mother's natal pooling unit and others. At the same time, the groom's pooling unit sent bride wealth to the bride's pooling unit. In the three cases for which I have this type of information, this was done.

I was told that the girls who ran away were not secluded but only had pig grease rubbed on them and were given a few skirts. No dowry was given and the groom's pooling unit gave no bride wealth. I know of two such cases in Auyana , and no dowry or bride wealth were given as far as I could determine. Both these cases involved girls marrying men who already had wives, which may have had something to do with the absence of ceremony.

When a girl married a man who was already married or who had once been married, it was said that both parties did the same things as they would have done if the man had not been married. This was true for the six cases I recorded, except that only a subdivision of the pooling unit participated in gathering the bride wealth.

When a previously married woman married a man who had not been married, the marriage was treated as though both had been married in that nothing special was done for the woman. She simply took up residence with the man. The only difference was that bride wealth might be given to her ex-husband's pooling unit—but not to her natal pooling unit. I was initially told that all the men in the groom's pooling unit would help him gather the bride wealth and that bride wealth was always given to the ex-husband's pooling unit, as they would be angry otherwise. This bride wealth was said to be smaller than bride wealth for a girl who had never been married. The latter statement was true. The other two statements had numerous exceptions. First, only a subdivision of the pooling unit helped the man gather the bride wealth. In this sense, the marriage was analogous to the situation where a man already had a wife and married an unmarried girl. Second, in the case of an unmarried man who married a once-married woman, a smaller bride wealth was demanded, and therefore only subdivisions were needed to collect the wealth. However, if only a subdivision was involved when a man got his *first* wife, this indicated that someone had been reluctant to buy him a wife in the first place, and he could not summon the support of the entire pooling unit.

A man who already had a wife gave the regular amount of bride wealth for any previously unmarried girl. I think the reason for the involvement of only a subdivision in pooling the wealth was that others in the pooling unit would not help in buying second or third wives. That is, it was an individual affair, and if the man could get someone to help him, fine. If not, then he was left with one wife. As this implies, when a woman's husband died and she remarried a man who already had a wife or who had once had one, whether her ex-husband's pooling unit would get any wealth was extremely problematical.

The next life-crisis event to be considered is that of birth. One set of transactions centered on the pregnancy and the other on the period immediately following the birth. When it was evident that a woman was pregnant, the natal pooling unit of the woman got together some bark cloth capes and sent them to her so that she might cover her protruding stomach. In return, her husband's pooling unit cooked some vegetables and sent them to her natal pooling unit. The allowed exceptions to this were that in addition to his wife's natal pooling unit, the husband might send a gift to those in another pooling unit as though they were his wife's natal pooling unit.

When a child was born, it was said that the mother's natal pooling unit cooked vegetables and sent them to her while she spent three days to a week confined to the birth house (which was also the menstrual house). This giving was called *auwi'wi*. Sometime after she left the birth hut and returned home, the new father's pooling unit killed several marsupials or, if lucky, a cassowary to cook and gave it to the mother's natal pooling unit. This giving was called *taina*. However, this was not done for every child.

The third life-crisis event to be considered is the piercing of the septum of a child. It was said that this was done for every child. I would guess that it occured around the ages of five or six. For little girls there was no special ceremony accompanying the piercing. For every boy, someone in his mother's natal pooling unit (but never his mother's brother) pierced his septum with a piece of bamboo which was left in and turned periodically until a hole was formed. The boy's pooling unit pooled vegetables and one of them would kill a pig, and the pig and vegetables were given to the mother's natal pooling unit.

The next life-crisis event to be considered is that of a girl's first menstruation. When a girl first menstruated, she told her mother, who took her to the women's menstrual house. When the menstrual period ceased, she returned to her mother's house. It was said she then underwent a ceremony similar to "changing clothes" at the time of marriage. Reportedly, two or three of her girlfriends would join her and all of them would be given special foods and have pig grease rubbed on them for a couple of days. However, she received no instruction at this time, nor were any skits put on for her, and initiated men were not prevented from coming into the house. People from her pooling unit and other friends would drop in and visit with her for a while and generally everyone had a good time except at one point. It was said that on the second or third day of seclusion, initiated unmarried males in her pooling unit would come in the house and drag her and her companions outside, although the girls tried to fight them off. Once outside, pieces of stiff grass were jammed into their nostrils to make them bleed and the girls were beaten with bundles of a vicious stinging nettle. The bleeding and beating were to make the girls strong. Following this, they were returned to the house. The next day, the girl's pooling unit pooled vegetables and killed one or two pigs. As the meat was cooking, the girls were brought outside, were given new clothes, and had armlets or other ornamentation put on them and pig grease rubbed on them. Following this, they circled the earth oven and then went off to sing and dance at other hamlets within the sovereignty and those in neighboring friendly sovereignties. The members of the girl's pooling unit meanwhile gave the pig and vegetables to various people, but some of it always went to the girl's mother's natal pooling unit.

I have already pointed out that this ceremony was not performed for 44 percent of the women, but have no evidence about whether this exact sequence was performed for the remaining 56 percent. I saw two such ceremonies in 1962, and the sequence was performed as described above except that in neither case were the girls' noses bled, although they were severely beaten with nettles. In Chapter 6, I will discuss who donated the pigs and to what extent entire pooling units were involved in these ceremonies.

The next life-crisis event to be considered is that of male initiation. As initially presented, there were three stages to male initiation and every male went through all three: *ma'eni, kumara,* and *ipo'a.* The major exception was that not all males went through all three stages, and two stages might be performed simultaneously. One consequence of these exceptions was a reduction in the number of times wealth was given, as a man could have two sons in different stages simultaneously and one giving would suffice for both of them. I will present only a skeletal outline of the three stages and will not discuss the variations except as they pertain to the giving of wealth.

*Ma'eni* was said to be essentially a means of moving a boy from his mother's house to the men's house about the time he reached puberty. The members of the boy's pooling unit collected vegetables and one of them killed a pig, which was given along with the vegetables to his mother's natal pooling unit. The boy was given a different type of clothing to wear and slept thereafter in the men's house.

*Kumara* was presented as the main initiation stage. It was performed when the boy was around fourteen to sixteen years old. This was a large affair, as several boys from a pooling unit were initiated at one time. The boys were first taken to a stream where an area had been prepared. There, they were beaten with small branches and clublike succulents by all the initiated male members of their pooling unit except their fathers and brothers. After they were beaten, each boy was held by someone from his mother's natal pooling unit while someone else from his mother's pooling unit jammed swordlike grass leaves into his nostrils, severing the blood vessels and causing his nose to spew blood. Following this, the same men pulled out his tongue and made three incisions near the base. Ginger and salt were rubbed into the incisions. Next, they pulled back the foreskin of his penis and made several deep cuts in the glans penis. Pieces of U-shaped cane were then forced down his throat, causing him to vomit violently. It was said that the reason those from the boy's mother's natal pooling unit mutilated him rather than those from his own pooling unit was that the former went easy on him, whereas the latter might have killed him.

The boys were then stripped of their clothing, herded together, and, surrounded by singing, chanting men holding branches to hide the boys' naked bodies, were taken back to the village and put into the men's house. Along the way, the men were attacked by the women, who threw stones and roots at them and who might wrestle with them in an attempt to prevent them from putting the boys into the men's house. Both men and women were sometimes hurt doing this. The boys were then kept in the men's house for three to four days. During this time, they were allowed outside only for toilet purposes. They were not allowed to drink water or eat sugar cane or anything juicy. They were forced to sit close to a large fire which was kept burning continuously. As long as any man was awake, the boys were not allowed to sleep and had to sit upright all the time. They received lectures principally involving relations with women and fighting, accompanied by punches to make sure they got the point. They were shown flutes and the bullroarers used to make the sounds, which until this time they had been told were caused by wild anthropomorphs (see the earlier discussion of *upaema*), and were told how men first got the flutes and bullroarers by stealing them from the women. On the day when the boys were presented to the village, members of their pooling unit killed pigs and prepared earth ovens. The boys were given special clothes, a special feather headband, and other ornamentation, and were decorated with grease, charcoal, and other paints in special patterns. They spent the day parading in the village while the women admired them and the young children ran screaming into the houses because of their fierce appearance. The pigs were divided and some were given to the natal pooling unit of the mother of each boy.

*Ipo'a*, the last stage, took place just before the boy was to marry. Again, several boys would participate in this ceremony at the same time, and both the *ipo'a* and *kumara* ceremonies might be done concurrently. At *ipo'a*, the boys were not beaten, but their noses were bled, their penises were cut, and they "swallowed" cane. They were also secluded for three to four days and could have neither water nor juicy food. But they were not continually harrassed and lectured. They were given special clothing and ornaments and were painted in a particular pattern and presented to the village. Pigs were killed by those in their pooling unit and given to those in their mothers' natal pooling unit.

The next life-crisis event to be considered is death. First, I will consider what was done about the death of an unmarried girl or a boy who had not yet been initiated. There were exceptions to the exact sequence as it was initially pesented but they are not of primary concern and will not be discussed here. The first step was to prepare the body to be mourned (*amambe*). This was done by those in a subdivision of the dead child's pooling unit. Preparations consisted of washing the body, putting ornaments on it, and laying it on a bamboo stretcher. The stretcher was then propped at an angle either inside the child's mother's house or just outside. Mourning (*kum*) consisted of singing and sobbing, which were to help the ghost find the road to ghostland. Those in the child's pooling unit, his mother's natal pooling unit, and married women from his pooling unit and their children were the principal mourners. There were the other mourners who were in some way closely associated with the child's parents. Mourning continued day and night for several days. During this time, the mother of the child might cut off part of a finger or part of her earlobe, and the child's father or brother might slice off part of an earlobe. Others did not mutilate themselves. On the day the child was to be buried, some of those in the mother's pooling unit dug the grave and buried the child. During this time, the members of the dead child's pooling unit pooled valued items. Pigs were killed and prepared in earth ovens. After the child was buried, the earth ovens were opened and the pig and valued items (*asi'e*) were given to those in the dead child's mother's natal pooling unit. At the same time, those in the dead child's pooling unit divided among themselves pig provided by one of the married women from the pooling unit. Two to three days after the burial, the father of the dead child killed a pig and distributed it to all those in his pooling unit (an event called *musa*). Not long after, those in the pooling unit got together special vegetables, cooked them, and gave them to those individuals outside the pooling unit who were in some way especially helpful during the funeral (called *kanta*).

For a married woman, the sequence of preparation, mourning, burial, wealth giving, postburial eating, and feeding special helpers was the same as for a child. However, it was said that more mourners came than for a child. Also pigs might be killed during the mourning and fed to the mourners. Further, the pig and valued items were not given to the dead woman's mother's natal pooling unit but to her own natal pooling unit. Her brother might cut off his earlobe or the earlobe of one of his children and receive in return a special portion of pig from her husband's pooling unit.

For an initiated or married male, the sequence remained the same, but the magnitude of the event was greater and the distribution of wealth different. Funeral attendance for an initiated unmarried male or a young married man was said to be as great as for a married woman in her prime. For a man in his prime (late twenties to late forties), it was said that people came from all over, that anyone who could trace any common ancestry or was a friend of the man or a friend of others in his pooling unit would come to mourn. For all men except old ones, it was said that the dead man's sisters (married or unmarried) would cut off a finger, that his mother's brother's son and his father's sister's son might cut off part of an ear, and that others who considered themselves close to him might cut off a finger (if female) or an ear (both sexes). In fact, females had a finger cut off when they were small if some adult male close to their parents died. Rarely did a woman cut off any of her own fingers. All of the mutilated individuals were given a special portion of pig following the burial. It was said that several pigs were killed during the mourning itself and given to the mourners. The pig and valued items given after the burial were still given to the mother's natal pooling unit, but they were also given to the dead man's father's sister's son and the dead man's sister's son. In addition, they might be given to any pooling units with whom the dead man's pooling unit was particularly friendly.

The above constitute the recurrent life-crisis events at which pooling units gave and received wealth. The actual distribution of wealth at these events is discussed in Chapter 6.

*Pooling unit attribute number nine was that they could refer to themselves as one aparawainonda. Aparawai* meant those who were initiated together, age-mates. *Onda* meant any *unordered* grouping of objects. Those in the pooling unit, then, were a collection of age-mates. Given that boys from the same pooling unit were initiated together, this was roughly true. Note that this makes it quite clear that women were not considered full members.

The next attributes to be considered were used at the sovereignty level and lower levels as well.

*Pooling unit attribute number ten was that they would refer to themselves as one akum or anda.* Unlike the sovereignty level, at the pooling unit level and lower levels, the *akum (anda)* could be referred to as a specific person's *akum (anda).* For example, one of the pooling units in Auyana was referred to as Kompi's *anda (kompi ai anda).* In addition, as initially presented to me, pooling units were not named and hence there was no possibility of referring to them as a particular named *akum (anda).* In fact, they did have names, and the significance of their unwillingness to present this to me initially is discussed at the end of this chapter.

*Pooling unit attribute number eleven was that when the sovereignty sent wealth to those who gave war aid (or those who they hoped would give it), those in a pooling unit initiated the pooling and contributed the most whenever the fight started over an offense against, or by, one of their members.* To my knowledge, there were no exceptions to this presentation.

The remaining attritutes are those involving prosecution and the pooling unit as a legal unit.

*Pooling unit attribute number twelve was that members of a pooling unit demanded and received help from other members in prosecuting any of the following offenses committed against them by someone from another pooling unit, whether the offender was in the same sovereignty or not.*

1. When a girl attempted to marry some man other than the one intended by the pooling unit, all those in the pooling unit would go to get her back from the place to which she had fled. If she was not turned over to them on demand, they would take her by force. Such confrontations were obviously very touchy situations which could erupt easily into fights. But, in the cases I collected, the extent of fighting was that a few blows were exchanged and then both sides withdrew.

I have no systematic record of whether they always attempted to retrieve a runaway girl. I know there were cases where no such attempt was made. One involved a girl who went to a distant group, and in another case a girl fled to a traditional enemy. It seems likely that retrieval attempts were made only when the sovereignties involved were on fairly good terms.

2. When a certain size bride wealth had been promised and the girl had her "clothes changed" and was sent to her husband's place only to find out that the bride wealth was smaller than promised, then all those in the pooling unit went to lend at least their physical presence to the demand that more be given and to take back the girl by force if necessary. I do not know if all those in the pooling unit went in such circumstances. Fights were rarely started over reneging on bride wealth. I elicited only one over a twenty-five-year period.

3. When a pooling unit did not receive wealth at those times it should have (see pooling unit attributes seven and eight), then all those in the pooling unit would go to demand the wealth. I do not know the frequency or result of such demands, but there were no fights started as a result of this offense for the twenty-five-year period for which I have records on fighting.

While the pooling unit might act as a prosecuting group in the above cases, it is obvious this prosecution rarely involved fighting. More often, it apparently resulted in an unwillingness to give wealth to the offending group. This, of course, could result in a cycle of withholding rewards. Also note that in these cases there was no demand for others in the sovereignty to help the pooling unit prosecute initially. This might have been a major reason why fights did not often result from such disputes, since the prosecuting pooling unit would most often be some distance from home in another sovereignty and, if a fight erupted, the other pooling unit could get help much sooner. It would have been clearly unwise to start a fight in these circumstances.

*Pooling unit attribute number thirteen was that those in the pooling unit demanded and received help from one another when the following offenses were committed by someone from another pooling unit in the same sovereignty: (1) adultery, or (2) a dispute that erupted into a "big" fight and became subject to the escalation clause.*

Pooling unit attribute number twelve shows that there were a few offenses for which whole sovereignties were not prosecuting groups but pooling units were. Pooling unit attribute number thirteen points out that of those offenses for which sovereignties were prosecuting groups, there were only two for which pooling units were prosecuting groups when the offenders were from the same sovereignty. This was because the remainder of the offenses were ones which, as initially presented, were either not committed by members of a sovereignty against one another or were not prosecuted in the same way if they were. Homicide, soul assassination, attack from hiding, and burning houses constituted the former. Pig theft and robbing a house were the only examples of the latter. It was said that if a person caught someone from another pooling unit in his sovereignty stealing his pig, then he might or might not attack him. In any case, this was an individual affair and became larger only by invoking the escalation clause.

In the cases of homicide within the sovereignty, they were all committed by those in different pooling units, and in each case the pooling units served as the prosecuting groups. But I could find no cases in which anyone was caught attempting to harm someone's soul or burning houses, and there were no cases of attack from hiding except when an adulterer was ambushed as he came out of the men's house in the morning. These attacks from hiding did not automatically involve entire units. The whole unit became involved only by the escalation clause, which was frequently invoked in such cases, and the adulterer would wind up with a couple of arrows in his leg if the husband was successful.

*Pooling unit attribute number fourteen was that no member of a pooling unit helped those in another pooling unit against his own pooling unit* (see sovereignty attribute number thirteen). This occurred rarely and those who did it were unable to remain as members of the pooling unit.

Pooling units were legal units in a different sense than sovereignties. Within a sovereignty, offenses such as adultry and theft were prosecuted against individuals. The escalation clause meant that entire pooling units could become involved and once involved would be attacked. But the only consequence of this was that if one joined in a fight he would be attacked by the other side, which is a rather weak sense of "joint responsibility." The only cases in which all the members of a pooling unit were pressured to participate were those in which one pooling unit was prosecuting another over one of the items listed under pooling unit attribute number twelve. In these cases, the pressure consisted mostly of diffuse anger and a general unwilling-ness to further cooperate with those reluctant to become involved.

Apart from offenses within the sovereignty, the pooling unit was indeed a legal unit. It was said that when men attempted to revenge a death, they would try to get the killer and, if not him, then someone close to him. This meant that while the entire sovereignty was a legal unit, the pooling unit members were more jointly responsible. However, I have no evidence that this was true *inside* the sovereignty in cases of homicide. Rather, it seemed that only lower levels were held jointly responsible, but not the entire pool-ing unit of the killer.

### SUBPOOLING UNIT ATTRIBUTES

I will refer to the subdivisions within pooling units as subpooling units. Each pooling unit was said to have two of these. The earlier discussion of the relationship between sovereignty attributes and pooling unit attributes ap-plies here as well. In addition, subpooling units exhibited an intensification of pooling unit attributes one through nine in the same sense that pooling units exhibited an intensification of sovereignty attributes five through nine. With this in mind, I will first consider the two attributes distinctive of the subpooling unit.

There was a special ceremony *apemba* performed for a new husband fol-lowing his bride's first menstruation after she moved to his hamlet. *Subpool-ing unit attribute number one was that they organized and pooled the goods for this ceremony.*

*Subpooling unit attribute number two was that they were given goods at this ceremony when the new husband was the child of a woman from their unit.* The name for the ceremony was taken from a type of banana which was the main vegetable used. The banana was ground into a paste and laid on long strips of banana leaf. Pieces of pig, wild marsupial, tree slugs, salt, and spicy bark contributed by the groom's subpooling unit were placed on top of the banana. The leaves were folded over and placed inside a bamboo tube which was cooked over an open fire. When done, it was distributed to the natal subpooling unit of the groom's mother. The remainder of the ceremony consisted of a little skit put on for him by his subpooling unit and his mother's natal subpooling unit which was intended to dramatize the dangers of adultery and intercourse with a menstruating woman.

The next two subpooling unit attributes were in a sense simply intensifica-tions of pooling unit attributes. I include them here because members of Auyana talked about them as being unique attributes rather than only in-tensifications.

*Subpooling unit attribute number three was that those in the subpooling unit of the person(s) most directly involved initiated and contributed the bulk of the goods to any pooling which was the responsibility of a pooling unit* (see pooling unit attributes seven and eight). This was the same criterion used in pooling unit attribute eleven and was also used *within* the subpooling unit. To what extent it was true will be considered in the later discussion of wealth and warfare in Chapter 6.

As a subsidiary attribute, members of a man's subpooling unit were those with whom he first consulted if he wanted to organize any of the pooling events. Indeed, he might not have to consult with any others in his pooling unit, as the subpooling unit contributed the bulk of the wealth. Only if others in the pooling unit were for some reason opposed to his attempt would he and those in his subpooling unit need to consult with them.

*Subpooling unit attribute number four was that those in the subpooling unit carried out the negotiations for either getting or giving a girl as a bride and were allowed by others in the pooling unit to proceed as they pleased in the absence of strong objections.* This was true as far as the cases I gathered; however, subpooling units got into disputes over exactly which of them was to negotiate for a given daughter or son.

The remaining attributes are by now quite familiar.

*Subpooling unit attribute number five was that they referred to themselves as one aparawainonda.*

*Subpooling unit attribute number six was that they referred to themselves as one akum (anda).* Subpooling units were like pooling units in that they could be referred to as a specific person's *anda*. Also, as initially presented to me, subpooling units had no name. And, unlike pooling units, I was never able to elicit a name for them.

*Subpooling unit attribute number seven was that those in the subpooling unit demanded and received help from one another when the following offenses were committed against them by someone from another subpooling unit in the same pooling unit: (1) adultery, or (2) a dispute subject to the escalation clause.* As this implies, I was told that there were no situations in which the subpooling unit alone prosecuted offenses outside its own pooling unit or sovereignty.

*Subpooling unit attribute number eight was that they did not help those in another subpooling unit against someone in their own subpooling unit.* There were no exceptions to this in the cases I gathered.

The cases I was able to record do not establish whether the subpooling unit was a legal unit. As previous discussion implies, the subpooling unit was the preferred target for homicide revenge by those outside the sovereignty. I earlier cited a single case where a lower level within the pooling unit (i.e., a subpooling unit) was held responsible for a homicide within the sovereignty. In another case of homicide within the sovereignty, the person attacked in retaliation was a brother of the killer.

BROTHERS AND INDIVIDUAL FAMILY ATTRIBUTES

Below the subpooling unit, the only subdivisions presented to me were those of pairs of brothers and individual families comprised of a man and his wife. Brothers were presented as having two distinctive prohibitions: they could not take any of the bride wealth received for their sisters, nor could they remarry one another's wives. The other attributes brothers possessed were ones also applicable at all other levels (i.e., sovereignty attributes eleven through fourteen). They could be referred to as one *aparawainonda* and one *akum* (*anda*). These were a prosecuting group and legal unit in the same sense as were those of a subpooling unit. Brothers were further distinguished only in terms of intensification of attributes exhibited at higher levels. For example, they were presented as *always* contributing larger amounts of wealth than anyone else whenever the pooling involved any of their children or wives.

From this and the earlier sections of this chapter, it can be seen that, as initially presented to me, every pooling had a single man who initiated it and contributed the most wealth to it. A man's brother was said to contribute the greatest amount, those in his subpooling unit the next greatest, and others in his pooling unit the least. This was roughly the pattern of donations, as discussed in Chapter 6. I will refer to the man who initiated and donated the most to the pooling as the major sponsor. Others who donated particularly large amounts will be referred to as cosponsors.

A man and his wife were a social unit. If a man had more than one wife then he and each wife formed a social unit, but not he and all his wives. Nor did co-wives form a social unit distinct from their husband. A woman and her husband were the basic unit in the production of food and the woman's housing. They also did almost all of the feeding, housing, and caring for their children. A man was also pressured to initiate and donate most to poolings for events centered on his children, and he usually did so. I discussed earlier the extent to which women were actually involved in the allocation of food and wealth outside the family. A man and his wife, then, were a production unit, a child-rearing unit and, to a certain extent, a pooling unit.

Children controlled no wealth independent of their parents' wealth, and in this sense they did not contribute to the wealth gotten together by a man and his wife to be put into a pooling. However, after a boy was initiated his father might make some gifts in his name at a distribution and in this way begin to provide him with paths for wealth after he was married. As they became older, girls would be given younger siblings to care for and would be urged to help their mother in her gardens. At some point, then, girls became a part of the husband-wife group which repeatedly performed a task. However, there was no term or any special behavior distinguishing this group from the husband-wife team. Given my definition of social units, girls did not form a social unit with their parents. Boys participated with their parents in even fewer tasks than girls, and there were no special terms or behaviors that specifically associated them with their parents.

Parents and their children were, however, a quasi-legal unit in that parents were held responsible for what their children did until after the children had married, although children were not held responsible for their parents' actions. The extent to which a husband and wife, apart from their children, were a legal unit was unclear. It was said that women did not steal and make trouble except for adultery and menstrual soul harm, and I could find no cases in which a woman had stolen or destroyed something. Menstrual soul harm was directed only against a woman's husband or lover, and therefore it did not involve anyone outside the husband-wife unit or, when directed against a lover, it was said that if he retaliated at all, it would only be against the woman. Men were held responsible for exchanges of wealth and other public events. There were, however, occasions (other than homicide) in which a woman might be attacked for something her husband had done. There was one such case during my stay. A man refused to divide a bride wealth among the subunit of his pooling unit, and one of the members of the subpooling unit attacked the man's wife with a fence post. A couple of his friends said it was because she argued with him when he publicly accused her husband of being a "crook." They also said that he was angry over not being given some of the bride wealth, not over her arguing with him. They also said that she encouraged her husband to withhold the wealth from him and instead give it to some of her family friends (kin). They said he would not otherwise have attacked her.

Excluding the husband-wife unit, the members of Auyana presented themselves as being organized in classic segmentary fashion with four degrees of inclusivity: sovereignties, pooling units, subpooling units, and brothers. Table 4 summarizes the attributes for the units. Wherever an attribute was presented verbally one way and observed to be another way, I have given a no/yes answer.

As will be discussed later, membership in social units was sometimes ambiguous or shifting. This makes it misleading to give exact figures for the number of members. Auyana had about 50 married men with a total of 220 men, women, and children (see the Appendix for a precise breakdown of Auyana demography). Based on Australian census figures and Auyana estimates, other sovereignties speaking the same language as Auyana ranged from about 25 married men to about 95 married men, the average sovereignty being about 60 married men with a total of 275 men, women, and children. The distribution of sizes, however, showed about as many at the extremes as around the average (see Table 29).

One of the two pooling units in Auyana was divided into three subpooling units, the other had two subpooling units. The pooling unit with three subpooling units had thirty-one married men, with subpooling units of ten, fif-

TABLE 4
AUYANA ATTRIBUTES AT VARIOUS SOCIAL LEVELS

| | Sovereignty | Pooling Unit | Subpooling Unit | Brothers |
|---|---|---|---|---|
| 1) Name | yes | no/yes | no | no |
| 2) *Upaema* | one/more | one | one | one |
| 3) One forest, one ground | yes | no/yes | no | no |
| 4) Live at one place | yes | no | no | no |
| 5) One *akum* | yes | yes | yes | yes |
| 6) One *aparawai-nonda* | no | yes | yes | yes |
| 7) Fights | Arrows—not to kill | sticks | maybe sticks | maybe sticks |
| 8) Soul attacks | no soul assassination | no soul harm | none | none |
| 9) Help against one another | no | no | no | no |
| 10) Peace-making | sometimes | always/ sometimes | always | always |
| 11) Gifts to killer who revenges death | wealth | pig | no | no |
| 12) Gifts to helpers | wealth | pig | no | no |
| 13) Victory feast | hold together | hold together | hold together | hold together |
| 14) Prosecuting unit: | | | | |
| a. forest | yes | no/yes | no | no |
| b. homicide or attack from hiding | yes | no | no | no |
| c. soul assassination | yes | no | no | no |
| d. arson | yes | no | no | no |
| e. pig theft | yes | no/yes | no | no |
| f. wealth theft | yes | no/yes | no | no |
| g. adultery | yes | no/yes | no/yes | no/yes |
| h. garden land | yes | no | no | no |
| 15) Legal unit | yes | yes | yes | yes |
| 16) Exogamous | no | yes | yes | yes |
| 17) Daughters for exchange | no | yes | yes | sometimes |
| 18) Levirate | no | yes | yes | no |
| 19) Miscarriage ceremony | no | yes | yes | yes |
| 20) Life-crisis pooling | no | yes | yes | yes |
| 21) Life-crisis dividing | no | yes | yes | yes |
| 22) Groom ceremony (*apemba*) | no | no | yes | yes |
| 23) Bride negotiations | no | no | yes | yes |

teen, and six married men. The other pooling unit had eighteen married men with subpooling units of seven and eleven married men.

I do not know the size of the pooling units in most other sovereignties. One small sovereignty comprised of about twenty-five married men was said to be, and claimed themselves to be, exogamous and also to be a pooling unit. In a survey of other sovereignties, I made an attempt to determine the exogamous collectivites within each sovereignty. These seemed to be around the same size as the pooling units in Auyana, and I assume they represented pooling units.

I do not know the size of subpooling units in other sovereignties. At the largest extreme, sovereignties had a level of organization not present in Auyana. These sovereignties were divided into two units which were said to be protection and legal units. It was said they lived intermixed except that most of each unit lived in a particular part of the sovereignty's territory, and while there was a common forest, most of those in each unit used their own particular section of it. These units were said not to be pooling units, nor were they exogamous. It was as though two sovereignties the size of Auyana got together and agreed to share a forest and land to live on and to give one another mutual protection. I do not know what enabled the largest sovereignties to grow. They were all located in the most recently gardened areas and were therefore the most recently established, but I am not sure what this had to do with their size.

All units were "one rope," were nonhomicidal internally, were legal units, and acted as prosecuting units. All were "security" groups, and sovereignties acted cooperatively only as a security group, including mutual protection of land. Sovereignties were also related to the land by having their members live separately from other sovereignties. Sovereignties, then, were the units sharing the most important resource—land—and were the level beyond which fighting became homicidal. The sharing of land, both to dwell on and live from, was possible only if aggression were controlled. Aggression was tolerated, but uncontrolled aggression was not. Sovereignties were, in Hogbin and Wedgewood's (1953) scheme, "parishes." However, the parishioners were peaceful only to the extent that they were expected to refrain from killing each other, no matter how angry they got.

The distribution of wealth and women was the task of pooling units and smaller. These units were also prosecuting units. They were not residential units, nor did they control and share forest land. The control and use of land was accomplished by the largest and smallest social units: sharing forest land was done by the largest unit, the sovereignty, and sharing gardened land was done by the smallest unit, a pair of brothers. Distribution of the land's resources was accomplished by the medium-range social units.

As will be discussed in the following chapter, social units were presented as being descendants of a pair of brothers whose male descendants (sons' sons) were the present men. If control and use of a piece of garden land was always accomplished by brothers and their sons, over several generations a portion of that land would be held by all those who were said to be agnates. I have already discussed how this was not true of a piece of gardened land, and in the next chapter I will discuss how it was not true of the genealogies.

## SUMMARY

The definitions of Auyana social unit attributes presented up to this point can be summarized by saying they involved marriage, pooling and receiving wealth, offenses, a few verbal-symbolic items (e.g., "one name"), and the allocation of territorial resources. A full member would have been someone who possessed all these attributes. In fact, there were no full members. There was no one who always helped with pooling, always helped prosecute offenses, always lived there, and so forth. A significant question is how much a failure to perform demanded tasks was related to an inability to make demands on others. I have tried to indicate some of the parameters of this relationship and more will be examined, but my primary focus now will be on those who at least some of the time met the demands placed on them and at least some of the time had their demands met. If this was the case, and if those living in Auyana in 1962 also said that such a person was "one *akum (anda)*" with those in Auyana, I will refer to that person as a "member."

# 4. Social Units and Common Ancestry

ELUSIVE ANCESTRY

It is interesting to note that none of the social unit attributes described in Chapter 3 directly imply anything about the mode of recruitment into those social units. Only if it were assumed that boys would stay with those who initiated them and bought their wives would social unit attributes have any consequences for recruitment. Given this assumption, the attribution of the tasks of initiation and buying a wife to the pooling unit of a boy's father, and the definition of the pooling unit as being composed of those who remarry one another's wives, or at least take one another's children, would then generate biologically agnatic social units. This was the way the members of Auyana first presented themselves to me.

The first reference to what I later came to know as a social unit occurred on the second day after I had arrived in Auyana, when I asked someone who a certain man was. The answer given me in pidgin was that he was a man in Pawe's "line" (*lain bilon Pawe*). When I asked who was in Pawe's line, I was told those living in the hamlets along the highest ridge in Auyana (see Map 5), plus some of those living down below, e.g., in hamlets A and B. I was told that the rest of those living down below were the line of an old *luluwai* (government-appointed official). In this way, I was first presented with the bipartite division of Auyana into two pooling units.

For several weeks I did not ask about the genealogical nature of the groups. However, I did begin to get a genealogy from my interpreter. Eventually, some anomalous information turned up: one man married his own sister if what I had been initially told about his ancestry was correct. I was working sporadically, attempting to make some sense of all this, when some men decided to have a small feast and present me with some food, because they were pleased that I had come to live there. Since most people in the sovereignty attended, I thought that this might be a chance to get the older

*107*

men together and see if I could reconcile some of the apparently contradictory genealogical information I had been receiving.

I was then working exclusively through an interpreter, and although I was given specific Auyana terms for some of the things I asked about, the only meaning they had for me was their pidgin translation. The first thing I asked was whether those in Auyana had one *tumbuna* (ancestor). I was told that they did but that no one knew his name and no one knew what children he had. It was just said that all those in Auyana came from one "old man." I next asked for the ancestor of Pawe's line, and was given the name of the person labeled A in Figure 1. As illustrated in the diagram, he was said to have had six sons and his sons' sons comprised the older living men in Pawe's line. I then asked for the ancestor of the "old *luluwai's* line." After a great deal of discussion among themselves, I was finally given the name of the person labeled B in Figure 2. He was said to have had two sons, who in turn had two sons each, and the sons of the latter comprised the older living men in the old *luluwai's* line. At this point, I thought I had an instance of the classic patrilineal clan divided into two lineages.

I then began asking about specific individuals I knew, in order to find out which of these lineages they were in. What I found out was that there were a number of nonagnates in Auyana and that the supposed lineages were genealogically more like clans (i.e., they could not trace known ancestry to a common ancestor). For example, I found that one segment in Pawe's line were not descendants of A or B. Rather, a daughter (labeled D in Figure 3) of B in Figure 2 had married someone from another sovereignty. Her married son had moved to Auyana for unknown reasons and died there when his children were young. The latter were taken by one of the descendants of A and thus were part of Pawe's line. Furthermore, one segment of the old *luluwai's* line was also not comprised of agnatic descendants of B. Rather, another daughter of B (labeled C in Figure 3), had married a man who moved to Auyana from another sovereignty as an initiated boy, and it was said that she was given to him for free as they wanted to keep him in Auyana. This man's sons' sons comprised many of the members of the old *luluwai's* line.

The last addition was not a case of nonagnates, but a segment in the old *luluwai's* line who could not trace ancestry to B. Rather, it was said that their ancestor (labeled E in figure 3) was a man in B's son's generation whose father and B were said to be the sons of two brothers. However, they knew no names and could not definitely state that they were the sons of two brothers, admitting they might not have been, but in any case asserting they were one *anda* (my first elicitation of this attribute).

Figure 3 summarizes how the situation was presented to me by the end of my discussion with the older men. Besides their obvious desire to present themselves as biological agnates, what also intrigued me was their repeating how the descendants of female D had been raised by them and hence were

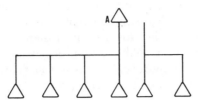

Figure 1. Pawe's line

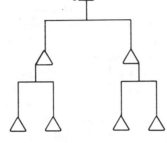

Figure 2. Old *luluwai*'s line

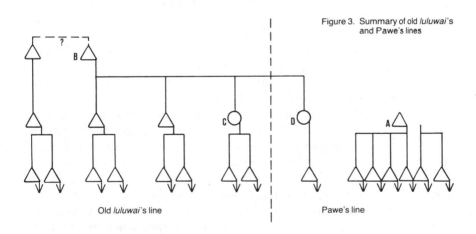

Figure 3. Summary of old *luluwai*'s and Pawe's lines

Old *luluwai*'s line                    Pawe's line

in their line. That is, after discontinuing their insistence on biological agnation, they insisted on sociological agnation.

The day after the session with the older men, I asked my interpreters and one of my neighbors whether children stayed with their fathers after they married or moved elsewhere. They said that boys stayed with their fathers and girls moved to live with their husbands when they married. I asked them what happened when a man died and elicited a statement of the levirate. But when I asked for cases, it turned out that the levirate by no means operated and furthermore that women might take their children with them when they remarried to another sovereignty. I then asked what would happen to these children and was told that their original father's line would get them back. More questioning revealed this was not always true either, but only part of a consistent attempt to initially present themselves as biological agnates.

This attempt to present themselves as biologically, or at least sociologically, agnatic manifested itself in the genealogies as well. In order to discuss this it is necessary to first consider their distinction between biological and sociological parenthood. It was said that the man's semen and the woman's fluids (mostly blood) gradually built up a fetus through repeated intercourse. One of the consequences of the belief that procreation required repeated intercourse was that the progenitor of a married women's child was almost always said to be the woman's husband. I have only one case in the genealogies in which a pregnancy was attributed to adultery. This case was collected from a woman who said she killed a daughter immediately after birth because her husband had accused her of being pregnant by another man and was angry. She said she killed the child because she was afraid her husband would be even more angry if he saw the child and might kill her and/or the child. In 1962, a married woman was discovered to be carrying on with a man, and when it was discovered that she was pregnant, her husband beat her with a hammer. The child, a girl, was kept by the husband, and in 1965 he seemed quite affectionate toward her.

On the basis of these two cases and the general attitude towards adultery, I attribute the fact that I found no other cases of illegitimate children to a failure to tell me about them. At the same time, it is possible that such instances were rarely perceived. For, if it takes several acts of intercourse to produce a child, then a woman would have to carry on with a man for some time before it would be thought that her pregnancy was not her husband's. But this sort of adulterous liaison was said to be infrequent. My primary source of information for this was a man who in 1965 told me of all the married women he had had intercourse with since he was married, including most of those in Auyana. According to his brother, the man was partly bragging. Still, he claimed that men told one another about those women who would commit adultery and those who would not, and a man might try to have intercourse with any of them if given the opportunity. This alone would result in few steady liaisons. Further, he said that men tried to avoid repetition simply because of the danger of detection.

In any case, my genealogical information on progenitors is, in the strictest sense, information on whether the child was born to a woman while she was married to a man, as her husband was invariably said to be the one who "made" the child.

In compiling the genealogies, I encountered no instances of children born to women who were not married. Although there were two such cases between 1962 and 1965, the members of the Auyana said this was because of unusual circumstances resulting from the arrival of Australians. Both the mothers involved were betrothed to men who were working at the coast as laborers. This meant that for two years these girls, while in their adolescent prime, were to refrain from sex. Members of Auyana said that this was obviously a hardship and that in the past this would never have happened as a girl would have been immediately sent to her intended husband. Given that girls were married at a fairly young age, it is quite possible that children born to unmarried girls were at least rare.

There were three senses in which a man or woman might be said to be "raising" a child (i.e., by sociological parents). The Auyana term *auwiyai* was used to refer to any activity in which someone took care of (or looked after something). The major distinction of *auwiyai* with respect to children was the following: If a woman fed and took care of a child, then she and her husband would be said to be looking after the child. I will refer to this as raising the child. It was possible for two or more women to do this by having the child alternately live with them. Thus, two men might be said to be raising a child at the same time.

A modified version of raising was when a man and his wife "marked" (*paiwai*) a child. This meant they wanted to help raise the child and would send food to it periodically. This was the phrasing, at least. In practice, this meant they acted as cosponsors or sent a gift of wealth to the man and woman with whom the child was living. Marking could develop into raising if the child occasionally went to live with those who had marked it.

If a man acted as the major sponsor for a child at the life-crisis events of menstruation and "changing clothes" for a girl, and initiation and getting a wife for a boy, he could be said to have looked after the child. I will refer to this as simply major sponsoring.

How, then, was the emphasis on biological agnation maintained in the genealogies? First, for almost the entire period of my stay I kept finding that the man initially presented as a person's biological father was not his or her biological father at all, but had only raised and sponsored the person. I still do not know if I uncovered all these cases. In any case, out of eighty-nine married men who were said to have been members of Auyana, twenty-three (26 percent) were cases of this sort. Twenty-one of the twenty-three were men whose biological fathers were from a sovereignty other than Auyana. In only two cases were the men's biological fathers from Auyana. Biological ancestry, therefore, was forgotten—or hidden—whenever it specifically involved foreign agnatic ancestry.

Another skew involved cases where it was initially presented that the man who raised and sponsored the child was not the biological father and had taken the child as an infant, when in fact the child was older when adopted. There were four such cases. All involved men whose biological fathers were not from Auyana. In addition, these four cases were the only ones in which I was initially told the biological father of a man when the biological father was not from Auyana. Of the twenty-five men with biological fathers not from Auyana, in twenty-one cases I was not told their biological fathers. In the remaining four, I was not told how old the child was when he had been adopted. In the twenty-one cases cited above, when I eventually discovered the real biological father I was further misled in eighteen cases by being told the child had been adopted as an infant, when in fact he had been adopted at a much older age.[1] Therefore, I first perceived members of Auyana as biological agnates, with only a few exceptions, and later discovered that there was only a core of biological agnates, with many exceptions.

It was, then, possible to become a member of Auyana by moving there after marriage. The low percentage of such cases which I encountered, however, suggested that something was limiting this possibility. On the other hand, the rather high percentage of children whose biological fathers were from another sovereignty and who had been raised and sponsored by someone in Auyana and had become members of Auyana meant that a person could become a full member even though he was not raised and sponsored by his biological parents. However, this does not explain why I was not told when I asked about the biological ancestry of "foreign" people. It obviously was not simply an irrelevant oversight.

To determine the nature of its relevance I will first examine more carefully the various processes by which it came about that social units were not biologically agnates. I will consider how a sample comprised of the married male members of Auyana beginning with the generation immediately preceding the older living men in 1962 came to be members of Auyana, in order to give an idea of at least the relative importance of the different processes. My reason for choosing only those from Auyana is that these men are the only ones for which I have this information. I have excluded females because, as discussed earlier, they shifted their membership when they married and consequently their patri-ancestry was primarily relevant for determining which pooling unit could demand wealth at the life-crisis events of their children and at their deaths.

I have begun with the generation immediately preceding that of the older living men in 1962, because there was little information available for earlier periods. Figures 1 through 3 show that a man could, at best, trace as far as three generations above him. However, very little was known about those in the second generation above him except as they were known to be the ancestors of social segments. Hence, the only generation for which a person usually had reasonably good knowledge was his or her parents' generation. Even here one might suspect selective oversights and misrepresentations to pre-

---

[1] This occurred regardless of whether the boys' mothers were from Auyana or not. I did, however, more readily find out about those whose mothers were from Auyana.

sent a different story from that which actually transpired. Such oversights might be expected to increase over time and so I have divided the total sample into three subsamples in order to see if there are any such trends.

The first subsample includes those in the generation before the older living men and will be called the Old sample. The second includes those younger than the Old sample but married prior to the arrival in 1950 of the Australians and will be called the Middle sample. The third includes those married since the arrival of the Australian government and will be called the Young sample. The total sample has 140 married men: 21 Old, 84 Middle, and 35 Young.

I will first consider the number of men who were raised and sponsored by someone in another sovereignty and who then moved as adults to Auyana and became members. There were no Old, five Middle, and no Young. However, these figures are misleading with respect to the amount of adult movement. They do not include entire sovereignties or subdivisions of sovereignties which moved into Auyana—these will be considered following the description of warfare. Nor do they include various individuals who moved into Auyana. For example, one Old and eight Middle moved to Auyana for a while but were not included because Auyana members disagreed over whether they had become "one *akum*" with Auyana. There were also one Old and twelve Middle who moved into Auyana and lived there long enough to build a house and make gardens but who were said to have not been "one *akum*" with Auyana. In any case, moving as an adult did not necessarily lead to smaller percentages of biological or sociological agnates. For, if the person who moved in was a biological agnate raised elsewhere, then the diversity of agnation was decreased. This was, however, the case with only one of the five men. I will later present evidence that this figure is probably low and that those biological agnates who had been raised and sponsored elsewhere and moved to their biological father's sovereignty chose to "forget" where they had been raised. Still, the immediate effect of adults moving was to increase agnatic diversity.

Next I will establish some parameters for raising, marking, and sponsoring. I will ignore cases where two men were said to be raising a child simultaneously, because information for this was extremely unreliable. Instead, I will consider only whether a man began raising a child and then stopped and someone else raised the child. Table 5 contains the number of raisers per child. The 5 cases of men who moved in after marriage are not included in this table as my data on who raised them is not complete; hence the total is only 135. There were no cases in which more than 3 men raised a male child, and the number of cases in which 3 men raised a child was quite small—7 of 135, or 5 percent. Given the obvious skewing of the Old sample toward having only one raiser per child, let me drop it. The number of male children with 3 raisers, then, becomes 7 of 114, or 6 percent, which is still about the same percentage as for the total sample. I interpret the fact that the percentage of those raised by 3 men is highest for the Young sample, next highest for the Middle sample, and zero for the Old sample to mean that such cases were routinely forgotten and converted into cases where the person had two raisers. And, if the skewing of the Old sample from the other two in the proportion of those raised by one man is any indication, eventually most of the Middle and Young samples will be converted into individuals said to have had only one raiser.

TABLE 5
FREQUENCY OF ADOPTIONS

| Number Who Serially Raised a Child | Old | Middle | Young | Total |
|---|---|---|---|---|
| 1 | 16 | 33 | 17 | 66 |
| 2 | 5 | 43 | 14 | 62 |
| 3 | 0 | 3 | 4 | 7 |
| Total | 21 | 79 | 35 | 135 |

Ignoring the Old sample, the proportion of those raised by one man and by two men is about the same. Of the Middle sample, 41 percent (33 of 79) were raised by one man and 54 percent (43 of 79) by two men. Of the Young sample, 50 percent (17 of 35) were raised by one man, and 40 percent (14 of 35) were raised by two men. The totals for the two categories show 44 percent (50 of 114) raised by one man and 50 percent (57 of 114) raised by two men.

To have been raised by one man means that the person was raised by his biological father. This brings up the question of whether those raised by their biological father were also sponsored by him. Let us analyze the Middle and Young samples since, in the case of the Old sample, each biological father who raised a boy was said to have sponsored him. Of the thirty-three Middle men raised by their biological fathers, two had another man as their major sponsors. In one case, the boy's father died just after his first initiation and an older brother acted as his major sponsor for the remainder of his initiation and for securing his wife. In the other case, the boy had been marked by another man, who became the major sponsor for his initiations (the boy's biological father was the cosponsor) and cosponsored, along with the boy's biological father, the securing of the boy's wife. Of the seventeen Young men, two had another man as a major sponsor. In both cases, the boy had been marked by another man, who was the major sponsor at his initiations (the biological father was a cosponsor) and cosponsored, along with the boy's biological father, the obtaining of the boy's wife. Hence it can be said that if the biological father raised the boy and remained alive, he would almost always be the major sponsor for the boy's initiation and for obtaining him a wife. In those few cases where the father was not the major sponsor, he would at least be a cosponsor.

If it was the case that when a biological father raised his son, he sponsored him, how was it that a biological father did not raise his son? A biological father might give the child to those in a group with which he traded, in order for the child to learn the group's language. This invariably involved someone in the other group sending another child in exchange. I use "invariably" here because this occurred in the only two cases I was able to obtain. Both cases involved those in the Middle sample. One was briefly mentioned in a discussion of the larger context within which Auyana lived. There it was mentioned that several boys from Auyana went to the village of Abi'era in Uwara' (Tairora) for a few years while several boys from Abi'era came to Auyana. Of the three Auyana boys who went to Abi'era, only one stayed more than a year. The one who stayed several years was sent by his biological father. However, the other two were boys whose biological fathers had died and who had been adopted. That is, while these were cases of a man giving away a male child he was raising, they were not usually his biological sons. In any case, all the boys returned to their natal village to be initiated and to have their wives bought, and none attempted to become members of the visited sovereignty. The other case involved an exchange of one boy from Auyana for a boy from a southern Uwara' village. In this case, the boys were sent at about the age of six or seven and both remained and died in the group to which they had moved.

I conclude that although the exchange of boys for trade purposes was practiced, it was not done often and did not necessarily mean a boy would remain in a foreign sovereignty. This, therefore, was not a significant reason for Auyana being other than a biologically agnatic group.

A biological father might give a male child as an infant to someone to raise and keep. When boys were exchanged for trade, they had to be old enough to know their natal language well enough not to forget it. It was also hoped that they would remember their biological group and be friendly towards it. However, in the giving away of an infant, the purpose was not to establish ties through a child, but to relinquish the child to someone. An example of this which was not included in the sample because it involved a child born around 1960 will perhaps make clear the intent of this transaction.

Ako was a man in his late forties or early fifties. Although he had successfully raised several sons by his first wife, two sons by his second wife died shortly after they were born. During his second wife's third pregnancy in 1960, Ako dreamed that the child was a male and that it would also die if he kept it. Ako's oldest daughter, about twenty, was one of the wives of a promising young man in the community. Ako arranged for his daughter to take his son when it was born and to give him a newly-born daughter of hers in return. His child was indeed a son and the transfer was made. In 1962, both children were completely accepted as part of their adopted parents' families, especially the little boy, as he was an active, assertive child and his adopted father was obviously quite proud of him. I did not find out about this case until I had been there about eight months. Until that time, I had been told the little boy was his adopted father's biological offspring and, judging from their interaction, had assumed this was true. It was said that the biological parents would not make any attempt to reclaim the child they had given away. Nor would Ako's other sons make any attempt to claim the little boy as their brother.

There were three such cases in the Middle sample and one in the Young sample. I classified all these as cases in which more than one man raised the child. Of the forty-six Middle men who were raised by more than one man, only three (six percent) were given away by their biological fathers as infants. Of the eighteen Young men raised by more than one man, only one (six percent) was given away by his biological father as an infant. There are few similarities in the cases, however. One involved a man getting the infant son of another man in his subpooling unit; all the parties involved were dead in 1962 and no one knew the reason for the transfer. In another case, the sister of a woman came to help her at childbirth. The sister was fond of the newborn baby and requested that she be allowed to raise it. The mother allegedly said that she could take the child when it was older—which was a way of saying "no." The two sisters were married to men in different but adjacent sovereignties, and the one continued to pester the mother to let her have the child. The mother finally consented, but when the child was ready to be initiated he returned to Auyana where his biological father sponsored his initiation and purchased his wife.

Another case has the ring of fantasy to it, but the man involved was alive in 1962 and swore it happened. Apo was a man in his late sixties or early seventies in 1962. When he was younger, he had a fierce reputation and was widely feared as a killer. Once, when passing through a Tau village, he saw a small boy just learning to walk and took a liking to him. Apo told the father that he wanted the boy and the father said he could have him in return for a pig and some wealth. The exchange was made and Apo raised the boy, initiated him, and got his wife. The boy remained in Auyana and was a man in his late forties in 1962. This case is questionable for several reasons. It was the only case anyone knew of in which someone bought a child. Further, he was obtained from an entirely different language group and one with which there was trade but few other transactions. However, the case may be indicative of the amount of power wielded by a true man of renown in Auyana.

The last case is that of a Young man and involved a man from another sovereignty who moved to Auyana for a brief period. While there, his wife gave birth to a son. The man's sister, who was married to a man in Auyana, came to assist at the birth and then demanded and received the child. She and her husband raised the boy until her husband died, and then someone in her husband's pooling unit completed the raising and acted as his sponsor. In this case, the main parties involved were alive in 1962, but the reasons given for the transaction differed.

Whatever the reasons for these transactions, the main point is that fathers rarely gave away their sons, either as trade intermediaries or as infants for someone else to keep and raise. There were only four given for trade (of which , two were biological sons), and four as infants.

The third means by which a man might lose a son was for his wife to leave him, taking her children with her. In the sample, there were only two cases of this. They were brothers, a Middle and a Young, whose mother left their father in a sovereignty adjacent to Auyana and took her sons along with her when she remarried to an Auyana man, who raised them.

By far, the most common reason a boy was not raised by his father was because of his father's death.[2] In 56 (88 percent) of the 64 cases of Middle and Young men who were raised by more than one man (i.e., who were raised by someone other than their biological father), their biological father had died and someone else had raised them. From another angle, this shows that adult males often did not live long enough to raise all their sons. Of the 114 Middle and Young men, 58 (50 percent) lost their biological father before they were initiated. Of course, this fact alone would not mean that groups would not remain agnatic. If someone in the father's sovereignty were to raise the child, then the group would remain agnatic. But, if we cross-tabulate the 56 Middle and Young men who were raised by more than one person *and* who were not given away by their biological fathers, Table 6 is the result.

TABLE 6
TYPES OF ADOPTION

|  | Father's Pooling Unit | Father's Sovereignty | Outside Father's Sovereignty | Total |
|---|---|---|---|---|
| Middle | 13 | 2 | 25 | 40 |
| Young | 7 | 4 | 5 | 16 |
| Total | 20 | 6 | 30 | 56 |

For the Middle men, only fifteen of forty (37 percent) were kept by someone inside the sovereignty after the child's biological father died. For the Young men, the percentage is about twice as high, eleven of sixteen (70 percent). The total is twenty-six of fifty-six (46 percent).

Why was there such a higher percentage of the Young sample who were kept inside their father's sovereignty? This could have resulted from the gen-

[2] It was also said to be possible for a boy to run away from his biological father and try to get some other man to raise him, but I have no cases of this.

eral decline in the number of adoptions outside sovereignties, perhaps because of the cessation of warfare and consequent reduction in dislocation. I
have no data from other sovereignties and so cannot speak to this question.
There is another possibility. The first thing to consider is that in all but three
of the thirty cases (twenty-five Middle, five Young) where a child was obtained by someone outside his biological father's sovereignty, adoption was
brought about by adults moving with the children to another place, not by
the child simply being transferred from one adult to another without the
initial parent changing residence. This occurred in three ways: (1) a man
moved with his wife and children to another sovereignty, died there, and
those in that sovereignty took his children; his wife may or may not have
remarried there; (2) a man died and his wife moved to her natal sovereignty
before remarrying; while there, here brother or someone in her subpooling
unit took her children and kept them; (3) a woman remarried a man in another sovereignty and moved there, taking her children with her. The recruitment of "foreign" children was dependent on the ability to attract "foreign" adults to coreside for at least a while. I believe that this ability
depended partly on the adults' being convinced that they would be safe
while there and might not be safe elsewhere. Evidence will be presented
later that Auyana was in a period of great strength just prior to the arrival of
the Australians and this might account for why so many Middle men were
acquired from other sovereignties.

Whatever the reasons for the discrepancy between the Middle sample and
the Young sample, it could be argued that even though someone outside the
sovereignty assumed responsibility for raising a child, this did not mean that
he had to sponsor the child. He could have sent the child back at some point
before adulthood. However, for all but one of the twenty-five Middle men
and one of the five Young men raised outside their biological father's sovereignty after his death, the man who raised them was also their major sponsor. In both exceptions, after their first initiation the boys moved to their
biological father's sovereignty where their initiations were completed and
their wives acquired by those in that sovereignty.

I will summarize the discussion to this point. The total of those in the
Middle and Young samples is 114.

1. Fifty (44 percent) were raised and sponsored by their biological father.
2. Sixty-four (56 percent) were not raised by only their biological father.
    a. Four of them were boys exchanged for trade intermediaries. Three
    of these four returned to their original sovereignty for their initiations
    and to have their wives bought.
    b. Four were given to someone to keep as infants. One of these re-
    turned to his biological father's sovereignty to be initiated and to have
    his wife bought.
    c. Two were obtained through divorce and were raised and sponsored
    by their adopted father.

d. Fifty-six were obtained by another man when their biological father died.[3]

(1) Twenty-six were raised and sponsored by someone from their biological father's sovereignty.

(2) Thirty were raised by someone outside their biological father's sovereignty.

(a) Two of these thirty returned to their biological father's sovereignty to be initiated and to have their wives bought. The remainder were initiated and sponsored by their adopted father.

(3) The total of those who were at least sponsored by their biological father's sovereignty was eighty (70 percent). Of the three boys given for trade who returned, two were already adopted by someone from outside their biological father's sovereignty and are not included in this total. Fifty (44 percent) were sponsored by their biological fathers, and thirty (25 percent) were sponsored by someone from their biological father's sovereignty.

As for the fate of the seven boys raised by three men, two of them were the adopted boys sent as trade intermediaries. They returned to their adopted father. The other five were cases where the adopted father of the boy died and the boy was then acquired by a third man and sponsored by him.

Although 67 percent of the men were sponsored by their biological father or someone from his sovereignty, this does not mean that 67 percent of those in Auyana were biological agnates. For, if a person's biological father's biological father was from another sovereignty, but the person's biological father had been raised and sponsored by someone in Auyana and the person had been raised and sponsored in Auyana, then he would be included in the 67 percent. My concern with these percentages has been to give an idea of how boys came to be raised and sponsored by someone other than their biological father. I have argued that this was primarily due to the biological father's death. In this sense, one can say that members of Auyana were extremely agnatic; that is, a man rarely relinquished his sons except at his death. Further, once another man obtained a boy, he almost invariably sponsored him. Although later data will show a great deal of movement in and out of Auyana, and although the percentage of children raised by more than one man was high, it was not true that children were shuffled around from one set of parents to the next. Once a couple started to raise a child, they attempted to keep the child until he reached adulthood. That they often failed to do this is another matter. The main sense, then, in which members of Auyana were not "agnatic" was in their inability to control the movements of women or children after a man had died. At the same time, they were

---

[3] Included among the ten who were given away were two who had been previously adopted. These two are included here to make a total of fifty-six rather than fifty-four.

extremely "agnatic" in that a boy almost always joined the group of which-
ever male had raised and sponsored him.

## Membership and Ancestry

While sociological agnation was a means to become a member in a social
unit, was the membership of such men as good or complete as the membership of those who were biological agnates? And did people who moved in
after they were married assume equal or lower standing than either of these?
To answer those questions, I will consider several social unit attributes as
they relate to these three types of members and will adopt the following
conventions concerning the various types of biological partri-ancestry possessed by the members of a social unit at any given time.

Numbers will be used to indicate the sovereignty of a boy's major sponsor
for his initiation and for purchasing his wife. This could also be phrased in
terms of pooling units rather than major sponsors, as a man did not act as a
major sponsor for such activities without the aid of his pooling unit. The
numbers for a person, his biological father, his biological father's biological
father, and his biological father's biological father's biological father will be
written in the following manner: #1-1-2-2#. The first number refers to the
person, the second to his biological father, and so on. The reason for including only four generations is that, as indicated earlier, actors did not know
genealogies beyond that depth. For convenience, "biological father" will be
shortened to "bio Fa" and the possessive suffix "s" will be dropped. For example, a man's biological father's biological father will be written "his bio Fa
bio Fa." In expressions such as #1-1-2-2#, the number referring to the subject's sovereignty will always be the number one. If a man's bio Fa was initiated and had his wife bought in the same sovereignty as the man, then he
will be given the same number. If not, then he will be given the number
two. The same will be done for the man's bio Fa bio Fa, and so forth. The
expression #1-1-2-2# means that the man was sponsored by someone in sovereignty one, his bio Fa was also sponsored by someone in sovereignty one,
his bio Fa bio Fa was sponsored by someone in a different sovereignty than
his bio Fa, and his bio Fa bio Fa bio Fa was sponsored by someone in the
same sovereignty as his bio Fa bio Fa. The expression #1-2-1-1# means that
the man's bio Fa was sponsored in a different sovereignty than he, but his
bio Fa bio Fa and bio Fa bio Fa bio Fa were sponsored in the same sovereignty as he.If Auyana were comprised only of males who were biological
agnates, the expression for each of them would be #1-1-1-1#. *Note that
these expressions make absolutely no reference to changes in residence.* If a
boy's bio Fa was sponsored in A, moved to B with the boy, and became a
member there and the boy was sponsored by his bio Fa and those in B, the
boy would be given the number one and his bio Fa the number two. But this
assignment of numbers would also be given if a boy's mother left his father,
taking the boy with her to sovereignty B where he was raised and sponsored.

The sample I will use to compare types of ancestry is the same as was used to analyze raising and sponsoring except that the five men in the Middle sample who move in as adults and became members have been excluded, as I will consider them separately from those raised in the sovereignty. In addition, two men have been added to the Middle sample who moved out of Auyana almost immediately after marriage and consequently were not included in the sample in Table 2.

Ten types of agnatic biological ancestry were found in the Auyana sample:

type  1   #1-1-1-1#
type  2   #1-1-1-2#
type  3   #1-1-2-2#
type  4   #1-1-2-3#
type  5   #1-2-1-1#
type  6   #1-2-2-1#
type  7   #1-2-2-2#
type  8   #1-2-2-3#
type  9   #1-2-3-3#
type 10   #1-2-3-4#

Five types were not found in the sample: #1-1-2-1#, #1-2-1-2#, #1-2-1-3#, #1-2-3-1#, and #1-2-3-2#. The significance of the absence of these types will be dicussed below. The totals for all the types are included in Table 7. Types 1-4 are men who were sponsored in the same sovereignty as their bio Fa. The difference between them is in continuity of membership among their ancestors. Those in type 1 (#1-1-1-1#) are the only ones who could trace biological patri-ancestry through males sponsored in Auyana to an ultimate ancestor who was a member of Auyana. Although they could not all trace exact ancestry to their common ancestor (see Figures 1-3), they could at least presume they were biological agnates. They obviously comprised considerably less than the majority of males in Auyana.

TABLE 7
ANCESTRY TYPES IN AUYANA

| Ancestry Types | Categories | | | |
|---|---|---|---|---|
| | Old | Middle | Young | Total |
| 1  (#1-1-1-1#) | 11 | 15 | 12 | 38 |
| 2  (#1-1-1-2#) | | 9 | 6 | 15 |
| 3  (#1-1-2-2#) | 6 | 13 | 8 | 27 |
| 4  (#1-1-2-3#) | | 4 | | 4 |
| 5  (#1-2-1-1#) | | | 3 | 3 |
| 6  (#1-2-2-1#) | | 1 | | 1 |
| 7  (#1-2-2-2#) | 4 | 33 | 5 | 42 |
| 8  (#1-2-2-3#) | | 3 | | 3 |
| 9  (#1-2-3-3#) | | 4 | | 4 |
| 10 (#1-2-3-4#) | | | 1 | 1 |
| Total | 21 | 82 | 35 | 138 |

Types 7-10 I will refer to as having foreign origin, as *none* of their biological patri-ancestors were sponsored by those in Auyana. The difference between them is in the continuity of membership between their bio Fa and their more remote agnatic ancestors.

Types 5-6 are anomalous in that they were not in the same sovereignty as had sponsored their father, yet they were in a sovereignty which had sponsored a more distant biologically agnatic ancestor. One interesting point is the small number of individuals in these two categories, particularly since the types for which there were no cases in the sample are all variants of types 5 and 6. That is, they are all types where there would have been an alternation of membership. One conclusion which could therefore be drawn is that this alternation rarely occurred. Another interpretation is that it occurred but was "forgotten." I do not know which of these to accept. As I will demonstrate later, those in types 7-10 who moved, usually moved to their bio Fa sovereignty. If raised in that sovereignty, their children would then be type 5 or 6 or some alternating type. For example, if a man of type 7 (#1-2-2-2#) moved to his bio Fa sovereignty and his children were raised and sponsored there, then his children would be type 5 (#1-2-1-1#). It could be argued that his children could make little use of the fact that he was sponsored in another sovereignty and would choose to forget that fact in order to emphasize their agnatic continuity with the sovereignty in which they were sponsored. If this is accepted, then it would mean I have failed to discover the actual sponsorship of an unknown number of men's fathers. I am willing to accept that this may have happened to some degree, but I do not believe it happened often enough to account for the lower numbers in types 5 and 6 and their variants.

Another interpretation of the low numbers in these types is that Auyana, for some reason, differed from other sovereignties for the period covered by my sample. Assuming that I did uncover most of the actual sponsors, it could have been the case that while those in types 7-10 in Auyana moved out of Auyana to their bio Fa sovereignty if they moved, men whose bio Fa were from Auyana, but who were sponsored in another sovereignty did not move back to Auyana. The major reservation I have about this interpretation is that I cannot think of any difference between Auyana and other sovereignties which might have resulted in this discrepancy.

Related difficulties in interpretation are encountered when the numbers in types 1-4 and 7-10 are considered. The low numbers in types 8-10 as opposed to type 7 and types 1-4 may mean either that continually changing membership each generation was infrequent or was "forgotten." The low numbers of type 4 as opposed to types 1-3 may be similarly interpreted. Since the data needed to resolve this question is not available, I am unable to determine whether the numbers in the different categories meant that there was actual "short term" agnatic continuity or only the claim to it.

Another point to note is that the proportions of Old and Young in types 1-4 are about the same and are considerably higher than for the Middle sample. This is related to the discrepancy between Middle and Young in the precentages of children whose bio Fa died and who were sponsored by someone from outside the sovereignty. The significance of both these inconsistencies will be discussed later.

One would assume that if the lack of biological patri-ancestry had any social importance, it would be most apparent in those in types 7-10, as these were men who had no biological agnatic connection to Auyana. If this assumption is correct, we should find those with types 7-10 to be either excluded from some social unit activities or, if not, to be quantitatively discriminated against.

There were, however, no cases in which those with types 7-10 were excluded from any of the social unit activities—as long as they *resided* with those in Auyana. Not only were none excluded, but two of the most famous men in Auyana during the period just prior to the arrival of the government were men with type 7 ancestry and between them they almost single-handedly built one of the present pooling units in Auyana. If there was discrimination on the basis of one's biological patri-ancestry, it was more subtle.

There are some indicators that there may have been such discrimination. I found that many of those in types 7-10 claimed not only the Auyana *upaema*, but also the *upaema* of their bio Fa's sovereignty. In this sense, they were symbolically set aside much like wives from another sovereignty except that, unlike wives, they could and did claim the Auyana *upaema*. Another indication was that the only two cases of a man marrying a girl from within his own pooling unit involved two men of type 7. In both cases, moreover, they were married to girls who were also adopted. Both men were in the Middle sample and were still alive in 1962. They had both remained members of their adopted father's pooling unit except when pooling units gave and received wealth. If they had been full members they would not have given to those in their own pooling unit at these times. But, at the same time, if they gave to their wife's natal pooling unit, they would be giving to their own pooling unit, assuming that the wife's natal pooling unit was the one which adopted her. I attended some events at which these men were major sponsors (both were active men with some renown), and they were given aid by those in their pooling unit. However, they solved their dilemma by giving some of the pooled wealth to one segment of their pooling unit and seeing that the remainder was then given through their wife to a different pooling unit as though it were the wife's natal unit. That is, they created a natal pooling unit for their wives by getting some men to agree to act as one. In one case, the created unit was that of the wife's biological father. In the other case it was not.

Two stronger indications of discrimination were the following. When boys were adopted at an early age, their adopted father would not tell them who their biological father was for fear that if those from the latter's sovereignty tried to lure the boy away (either before or after marriage), he would go with them. However, all adopted boys apparently found out that their adopted father was not their biological father either from other children or from adults in the sovereignty. This means that this sort of information was common knowledge for at least a generation and implies it was of some importance.

A stronger indication came near the end of my stay in 1965. Several men of type 7 had moved back to their biological father's sovereignty shortly after Auyana had been involved in a fight with that sovereignty. I often asked why they had gone back, and received various ambiguous answers. But one day my interpreter, who had been in the same subpooling unit with and was very close to a few of these men, said that one of the reasons they returned was that they feared soul assassination. He said that those in his pooling unit would not do it, but those in Auyana's other pooling unit might. An assassin might argue that the men were really members of their biological father's sovereignty and should be killed in revenge for deaths caused by that sovereignty.[4]

Besides the threat of soul assassination, men in such a position might have been discriminated against by not getting pooling aid, not being given any or a fair part of the wealth received by their pooling unit, not getting support in prosecuting offenses, or not being able to claim any or good used land. Unfortunately, I do not have records to demonstrate this type of discrimination. Indeed, such records would be extremely difficult to obtain unless one was continually living there, for they would involve people incriminating themselves or others, since it was claimed that adopted children were treated as well as biological children.

However, there are two items for which I have records which may give some indirect indication of whether such discrimination occurred and whether those with types 7-10 ancestry were in a more difficult social position than others. They are: (1) the readiness with which a wife was obtained for them, and (2) whether they moved out of Auyana after they were married.

As I mentioned earlier when discussing my interpreters, my younger interpreter claimed that those in Auyana procrastinated in getting him a wife. However, he said this was true for all adopted sons and cited several cases. He did not distinguish between those who were adopted by someone in their biological father's pooling unit or sovereignty and those who were not. He claimed this was because men thought of their biological children first and would only think of their adopted children after they had taken care of the former. To test this assertion, I will use only the Young sample, as I do not have good records on the readiness with which those in the Middle cate-

---

[4] The conditions under which this might happen will be discussed later. Mere possession of foreign ancestry was not enough.

gory obtained their wives. I will ignore types 5-6 due to their anomalous
nature and low numbers. Types 7-10 are combined on the basis that they
were all foreigners, and types 1-4 on the basis that they are all of the same
sovereignty as their biological father. I will distinguish between those who
were said to have not obtained their wives until long after the last stage of
their initiation and those who were said to have obtained them promptly. Of
the five boys in the Young sample in type 7 (see Table 7), two (40 percent)
got their wives quickly, and three (60 percent) did not. Table 8 shows the
figures for boys in types 1-4, subdivided on the basis of whether their biological father was alive at the time their first wife was obtained. As Table 8 reveals, the most important consideration in the rapidity with which one got a
wife was whether one's biological father was alive at the time. If he was, then
one would practically never have to worry about readily obtaining a wife. If
he was dead, one would have to worry. Further, the number of those in
types 1-4 whose bio Fa was dead at the time of their marriage yet who obtained their wife promptly was only four out of eleven (36 percent), which is
about the same percentage as those in type 7 who obtained their wives
promptly (33 percent). Unfortunately, the low numbers make it impossible
to tell whether the similarities in these percentages indicate anything more
than that in both cases a man might not get his wife quickly. However, I
conclude that there was no more discrimination against those in types 7-10
than there was against those in types 1-4 whose biological fathers were not
alive.[5]

TABLE 8
EASE OF MARRIAGE: TYPES 1-4

| Ease of Getting First Wife | Biological Father Alive at Marriage | Biological Father Not Alive at Marriage | Total |
|---|---|---|---|
| Delayed | 1 | 7 | 8 |
| Prompt | 14 | 4 | 18 |
| Total | 15 | 11 | 26 |

The other index which may indirectly reveal whether there was discrimination is the rate of movement to other sovereignties. There were several
reasons for a man and/or his family to move to another sovereignty. I will
consider only those cases in which the stay was long enough that a garden
was planted by the man and/or his family. This might be as long as several
months or as short as a week. The rapidity with which a garden was begun
apparently depended in part on why the person moved there. If a man took

[5] I believe that more cases would reveal that if a man had a married brother when his bio Fa
died, the man would have his wife bought just as quickly as if his bio Fa were still alive.

his family and fled his sovereignty because he was afraid of being massacred, he would probably build a house and begin a garden shortly after he arrived at his destination. On the other hand, if he intended to come back after a short period and then changed his mind and decided to stay, it might be a while before he would build a house and begin a garden. However, my reason for not dividing the types of moving on the basis of the apparent motive for the move is twofold:

1. I do not have reliable data. After ten years, various reasons might be given for why someone moved. Fighting between sovereignties precipitated many moves, as shown below. My impression is that fighting within the sovereignty also precipitated a great many moves. But, inasmuch as not everyone moved under these conditions, even if this was one of the reasons, it was neither necessary nor sufficient for moving.

2. Whatever the reason for a move, if those with foreign biological patri-ancestry were being discriminated against, then they should have been generally more willing to move, and therefore their rate of movement should have been higher. However, this is true if either the causes of moving (other than ancestry) were distributed randomly with respect to ancestry or they were more heavily concentrated in those with foreign biological patri-ancestry. I have no way to distinguish which was the case, but fortunately for the argument here, this distinction is irrelevant.

There is an additional argument as to why those with foreign biological patri-ancestry might have had a higher rate of movement: They may have been more rapidly assimilated into their biological father's sovereignty than someone who moved to a group with which he had no biological agnatic connections, even though he might have had cognatic or affinal ones. I will not systematically examine this as, again, the data are extremely elusive. However, several cases indicate the validity of this argument.

Komo was captured by an enemy group when he was about eight to ten years old. He had gone to watch a fight with the enemy group and was standing in the rear holding extra bows and arrows for his father. The enemies made a massive charge and overran Auyana, killing Komo's father in the process. Komo hid in the bushes but was discovered. For some reason, instead of killing him the enemies took him back and raised him, sponsored him, and bought him a wife. He was there for several years after his marriage and had a boy about a year old when the group again got into a fight with Auyana. Komo left his wife and son and crept over to the Auyana side. They welcomed him and he then fought against the group he had just left. The most significant point for the immediate discussion is that he apparently had little trouble getting those in Auyana to help him buy another wife. She was a woman from Auyana whose husband had died not long after their first child had been born, and she had come back to Auyana to live with her brother. Hence, the wealth given was not large, but Komo was able to get help even after moving over from an enemy group.

A contrasting case involved a man, Kasari, who moved from Auyana to a neighboring sovereignty not long after his marriage. He stayed there about fifteen years. During this time, he acted as only a partial member of Auyana, participating in some poolings and receiving some of the wealth given to those in Auyana. Auyana then got involved in a fight with a sovereignty friendly with the one in which Kasari was living. It was said that Kasari became afraid that those where he was living might send some of his clothing to the warring sovereignty so the latter could assassinate his soul. That is, he was afraid he would be treated as a legal unit with those in Auyana. Whatever his reason, he moved to another sovereignty which was on uneasy terms with Auyana, but in which there was a segment of ex-members of Auyana. He had not been there long when he got into a fight with someone in that sovereignty and was shot and killed. Members of Auyana claimed that the fight had been a frame-up and that he was shot because the group they had been fighting had paid the sovereignty to which he had moved to kill him. Auyana then made raids on the sovereignty which had killed Kasari and initiated a major fight with them. This case illustrates the opposite of Komo's case—that is, the apparent difficulty of ceasing to be treated in some sense as a member of a previous sovereignty if one did not move to a group with whom one could trace some biological agnatic relationship.

TABLE 9
MOVES FROM AUYANA

| Ancestry Types | Old | | Middle | | Young | | Total |
|---|---|---|---|---|---|---|---|
| | Moved out of Auyana | | Moved out of Auyana | | Moved out of Auyana | | |
| | Yes | No | Yes | No | Yes | No | |
| 1 (#1-1-1-1#) | 4 | 7 | 8 | 7 | 2 | 10 | 38 |
| 2 (#1-1-1-2#) | | | 7 | 2 | 1 | 5 | 15 |
| 3 (#1-1-2-2#) | 3 | 3 | 3 | 10 | | 8 | 27 |
| 4 (#1-1-2-3#) | | | 3 | 1 | | | 4 |
| 7 (#1-2-2-2#) | 1 | 3 | 21 | 12 | 1 | 4 | 42 |
| 8 (#1-2-2-3#) | | | 3 | | | | 3 |
| 9 (#1-2-3-3#) | | | 2 | 2 | | | 4 |
| 10 (#1-2-3-4#) | | | | | | 1 | 1 |
| Total | 8 | 13 | 47 | 34 | 4 | 28 | 134 |

In any case, if it was true that those with foreign biological patri-ancestry had more options for movement, then not only would this have made their moving rate higher, it should have made their rate of return lower than those who moved to a place with which they did not have such connections. I will accordingly consider both the moving and the return rates. The few cases in which a person moved to a place and then moved again to another place without returning to the first one will be mentioned in the appropriate context.

Table 9 contains the figures for those sponsored by Auyana, except for types 5 and 6, who moved from Auyana at some point in their life after they were married. Types 5 and 6 are again excluded due to their irregular ancestry and their low numbers. As explained earlier, I have combined types 1-4 and 7-10. The overall rate of movement was 59 out of 134, or 44 percent. It is obvious from inspection that this rate was much higher for the Middle sample than for the Young and Old samples.[6] In Table 9, I have classified Young men as moving out only if they moved to another sovereignty for reasons other than to become an evangelist or to work for cash. If these last two categories are included as moving out, then 4 more would be classified as moving out, making a total of 8 out of 32 (35 percent), still a lower figure than the rate for the Middle sample. I believe this lower rate in the Young sample was due to the cessation of warfare and the concommitant cessation of other activities which might result in movement. In the case of the Old sample, I believe the lower rate was simply due to selective forgetting in situations where the appearance of stability was desirable. These arguments are pursued in more detail at the end of this chapter. At this point, I want to focus on the Middle category in order to determine at least what may have been operating in pre-contact times.

The moving rate for the Middle sample was forty-seven out of eighty-one (58 percent). An examination of Table 9 shows that the moving rates for those in types 7-10 were equal to or higher than this. However, types 1-4 show considerable variation. This variation does not seem to be clearly related to the recency of foreign biological patri-ancestry. If moving out was directly related to the recency of foreign biological patri-ancestry, then types 7-10 should have been about the same and should have had the highest rate, types 3 and 4 should have been about the same and had the next highest, type 2 should have had the next highest, and type 1 should have had the lowest. But, as Table 10 shows, this was not the case.

TABLE 10
RATES OF MOVEMENT: ALL TYPES

| Type | Percentage |
|------|------------|
| 7-10 | 65% (26/40) |
| 3-4 | 35% (6/17) |
| 2 | 78% (7/9) |
| 1 | 53% (8/15) |

If a man's biological father was sponsored by the same sovereignty, then how much further back one could trace biological ancestors might not have

---

[6] While many people moved in and out of Auyana, not everyone did. Of those in the Middle category, 42 percent stayed in Auyana, and of the 58 percent who moved, most moved only once.

been relevant for purposes of judging discrimination. If this was so, the differences between types 1, 2, and 3-4 may have been due to factors not related to ancestry, and types 1-4 *summed* should show a lower moving rate than types 7-10. Table 11 affirms this and the difference is significant, at ≤.05 level in the Chi square test for significance.

TABLE 11
MOVES: MAJOR TYPES

| Moved | Types | | |
|---|---|---|---|
| | 7-10 | 1-4 | Total |
| Yes | 26 | 21 | 47 |
| No | 14 | 20 | 34 |
| Total | 40 | 41 | 81 |

This provides some evidence that whether a man's biological father came from the same sovereignty as he did was important and, beyond that, what sovereignty his patri-ancestors belonged to was not important. Still, the high rate of movement (about 50 percent) for those in types 1-4 leads one to wonder what variables were operating. If claims of agnation were useful in making it easier to move into a foreign place, types 7-10 would have such claims, their biological father having been a member of another sovereignty. The only situation in which those in types 1-4 would have biological agnates in another sovereignty would be if a segment from their sovereignty had moved to another sovereignty and had become established there as a segment. There were three such segments from Auyana in the period considered here, all of them having moved prior to the period during which those in the Middle category lived. Inasmuch as it was extremely difficult to determine exact biological connections, if any, I decided to lump together individuals who claimed to be able to trace biological agnatic ancestry to a segment and individuals who claimed to have come from the same subpooling unit within Auyana as those who had moved. I will refer to such cases as those who had a close patri-segment in another sovereignty. If types 1-4 are then divided into those who had a close patri-segment in another sovereignty and those who did not, and this is cross-tabulated with whether they moved or not, the result is Table 12.

TABLE 12
MOVES: TYPES 1-4

| Close Subpooling Segment in Another Sovereignty | Moved Out of Auyana | | |
|---|---|---|---|
| | Yes | No | Total |
| Yes | 16 | 8 | 24 |
| No | 5 | 12 | 17 |
| Total | 21 | 20 | 41 |

If the rates of moving out for types 7-10 and the two categories of types 1-4 are compared, table 13 is the result. This tabulation supports more strongly the contention that patri-ancestry could make it easier to move to a foreign place and therefore was relevant in determining whether a person moved. Thus, if we just consider moving, it would appear that closeness of biological agnatic ancestry did not make much difference in whether someone moved, unless he had close biological agnates in another sovereignty.

TABLE 13
RATES OF MOVEMENT: PATRI-ANCESTRY

| Types | Percentage |
| --- | --- |
| 7-10 | 65% (26/40) |
| 1-4 with close patri-segment in another sovereignty | 66% (16/24) |
| 1-4 with no close patri-segment in another sovereignty | 29% (5/17) |

I will now consider types 7-10 and 1-4 separately in order to examine some other possible causes. I will first examine whether people with types 7-10 ancestry maintained contact with their bio Fa sovereignty, on the assumption that if they did they might be more suspect in their own sovereignty than if they did not. Twenty-seven of the forty (67 percent) of types 7-10 maintained contact with a pooling unit or a subpooling unit within their bio Fa sovereignty. By maintaining contact, I mean that they occasionally visited there, occasionally helped them with pooling, and were sometimes given a share of wealth received by a pooling unit in that sovereignty.

If we calculate the moving rate for those in types 7-10 who maintained contact and those who did not, Table 14 is the result.

TABLE 14
RATES OF MOVEMENT FOR TYPES 7-10: OUTSIDE CONTACT

| | Percentage |
| --- | --- |
| Maintained contact with bio Fa segment | 82% (22/27) |
| No contact with bio Fa segment | 31% (4/13) |

Of the twenty-seven men who maintained contact with their bio Fa segment, twenty-two moved. Whereas, of the thirteen men who did not maintain contact with their bio Fa segment, only four moved. It is clear that merely having foreign ancestors was not as important as whether contact was maintained with them. Twenty-two of the twenty-six men in types 7-10 who moved were men who had maintained contact with their bio Fa sovereignty. This figure, in combination with the figures for types 1-4 who maintained contact with outside biological agnates (see Table 13), raises the question of whether perhaps it was not agnatic biological ancestry which was relevant in moving but simply maintaining contact with those in another sovereignty regardless of whether one had common ancestry with them or not. But I have been unable to separate these variables. I collected the data on moves and maintaining contacts by examining the events at which wealth was pooled by those in Auyana and asking who helped and what they gave. If someone from outside Auyana was involved, I asked why they were there, and in this way got information on contacts outside Auyana. All men engaged in exchanges, gifts, trade, and visiting, but none of these activities involved the pooling of wealth. However, most men did have relationships with individual men outside Auyana in which they would help a man pool wealth and were given part of any wealth he received through gifts to his pooling unit. Usually they had such relationships with men in two or three different sovereignties. Fewer men had such relationships with several men in a single pooling unit in another sovereignty, and a man who had them was said to be a biological agnate of some member of the foreign pooling unit. Inasmuch as these relationships are the ones I am defining as maintaining contact, it is impossible to separate biological agnation and maintaining contact. Rather, it seems that if a man were going to maintain contact with a foreign pooling or subpooling unit he would do it with a unit with which he claimed biological agnatic ancestry. In any case, it would seem at this point that the combination of having a bio Fa from a sovereignty other than the one in which a man was raised and sponsored (i.e., types 7-10) and maintaining contact with those in that sovereignty quite frequently resulted in moving.

Still considering only types 7-10, I found one situation in which keeping up contact was particularly important: when the person's adopted sovereignty and bio Fa sovereignty got into a fight which either was precipitated by mutual accusations of soul assassination or resulted in homicide. I will refer to this as homicidal fighting. If the twenty-seven men who maintained contact with their bio Fa sovereignty are subdivided on the basis of whether homicidal fighting occurred between their adopted and bio Fa sovereignties, Table 15 is the result. While the overall movement rate for those who maintained contact with their bio Fa sovereignty is high (82 percent), the rate is higher for those whose bio Fa and adopted sovereignties engaged in homicidal fighting. In fact, homicidal fighting was practically a sufficient condition for moving.

This suggests that perhaps homicidal fighting between the two sovereignties would make a difference regardless of whether the person maintained contact with the bio Fa sovereignty. But if we examine the thirteen who did not maintain contact, we can see that, as Table 15 shows, the rate of movement was not affected by the existence of homicidal fighting between the two sovereignties when there was no contact with the bio Fa sovereignty.

TABLE 15
RATES OF MOVEMENT FOR TYPES 7-10 DURING PERIODS OF HOMICIDAL FIGHTING

|  | Percentage |
|---|---|
| Contact maintained with bio Fa sovereignty | |
| Homicidal fight between adopted and bio Fa sovereignty | 94% (15/16) |
| No homicidal fight between adopted and bio Fa sovereignty | 64% (7/11) |
| No contact maintained with bio Fa sovereignty | |
| Homicidal fight between adopted and bio Fa sovereignty | 33% (2/6) |
| No homicidal fight between adopted and bio Fa sovereignty | 29% (2/7) |

I suggest that there were three categories of movers within types 7-10, which were distinguished by their moving-out rates, where they moved, and their return rates: (1) those who had contact with their bio Fa sovereignty and homicidal fighting erupted between their adopted and bio Fa sovereignty; (2) those who had contact with their bio Fa sovereignty but no homicidal fighting occurred between the two sovereignties; and (3) those who did not maintain contact with their bio Fa sovereignty. Table 16 summarizes the moving out rates for these different types.

TABLE 16
RATES OF MOVEMENT FOR CATEGORIES OF MOVERS: TYPES 7-10

|  | Percentage |
|---|---|
| (1) Contact with bio Fa sovereignty; homicidal fighting between adopted and bio Fa sovereignty | 94% (15/16) |
| (2) Contact with bio Fa sovereignty; no homicidal fighting between adopted and bio Fa sovereignty | 64% (7/11) |
| (3) No contact with bio Fa sovereignty | 31% (4/13) |

In order to discuss where men of types 7-10 moved and whether they returned or not, I will consider the number of moves made, rather than the number of men making moves. Of the twenty-six men who moved out of Auyana, three moved more than once, giving a total of twenty-nine moves out of Auyana. I classified the sovereignties into which they moved on the basis of whether they were: (1) a bio Fa sovereignty; (2) a wife's natal sovereignty; (3) a mother's natal sovereignty; (4) a sovereignty in which there was someone with whom one could claim common ancestry through a woman from his subpooling unit (e.g., his father's sister's son); and (5) other sovereignties. Given that pooling units and not sovereignties were exogamous, these categories are not mutually exclusive. But, in cases where the sovereignty to which a man moved was his bio Fa sovereignty, people said that this was the reason he had moved there, not that his wife was from there. Thus, I will consider the latter to be an auxiliary reason when there is duplication, and a person will be classified in Table 17 as moving to sovereignties in categories two through five only if the sovereignty was not also his bio Fa sovereignty. Of the twenty who moved to their bio Fa sovereignty, eight moved also to a wife's natal sovereignty, and two to a mother's natal sovereignty. Of the four who moved to "other," all moved to places where they knew men with whom they had carried on transactions and were friendly.

TABLE 17
DESTINATIONS: TYPES 7-10

| Moved To | Percentage |
|---|---|
| Bio Fa sovereignty | 69% (20/29) |
| Wife's natal sovereignty | 17% (5/29) |
| Mother's natal sovereignty | — |
| Close common ancestry through woman | — |
| Other | 14% (4/29) |

Of those who moved to their bio Fa sovereignty, all were men who had contacts with that sovereignty. An obvious conclusion from Table 17 is that one did not move to a group where one did not have prior established contacts. Further, of the twenty-four moves involving men who had prior contacts with their bio Fa sovereignty, only four were not moves to the bio Fa sovereignty. If we take only the three categories of movers in Table 16 (adjusting for multiple moves) and analyze whether men in those categories moved to their bio Fa sovereignty or not, the result is Table 18. While the

TABLE 18
RATES OF MOVEMENT TO BIO FA SOVEREIGNTY: CATEGORIES OF TYPES 7-10

|  | Percentage |
|---|---|
| (1) Contact with bio Fa sovereignty; homicidal fighting between adopted and bio Fa sovereignty | 87% (13/15) |
| (2) Contact with bio Fa sovereignty; no homicidal fighting between adopted and bio Fa sovereignty | 78% (7/9) |
| (3) No contact with bio Fa sovereignty | — (0/5) |

difference between categories (1) and (2) in Table 18 is not striking, the tabulation supports the argument that these were different kinds of moves.

Of the twenty-nine moves away from Auyana, in seven cases (24 percent) the mover returned. If these cases are examined in terms of the three categories of mover in types 7-10 and where they moved, the result is Table 19. Most striking is the contrast between category (1) and categories (2) and (3) combined. The difference between (2) and (3) is suggestive but inconclusive because of the small numbers.

TABLE 19
RETURN RATES: CATEGORIES OF TYPES 7-10

|  | Percentage | |
|---|---|---|
| (1) Contact with bio Fa sovereignty; homicidal fighting between adopted and bio Fa sovereignty | 13% | (2/15) |
|     Moved to bio Fa sovereignty | — | (0/13) |
|     Moved elsewhere | 100% | (2/2) |
| | | |
| (2) Contact with bio Fa sovereignty; no homicidal fighting between adopted and bio Fa sovereignty | 33% | (3/9) |
|     Moved to bio Fa sovereignty | 33% | (3/9) |
|     Moved elsewhere | — | (0/2) |
| | | |
| (3) No contact with bio Fa sovereignty | 40% | (2/5) |

I will summarize my interpretation of types 7-10 to this point:

1. If one maintained contact with his bio Fa sovereignty and a homicidal fight broke out between his adopted and bio Fa sovereignty, he was almost certain to move out (Table 16). When he moved, he would almost certainly move to his bio Fa sovereignty (Table 18) and remain there (Table 19).

2. If one maintained contact with his bio Fa sovereignty and no homicidal fighting occurred between his adopted and bio Fa sovereignty, there was a high probability he would move (Table 16). If so, he would almost always move to his bio Fa sovereignty (Table 18) and would remain there about half the time (Table 19).

3. If one did not maintain contact with his bio Fa sovereignty, he was much less likely to move out than he would be in either of the above two cases (Table 16). He would never move to his bio Fa sovereignty (Table 18), and he would remain wherever he moved about half the time (Table 19).

To this point I have periodically mentioned that some members of Auyana were cognates although they were not agnates. It might be asked whether those who had cognates in Auyana but who had a bio Fa from another sovereignty moved away any less than those who had no cognates in Auyana. Considering the number of individuals who moved, rather than the number of moves, Table 20 compares the moving out rate for those of types 7-10 whose mothers were from Auyana and those whose mothers were not.

TABLE 20
RATES OF MOVEMENT FOR TYPES 7-10: MATRI-ANCESTRY

|  | Percentage |
|---|---|
| Mother from Auyana | 64% (9/14) |
| Mother from elsewhere | 65% (17/26) |

Nor does it make any difference if those whose mother or biological father's mother was from Auyana are combined, as illustrated in Table 21.[7] In addition, my inspection of the data does not indicate there were any special conditions (such as homicidal fighting) in which matri-ancestry might be particularly important for moving. Hence, I conclude that biological matri-ancestry made no difference in moving out for those in types 7-10.

TABLE 21
RATES OF MOVEMENT FOR TYPES 7-10: COGNATES

|  | Percentage |
|---|---|
| Mother or bio Fa mother from Auyana | 63% (12/19) |
| Other matri-ancestry | 67% (14/21) |

Let us now turn to types 1-4. Table 12 demonstrates that those who had a close patri-segment in another sovereignty were much more likely to move out than those who did not. However, the relationship of other variables to this is less clear than for types 7-10. In the first place, of the twenty-four men who had a close patri-segment in another sovereignty, twenty-two maintained contact (as defined on page 130). This, of course, leaves, only two who did not maintain contact, rendering it impossible to compare those who had close patri-segments in other sovereignties but did not maintain contact with those who did. Table 22 compares the moving rates for those who had contact with a close patri-segment in another sovereignty and those who did not, and, as would be expected, the figures are practically the same as in Table

TABLE 22
RATES OF MOVEMENT FOR TYPES 1-4: CONTACT

|  | Percentage |
|---|---|
| (1) Contact with close patri-segment in another sovereignty | 68% (15/22) |
| (2) No contact with close patri-segment in another sovereignty | 32% (6/19) |

---

[7] Table 21 is adjusted for the number of moves, not the number of individuals moving.

13. In any case, Table 22 is analogous to Table 14 (for types 7-10) and confirms the conclusion that those who kept up contacts with close agnates in another sovereignty were more likely to move. In addition, for types 7-10, homicidal fighting between two sovereignties in which there were close agnates who kept up contacts resulted in an even higher moving rate (see Table 13). However, Table 23 shows this to have not been the case for those in types 1-4. If anything, it was the reverse.

Before discussing the difference between types 1-4 and 7-10, I will consider where types 1-4 moved and whether they returned. Table 24 shows where those in Types 1-4 moved; the differences between this tabulation and Table 17 are obvious. Table 25 contains figures for whether those in subcate-

TABLE 23
RATES OF MOVEMENT FOR TYPES 1-4: HOMICIDAL FIGHTING

|  | Percentage |
|---|---|
| (1) Contact with close patri-segment in another sovereignty; homicidal fighting between own sovereignty and sovereignty of close patri-segment | 63% (12/19) |
| (2) Contact with close patri-segment in another sovereignty; no homicidal fighting between own sovereignty and sovereignty of close patri-segment | 100% (4/4) |

TABLE 24
DESTINATIONS: TYPES 1-4

| Moved To | Percentage |
|---|---|
| Close patri-segment in another sovereignty | 37% (8/22) |
| Wife's natal sovereignty | 32% (7/22) |
| Mother's natal sovereignty | 9% (2/22) |
| Elsewhere | 22% (5/22) |

TABLE 25
RATES OF MOVEMENT TO CLOSE PATRI-SEGMENT: CATEGORIES OF TYPES 1-4

|  | Percentage |
|---|---|
| (1) Contact with close patri-segment; homicidal fighting between own sovereignty and sovereignty of close patri-segment | 33% (4/12) |
| (2) Contact with close patri-segment; no homicidal fighting between own sovereignty and sovereignty of close patri-segment | 75% (3/4) |
| (3) No contact with close patri-segment | —   (0/6) |

gories of types 1-4 moved to a close patri-segment (cf. Table 18). Table 26 contains return rates for subcategories within types 1-4 (cf. Table 17).

TABLE 26
RETURN RATES: CATEGORIES OF TYPES 1-4

|  | Percentage |
|---|---|
| (1) Contact with close patri-segment; homicidal fighting between own sovereignty and sovereignty of close patri-segment | 58% (7/12) |
| Moved to close patri-segment | 75% (3/4) |
| Moved elsewhere | 50% (4/8) |
| (2) Contact with close patri-segment; no homicidal fighting between own sovereignty and sovereignty of close patri-segment | 100% (4/4) |
| Moved to close patri-segment | 100% (3/3) |
| Moved elsewhere | 100% (1/1) |
| (3) No contact elsewhere with close patri-segment | 67% (4/6) |

There is one further set of figures worth considering: whether people moved as part of a dispersal or not. By a "dispersal," I refer to a situation where most of the members of a sovereignty did not move but at least four men in a pooling unit moved within a few days of one another. Table 27 compares types 7-10 and 1-4 as to this kind of move.

TABLE 27
MOVES AS DISPERSALS

| Types | Percentages |
|---|---|
| 7-10 | 41% (12/29) |
| 1-4 | 59% (13/22) |

For types 7-10, all twelve of those who moved out as part of a dispersal did so when homicidal fighting broke out between their bio Fa sovereignty and Auyana. Further, all twelve had contact with their bio Fa sovereignty. The same conditions obtained for twelve out of the thirteen in types 1-4 who moved out as part of a dispersal. The one man for whom this was not the case moved out with others in his subpooling unit who had been keeping up contact. Hence, it could be argued that contact with close agnates in another sovereignty combined with homicidal fighting between the two sovereignties was a necessary and almost sufficient condition for dispersals. The twelve in types 7-10 who moved as part of a dispersal are twelve of the fifteen in Table 14 who kept up contact with their bio Fa sovereignty, and twelve of the thirteen in types 1-4 who moved as part of a dispersal are the twelve in Table 14 who maintained contact with a close patri-segment.

Following are summary statements for divisions within types 1-4 analogous to the summary for types 7-10:

1. Men who maintained contact with those in a close patri-segment that was part of a sovereignty which became involved in a homicidal fight with their own sovereignty moved away about 67 percent of the time (Table 23). They moved, as did those in types 7-10, as part of a dispersal (Table 27). Unlike those in types 7-10, they did not generally move to a close agnate (Table 25); nor did they remain where they moved. Rather, most of them returned to Auyana (Table 26).

2. Those who maintained contact with a close patri-segment in another sovereignty that was not involved in homicidal fighting with Auyana moved away even more often than those in category 1 (Table 23). In this regard, they were unlike types 7-10. They were like types 7-10 in that they moved out as individuals and not as part of a dispersal (Table 27), and they moved to live with close agnates (Table 25). Unlike types 7-10, however, they were almost certain to return (Table 26).

3. Those who had no contact with a close patri-segment were like types 7-10 in that they moved out only about a third of the time (Table 22), they moved out as individuals (Table 27), and they did not move to close agnates (Table 25). Unlike types 7-10, about 67 percent of those in types 1-4 returned (Table 26).

I will attempt to interpret the three categories of types 7-10 and 1-4. I view the first category as those who had to move because of suspected loyalties. One of the reasons previously mentioned for why certain of those in types 7-10 returned to Auyana was that they were afraid someone in Auyana might attempt soul assassination on them during a time when Auyana was fighting with their bio Fa sovereignty. The reverse of this was that those in Auyana were afraid that those with foreign ancestry would attempt soul assassination on or somehow betray Auyana. While I found no cases of this for types 7-10, I did record a case involving those with types 1-4 who maintained contact with a close patri-segment in another sovereignty. In the discussion of sovereignty attribute number seven, it was mentioned that there had been a fight within Auyana which resulted in homicide and later accusations of soul assassination. The fighting started over the presumed betrayal of Auyana by those in a subpooling unit which had a close patri-segment in a sovereignty with which Auyana was having a homicidal fight at the time. Others in Auyana accused the subpooling unit of giving material to use in assassinating souls to the enemy and claimed that this resulted in the death of an Auyana man from a relatively minor arrow wound. The accusers, who were in a different pooling unit from either the alleged betrayers or the dead man, attacked the traitorous subpooling unit, killing two of them. The survivors then fled, some going to the enemy group (these are the cases in Table 26, [1]). Three later returned to Auyana, and it was they and their sons who accused the other pooling unit of still trying to kill them by soul assassination. If two men of type #1-1-1-1# ancestry whose biological patri-ancestry was impeccable could have this sort of charge leveled at them and be killed for it, then those who had no such credentials would seem even more liable. But note that this liability occurred only when one maintained contact with outside agnates (or presumed agnates).

The point is that all men who maintained contact ran a constant risk that they would be placed in a tenuous position by the eruption of homicidal fighting. However, it is obvious that this position was more tenuous for those in types 7-10 than for those in types 1-4. The moving rate for those in types 7-10 was much higher (94 percent vs. 65 percent). The return rates support this as well, being 75 percent for those in types 1-4 and 13 percent for those in types 7-10. Further, it is no surprise that almost all of those in types 7-10 went to their bio Fa sovereignty under these conditions whereas few of those in types 1-4 went to an enemy sovereignty, even though they might have agnates living there. The fact that those in types 1-4 frequently returned after such a movement whereas those in types 7-10 never returned (compare Table 26 [1] and Table 19 [1]) may be taken as an indication that only biological agnates could compromise their loyalties and still be able to return as members.

Also, the fact that movement almost always occurred as part of a dispersal lends credence to my interpretation of this category. For it seems unlikely that the movement of entire units or large sections of units could be simply fortuitous coincidence. A widespread suspicion of those with common foreign ancestry seems more likely.

The interpretation of categories two and three is much less clear. A plausible explanation would be that these are cases where there was no single overriding consideration but a combination of considerations which resulted in movement. This interpretation might explain why overall the moving rate was lower and the return rate higher than for category one, and moving out was individual rather than part of a dispersal. Biological agnation was important, in that those who had contact moved to live with their biological agnates. It could also be argued that those in category two moved out more often than those in category three (those who had no agnatic contacts outside their sovereignty) and returned less often because biological agnation resulted in faster acceptance into another sovereignty. The fact that the return rate (33 percent) for types 7-10 was lower than that for types 1-4 (100 percent) could be taken as further evidence that biological agnation did give an advantage. The apparent exception to this argument is category two in types 1-4, which is based on only four cases.

If my interpretation of moving is correct, then the assertion that warfare serves to unite those on a team (Simmel 1955, Murphy 1957) is once again an oversimplification. The Auyana case would indicate that warfare split those who were only partly united. This finding would not surprise many Japanese-Americans, given their incarceration during World War II, and it would seem safe to assume that the process characterizing Auyana is a common one. In the Auyana case, where members could not be imprisoned, the result was that people were sometimes forced to leave during intensive fighting, but moving to live with another group might place a person in a position of suspicion. Paradoxically, warfare both weakened and intensified group boundaries.

Before considering other evidence concerning the importance of agnatic ancestry, some further comments on the moving rate in Auyana are needed. It was stated earlier that only 4 percent of the members of Auyana were men who had been raised and sponsored in another sovereignty and then moved to Auyana. However, the sample was based on whether the individuals were members, whereas the discussion of moving considered only whether they made a garden in another sovereignty, not whether they became members. If the criterion of making a garden is used in considering those who moved into Auyana, then 22 additional cases would be added to the 138 discussed earlier, giving a total of 160 cases. The total number of men who moved into Auyana as individuals and made gardens is, then, 27 out of 160, or 17 percent. This figure is still much lower than the 58 percent of those in the Middle sample who moved out of Auyana. Even if we consider only whether they remained where they moved, there is still a considerable discrepancy.

Of the twenty-seven who moved into Auyana, nineteen (66 percent) left Auyana. Of the twenty-six men in types 7-10 who moved away from Auyana, eight (38 percent) stayed away.[8] One reason for the discrepancy between those moving in and those moving out may be that I never found out where some men were sponsored. It could have been that some of those supposedly sponsored in Auyana were actually sponsored somewhere else and moved to Auyana. They may have been types 7-10 in another sovereignty and moved back to their bio Fa sovereignty. Another possibility is that men who came to Auyana and stayed for a while but did not become members may have been forgotten, whereas those from Auyana who moved out were remembered. However, I am inclined to attribute the discrepancy to the political position of Auyana during the period just prior to the arrival of the Australians. During this time, there were only four boys whose bio Fa was from Auyana and who were raised in another sovereignty. Interestingly enough, none of the four returned to Auyana. At the same time, large numbers of people were moving into Auyana in large segments (see Chapter 5). This indicates that during this time Auyana was in an expansionist phase and was recruiting, or attempting to recruit, large numbers of people, some of

8 Note again the discrepancy between types 7-10 and 1-4.

whom were adult men. More importantly, at least for explaining the discrepancy between the rate of adult men who moved into and became members of Auyana and those who moved out of Auyana, this phase could have resulted in Auyana's obtaining exceptionally large numbers of foreign children to raise. Earlier, I mentioned the three ways by which foreign children were obtained. One was when the bio Fa of the child moved to Auyana. The five men who moved into Auyana and became members contributed four of those in the Middle category of types 7-10. Seventeen more of those in the Middle category of types 7-10 were boys whose bio Fa moved to Auyana, stayed for a while, and died in Auyana without becoming members. The boys were then raised and sponsored by someone in Auyana. Of the forty in types 7-10, twenty-one had a bio Fa who moved to Auyana. It could be argued, then, that Auyana had an unusually large number of foreign children during this period because there were a large number of men moving there. This of course would mean that adults who moved in and became members would contribute a proportionately smaller percentage to the population than if there had not been so many children. It might further mean that the absolute numbers that moved out of Auyana would be higher than those in types 1-4 who returned to Auyana, and closer to the percentage of those in types 7-10 who returned to Auyana, because so many who moved into Auyana were types 7-10.

If the above interpretation is true, then my earlier dismissal of the importance of married men moving in as a source of divergence from a group being all biological agnates may only apply to certain expansionist periods for any group. But to check this would require data I do not have.

Returning to the question of the importance of biological agnatic descent, if it is correct that foreign children (even if raised in Auyana) were not fully trusted when they kept up contact with their bio Fa sovereignty, then one would suspect that entire segments which moved into a sovereignty might be even less trusted. Chapter 5 discusses a history of fighting for a period of about twenty-five years. As part of that history, I collected information on all those who had ever moved into or out of Auyana. It turned out that a large number of segments which were subpooling units or larger moved into Auyana during this time. The reasons for their moving, the length of time they stayed, and so on will be discussed in Chapter 5. The relevant point here is that every one of them eventually moved back. As far as this history of Auyana indicates, people became members of another sovereignty and remained there only if they comprised relatively small numbers (subpooling units were around five to ten married men). While more information might show this not to have been literally true, it is obvious that large segments did not become readily integrated into a foreign sovereignty, even though they might be peacefully living there for some time. Each of these segments that moved in maintained themselves as a social unit. Most were large enough to act as separate pooling units. When they could not, they would get some aid from those in Auyana, and, if it was close, some aid from the sovereignty they had just left. By this means, they maintained themselves as distinct entities within Auyana, and I think this made them even more suspect than individuals with a bio Fa from another sovereignty who kept up contact with the sovereignty, for at least the latter acted as members of an Auyana subpooling and pooling unit. But the relocated segments acted, at best, only as members of the same sovereignty as the rest of Auyana, in that they would help to prosecute offenses and were to some extent part of a legal unit.

However, members of Auyana denied that the relocated segment helped to prosecute offenses as much as others in Auyana, or that they were accepted as part of a legal unit by the others in Auyana. They said this was because those outside Auyana were afraid that if they killed anyone from the relocated segment, those in the sovereignty from which the segment had moved would attack them. As a result, relocated segments were still considered to be part of a legal unit with those in the sovereignty which they had left. All of this, then, indicates that the relocated segments did not forget their origins, nor did those in Auyana or others. The relocated segments are better viewed as allies of Auyana who lived with those in Auyana for a period of time. If nothing else, the position of these segments indicates that moving as an adult to another sovereignty and becoming a member there was plausible only if one maintained himself as part of a pooling unit comprised of others who had already been living there and acting as a pooling unit.

If it is granted that having a bio Fa from another sovereignty might place a man in a somewhat tenuous position, one would expect that if his descendants stayed in a sovereignty and remained full members, ultimately his foreign biological patri-ancestry would be forgotten. As remarked earlier, no one was able to trace ancestry back more than three generations. But what is interesting is that the most distant men to whom ancestry could be traced were always those whom I will call "eternal members." They were men who were said to have been born, raised, and sponsored by their bio Fa, who was a member of X sovereignty and whose own bio Fa had raised and sponsored him and had also been a member of X sovereignty. It follows that, given enough time, every person, if not forgotten, became converted into a biological agnate of those in his sovereignty.

But if foreign biological patri-ancestry might have placed one in an awkward position, why then was it claimed? Why, for example, did a man in this position claim the collective soul of his bio Fa sovereignty? There were several reasons for this.

First, others in Auyana might hurl his foreign origin at him as an insult when they were angry. This occurred twice to my knowledge during the 1962-65 period. In one case, the man who made the insult was in the other's subpooling unit. In the other case, the man who made the insult was in a separate pooling unit and was insulting the entire pooling unit. But although such insults would make it clear to people of foreign origins that their position was somewhat tenuous, it would not explain why a person would carry on transactions with foreigners or claim their collective soul.

Second, as mentioned earlier, those in a person's bio Fa sovereignty might initiate contacts with him and try to persuade him to come back. It was possible, of course, for a man to turn down such overtures. However, I will later argue that in the type of situation in which members of Auyana found themselves, a man needed any friend he could get in other sovereignties. To turn down such overtures would be to pass up an opportunity to acquire such friends.

Third, a man might use his bio Fa origin as an initial claim to develop a relationship with someone. In order to examine this, it is necessary to consider the different sovereignties with which Auyana carried on transactions.

Rather than overwhelm the reader with a plethora of foreign names, I will adopt the following conventions. First, those from sovereignties which speak a different language than Auyana will be referred to by the name given to the largest grouping of which they were a part (see Map 4). For example, sovereignties in Tau (Fore) will be referred to as a "Tau sovereignty." If it becomes necessary to distinguish between such sovereignties, I will assign them numbers. Secondly, Indona will be referred to as Indona. The remaining groupings (Arora, Kawaina, and Opoimpina) are each divided into sovereignties. On Map 6, the rough territorial boundaries of these sovereignties, are defined by the solid lines. The first letters of each will be used in the text. Table 28 contains the names Auyana members gave to the various sovereignties.

TABLE 28
AUYANA NAMES OF SOVEREIGNTIES ON MAP 6

| Abikara | = A | Arora | = Arora #1 |
|---------|-----|-----------|-------------|
| Omuna | = O | Sepuna | = Arora #2 |
| Nankona | = N | Aunkapia | = Arora #3 |
| Waipina | = W | Kosena | = Arora #4 |
| Anokapa | = K | Kawaina | = Kawaina #1 |
| Amaira | = R | Kawaina | = Kawaina #2 |
| Sinkura | = S | | |
| Abia | = V | | |

Note that the two sovereignties within Kawaina do not have separate names. This is because Kawaina had only recently divided into two sovereignties. Also, sovereignty S (Sinkura) within Opoimpina was in the process of dividing into two sovereignties when the government arrived in 1950, and by 1962 was recognized as two sovereignties. However, as I am primar-

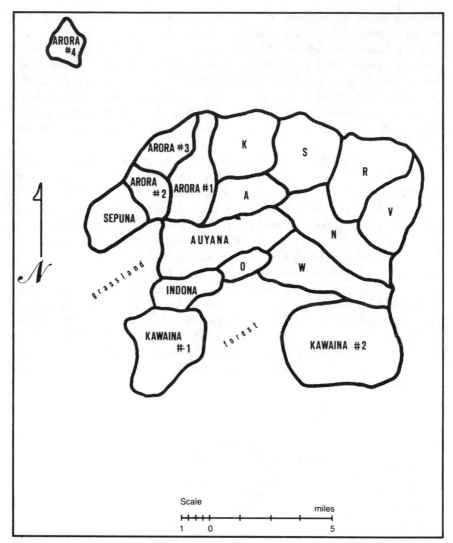

Map 6.  Sovereignties

ily concerned with the period prior to 1950, I have listed it as one sovereignty.

   One of the cases of using foreign agnatic claims in order to initiate relationships was mentioned in the discussion of Uwara' (Tairora). Some members of
Auyana claimed that they and some in Uwara' had come from men who lived
in Arora #1. The genealogical depth at which each claimed origin from Arora
#1 varied, however. For some men, it was apparently two generations

above them; for several, it was their bio Fa. If true, this means that there had been movement out of Arora #1 over at least two generations and that to some extent those who moved out were kept track of and used. A man in Auyana whose bio Fa was from Arora #1 had also used this to initiate an exchange relationship (not trade—see Chapter 6) with a man in Indona whose bio Fa was said to have been a member of Arora #1.

Other cases involved a man using such claims in order to set up transactions with a woman as though she had come from his pooling unit. That is, she was used as the channel for giving and receiving wealth. As will be discussed in a later section, there were many such cases, and I will only give one to illustrate.

Ane was a man whose bio Fa was from K and who had moved, along with several others from K, to Auyana. After a brief stay, all except Ane's bio Fa returned to K. After a year or so in Auyana, he died. Ane and his siblings were still quite young at the time of their father's death. Their mother remarried a man who was a member of Auyana and he raised and sponsored Ane and his brother. Ane kept up some contact with those in K, but he never moved there. However, there was a woman from K who was married to a man in A and Ane, using the claim that he was from K, developed a relationship with her and her husband in which she was treated as though she were a woman from his pooling unit. This does not mean that such relationships were developed with women and their husbands only when one could claim mutual biological agnatic descent. However, from the frequency with which such relationships were established, I would gather that it did provide a means by which the relationship could be more easily initiated.

Although some of the above transactions involved social units within a sovereignty, most involved single individuals. In any case, when individuals were involved, the greatest genealogical depth ever used in claiming foreign origins was that of a person's bio Fa bio Fa. Claims to foreign origin at a greater genealogical depth were made only when there were several individuals within a sovereignty who could make the claim. For all the cases I documented, this occurred only when the claim to foreign origin was used to build a subdivision within a sovereignty. Otherwise, the claim would be ignored after the second generation.

The use of a claim to foreign ancestry to build subdivisions within a sovereignty was highly important in Auyana. Not only was it used for recruiting, but subdivisions could also claim special access to the forest of another sovereignty, a claim which could not be made by single individuals. In order to demonstrate this process, I will consider one of the pooling units in Auyana and how it was formed. Figures 4 and 5 contain the total members of the pooling unit. Each chart is a subpooling unit of the pooling unit. The three main actors have been given Auyana names and the other members have been assigned numbers. I will refer to this pooling unit as Ta's pooling unit, since this was the way it was most often referred to by members of Auyana. I

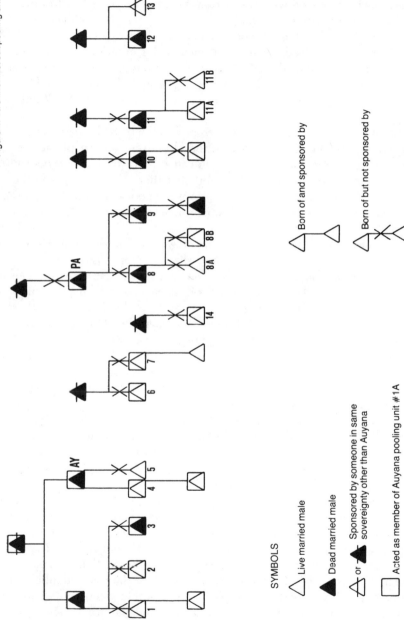

Figure 4. Ta's line: first subpooling unit

SYMBOLS

△ Live married male

▲ Dead married male

◁ or ◀ Sponsored by someone in same sovereignty other than Auyana

☐ Acted as member of Auyana pooling unit #1A

△—△ Born of and sponsored by

◁⊣▷ Born of but not sponsored by

Figure 5. Ta's line: second subpooling unit

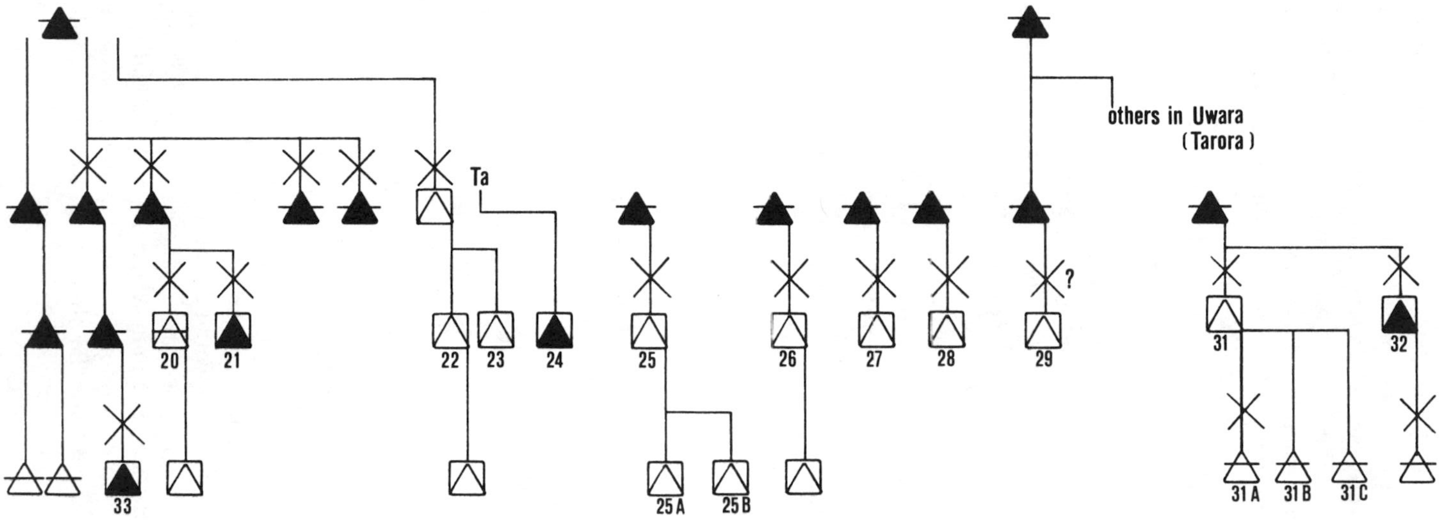

See Figure 4 for symbols

estimated Ta to be in his late sixties to early seventies in 1965.

Ay's father was said to have married a woman from Auyana and moved to Auyana from sovereignty N. Ta was not sure which pooling units existed in Auyana when Ay's father moved in. In any case, Ay's father became a member of an Auyana pooling unit and remained in Auyana until he died. He adopted and sponsored Pa. No one knew the circumstances surrounding the adoption. Pa's bio Fa was from sovereignty K. Pa then helped Ay's father to sponsor Ay and his brother. At this point there were supposedly two pooling units in Auyana. Pa, Ay, and his brother were all members of pooling unit #1, but with close ties to some in pooling unit #2. However, pooling unit #1 was in the process of division.

Ta's mother was from pooling unit #1 and married Ta's father, who was from Arora #1. Ta's father was killed, presumably during a fight within Arora #1, and Ta was brought as a nursing infant by his mother to live in Auyana. One of the men in pooling unit #1 raised and sponsored him. Ta and Ay very early began to act as though they were brothers. Shortly after Ta was married, Pa died, and Ay's brother took #8 and raised him, and Ta took #9 and raised him. Thus, what was eventually to become a pooling unit was at this time three married men, their children, and several adopted boys. Shortly after Ta was married, a severe fight broke out between the two sub-pooling units of pooling unit #1, both of which had been recruiting foreign boys. A split developed after the fight, creating, in effect, three pooling units in Auyana. I will refer to the pooling unit of which Ta and Ay were members as pooling unit #1A and the other pooling unit which derived from pooling unit #1 as #1B.

Both Ta and Ay had become near legends when they were still alive. Members of Auyana used two phrases to refer to important men: one was *kentaspomba*, and the other was *auwi'wasi*. *Kentasa-* meant "our" and *-po-* meant "post" (*-mba* is a nominative suffix). Members of Auyana said that a man who was called their "post" was like the center post of the men's house, the one who held them up. If he fell, they too would fall. From informal conversations, it seemed that in order to be a post, a man had to be a killer and also one who organized events, especially those involving the pooling and distribution of wealth. In 1962, I asked fifteen married men from each subpooling unit within Auyana who had been the posts in the past what it took to be a post. All agreed that one had to be a killer. All also agreed that although this was necessary, it was not sufficient, and a man who never spoke up in public and never organized exchanges and distributions might have fame as a killer, but he would not be a post.

*Auwi'wasi* meant a man who had a name. Members of Auyana used "having a name" in the sense of men whose reputations had spread a long way and whose names were therefore known by people far away. I also asked how people got a name and how far their name went (how widely known they were). Again, those who were killers and organizers had names that went the farthest. It was said that a killer's name went far, but not as far as those who were both killers and organizers. A man who was not a killer but who had lots of pigs and organized many exchanges might have a name that only went a short distance.

Everyone agreed that Ta and Ay had been the Auyana posts for the period of twenty-five to thirty years prior to the arrival of the government. Members of Auyana claimed their names had reached every group which Auyana knew about and which knew about Auyana. Stories abounded about their prowess in fighting, and Ta and Ay were clearly the two most dominant men in Auyana for the period considered here. Further, their reputations were established by the time they were young married men, since both had killed several men by then.

Returning to the history of the development of Ta's pooling unit, not long after pooling unit #1 was divided into pooling units #1A and #1B, Auyana had a homicidal fight with another sovereignty which lasted for several months. This was the fight during which the homicides within Auyana discussed on p. 113 occurred. Some of those in pooling unit #1B had contacts with a close patri-segment in the enemy sovereignty. Ta and Ay accused some in #1B of soul assassination against Auyana and attacked and killed two members of #1B. An intriguing part of this affair is that the person who died as a result of the soul assassination was not in pooling unit #1A (i.e., in Ta's or Ay's pooling unit), but in pooling unit #2. It would appear, then, that the internal fighting which led to the split of pooling unit #1 resulted in lasting grudges and eventually in homicide. In any event, most of those in pooling unit #1B fled from Auyana. Several eventually returned and joined with those in pooling unit #2 to form a single pooling unit. Meanwhile, those in pooling unit #1A were recruiting numerous foreign children.

Referring again to Figure 4, persons 1, 2, and 3 were raised primarily by Ay after Ay's brother died with both Ta and Ay cosponsoring them. Number 5 was a son of Ay who was taken while still a small child by his mother when she left Ay, and was raised in her natal pooling unit in sovereignty K. However, those in sovereignty K would not buy a wife for him and, as he would not move back to Auyana, neither would those in Auyana. He married a widowed woman who divorced him and in 1962-65 he had no wife. Nonetheless, those in Auyana in Ta's pooling unit occasionally had him help them pool wealth and occasionally distributed to him some of the wealth they received.

Numbers 6 and 7 were men whose father moved to Auyana as part of a large segment from Onkena (see Map 4). Their father died and Ay claimed the boys, raised them, and sponsored them. Both acted as members until the late 1950s. Then, #7 returned to Onkena and his son was jointly sponsored by those in Onkena and those in Ta's pooling unit in Auyana. Number 7 had little else to do with those in Auyana. Numbers 10 and 11 were both men whose fathers moved to Auyana as part of a large segment from sovereignty K and died while at Auyana. Both were raised and sponsored by those in pooling unit #2 but became members of pooling unit #1A after they were married.

Before considering the younger generation in Figure 4, let us look at those in Figure 5. Although Ta sponsored all his own sons, #23 was one of several boys sent to Abi'era in Uwara' (Tairora) for a while in order to be a trade intermediary. Number 25 was a man whose mother was from Auyana and who brought him to Auyana when he was still small after her husband died. Numer 25 remained in Auyana. Number 26 was the man named Ako, who as a boy had been "bought" by Ta. He also remained in Auyana. Number 27 was a man whose father was from Arora #1 (the sovereignty to which Ta's bio Fa belonged). When his father was killed, Ta helped Arora #1 avenge the death, despite the fact that Auyana and Arora were considered severe enemies, and then demanded that the boy be given to him. Number 27 had moved out of Auyana to Arora #1 twice, but returned both times. Number 28's father was from Indona; when the father died in Auyana where Indona was refugeed, Ta took the boy and raised him. He remained in Auyana, although in 1962 he was threatening to move back to Indona if those in Auyana did not buy him a wife soon.

Numbers 20, 21, and 29 were all men whose bio Fa were sponsored in Uwara' (Tairora) but who claimed to have derived from Arora #1. Number 20 said that after Ta's father died, #20's father was a child and was taken along when several fled to Uwara' (Tairora). He was raised and sponsored there and married a woman from Onkena, who returned to Onkena when he died. Her natal pooling unit then raised and sponsored #20. They bought him a wife from sovereignty W in Opoimpina. Number 20 then moved with his wife and unmarried younger brother (#21) to sovereignty W. When sovereignty W got into a fight with Auyana, #20 claimed that he could not fight against those who were from the same sovereignty as he (referring to the origin of Ta from Arora #1), and moved to Auyana. He stayed there and his son was sponsored by Ta's pooling unit. Number 21 was still unmarried when #20 moved to Auyana, and went with him. Those in Ta's pooling unit bought a wife for #21, but just after she moved to live with him, he was killed. Number 29 claimed much the same story as #20 except that he pushed the point at which his ancestors moved to Uwara' (Tairora) back to his bio Fa bio Fa . Further, #29 came in with the first government patrol as an interpreter and stayed. Those in Ta's pooling unit cosponsored the purchase of his wife. He had moved out of Auyana to Uwara' (Tairora) and then back again before 1962.

The remainder of Ta's father's children were taken by those in Arora #1 when Ta's father was killed. They all remained there, except for #33's father, who moved to Auyana and died there. Number 33 was raised and sponsored by #22 (Ta's son), but shortly after a wife was bought for him, he died.

Returning to the younger generation in Figure 4, #7's son was commented on above. Number 14 was the son of a man who moved in as part of an Anepa' (Awa) sovereignty and then died before Anepa' moved back. Number 14 was taken by #6 and raised and sponsored by him and acted as a member of Ta's pooling unit.

Numbers 8A and 8B are interesting cases in that they show the shifting that can go on within a sovereignty. Their mother was from pooling unit #2. When their father died, she moved to live with one of her brothers. At that time, #8A was taken by #4 and #8B was taken by her brother. Number 4 then sponsored the initiation series for #8A. But, before buying a wife, #8A moved to live with some people in pooling unit #2 and asked them to buy his wife, saying that he was mad at those in Ta's pooling unit. This so angered #4 and others in Ta's pooling unit that they refused to help buy his wife and had little to do with him. In the case of #8B, however, even though he was raised by a man in pooling unit #2 who was his major sponsor for his initiation and for buying his wife, #4 and some of the others in Ta's pooling unit contributed large amounts to both endeavors and made various attempts to recruit him into their pooling unit. They were unsuccessful, but he was young and there was still hope that they could recruit him.

When #9 died, his son was raised and sponsored by #22 in Figure 5. The boy acted as a member of the subpooling unit in Figure 5 until he died, not long after he was married. Number 10's son was raised and sponsored by #6 when #10 died, and acted as a member of that subpooling unit. Number 11A was sponsored by his father, with #22 acting as a major cosponsor, and thus #11A was not clearly in either subpooling unit.

Number 11B was a different case altogether. As an unmarried man, he was caught with another man's wife and was shot in the hip. When the wound did not heal, he was taken to the hospital at the nearest government patrol post. From there, he was sent to various hospitals. Afterwards, he decided to become a medical orderly. He underwent six months' training and was then stationed at various posts in the Eastern Highlands. During this time, he remained unmarried because he had been left a cripple as a result of the wound. In 1964, while he was stationed nearby, several from Auyana went to see him. Among them was a girl who had become pregnant but did not want to marry the man intended for her by her pooling unit. She convinced #11B to marry her. He paid for her in 1964, and she had gone to live with him by the time I returned in 1965. Number 11B never acted as a member of Auyana after he went to the hospital and it seemed unlikely that he ever would.

Numbers 31 and 32 in Figure 5 and numbers 12 and 13 in Figure 4 have not been discussed for several reasons. The most important one is that they were four of eight children (other than #25 in Figure 5) who were all obtained from sovereignty N at about the same time. The mother of #31 and #32 was a woman who was originally from Arora #1 but had set up a special relationship with Ta, treating him as though he were in her natal pooling unit. When her husband died, she moved to Auyana, and Ta took responsibility for raising and sponsoring #31 and #32.

Number 32 was a member of Auyana and his death precipitated a major fight between Auyana and Arora #1 (the latter was accused of killing him by means of soul assassination). When #32 died, his son was raised by #31 who was also a member of Auyana but maintained considerable contact with his bio Fa sovereignty. For example, he sent his oldest son, #31A, to a man in sovereignty N to be raised there. When Auyana became engaged in a homicidal fight with those in sovereignty N, #31 moved back to sovereignty N, taking #31B, #31C, and #32's son with him. Number 31 was acting as the major sponsor for all these boys. Those in Ta's pooling unit contributed only small amounts to buy the wives for #31C and #32's son. Both boys were younger than #31B and had not been initiated before they moved back to sovereignty N, which may be why members of Ta's pooling unit contributed little. In the case of #31B, who had been initiated in Auyana, Ta's pooling unit contributed about one-half of the bride wealth, and they continued to attempt to lure back both #31 and #31B.

Shortly after the mother of #31 and #32 moved back to Auyana, #12's father came there with his two sons. Number 12's father and #31's father had been in the same pooling unit in sovereignty N. Members of Auyana said that #12's father left sovereignty N because he was afraid others in that sovereignty would kill him by means of soul assassination, just as they had killed #31's father. Number 12's father remained in Auyana, although he retained considerable contacts with his original sovereignty, which contributed a fairly large share to buying the wife of #12. Before #13 could have his wife bought, Auyana got into the homicidal fight with sovereignty N. Numbers 12 and 13 and their father moved back to sovereignty N along with #31 and others. Although #13 had been initiated in Auyana, he and #12 fought against Auyana. Even so, those in Ta's pooling unit contributed a small amount to buy #13's wife. He married a girl in pooling unit #2 and attempted to move in with those in Ta's pooling unit after the homicidal fight had stopped, but he did not stay there long before moving back to sovereignty N, where he was in 1965.

The other four boys whose bio Fa were from sovereignty N are not included in Figures 4 and 5. They were raised by men in pooling unit #1A. These men were said to have been biological agnates of one another and those whose fathers were "eternal members" of Auyana. This means pooling unit #1A was initially comprised of those whose fathers were eternal members. During the time when Ta and Ay were building up a segment around them, these men were also building one and received considerable amounts of aid from Ta and Ay. The men had eight sons of their own and they raised and sponsored the four boys mentioned above whose biological fathers were from sovereignty N. However, unlike the Ta and Ay segment, they were not able to maintain themselves. Four of the eight sons died of illness, one was killed by homicide, and the four men with a bio Fa from sovereignty N returned there when the homicidal fighting with sovereignty N began. This segment was thus reduced in a short period of time to three men. One of these men became a member of pooling unit #2 and still was in 1962-65. The other two became more or less members of the subpooling unit in Figure 5. Partly as a result of the collapse of one segment of the pooling unit and partly because of the group which Ta and Ay had built, what started as a few people in a pooling unit had become a pooling unit of its own with the survivors of the original pooling unit being attached to one segment of the new pooling unit. I will return to this later.

Let us now reconsider the problem of how agnatic ancestry was used to build Ta's pooling unit. Those in Figure 5 were obtained primarily through Ta's own sons or through his adopted children, and biological agnation had little to do with the latter. However, #29, #20 (and his son), #21, and #23 were all obtained through men moving to Auyana and claiming common biological agnatic ancestry with Ta. This, then, is one sense in which agnatic ancestry was used. For those in Figure 4, however, there was not even this use of biological agnatic ancestry. Rather, it seems to have been simply a case of either adopting children or getting men to shift from one pooling unit within Auyana to another.

It is when we consider the relationship between those in Figure 4 and Figure 5 that the use of biological agnatic ancestry to build internal segments becomes more clear. I have already mentioned that Ay's father moved to Auyana from sovereignty N. However, Ta claimed that Ay's father was obtained as a boy by those in sovereignty N, and his bio Fa was a member of the same pooling unit in Arora #1 as Ta's bio Fa. Ta consequently claimed that he and Ay were biological agnates. This claim was used to distinguish those who came to form this pooling unit. Most were, of course, at least raised and sponsored by Ta and Ay. I also found that this claim included the name of the pooling unit. Late in 1962, I learned that Ta's pooling unit was named Manenamia, which was the name of the segment within Arora #1 in which Ta's bio Fa and Ay's bio Fa bio Fa had been members. It is significant, however, that I did not discover this name until late 1962. As mentioned in the discussion of pooling unit attributes, pooling units were initially presented as having no names, and I was repeatedly told this until fairly late in 1962, despite questioning about it in various contexts. Perhaps this reluctance to give the names of pooling units was because names referred to the sovereignty from which the presumed founder (or founders) originated. Just as Ta's pooling unit was named Manenamia, so pooling unit #2 was named Sinkura from the fact that the presumed founder was a man whose bio Fa was a member of Sinkura (sovereignty S on Map 6), but the founder had been obtained as a child by Auyana and raised and sponsored by them.

If a man was successful in raising and sponsoring large numbers of children, then these children and any others who had joined with the man could use his foreign biological origins to set themselves apart from others within a pooling unit. If the segment continued to grow, then this man would come to be viewed as the founder, and eventually an entire pooling unit would have a name referring to a foreign sovereignty. But if a man was not particularly successful in building a segment, then his foreign biological origins were not used and were not remembered. For example, those in the youngest generation in Ta's pooling unit thought that Pa (see Figure 4) was either Ay's brother or was simply a man from Auyana who joined with Ay, and only Ta provided me with the information in Figure 4.

The process of building and naming groups could result in a sovereignty eventually comprised entirely of foreigners. In the discussion of pooling unit attributes, I stated that members of Auyana initially presented Auyana as being divided into two pooling units. These two were the two mentioned above, Sinkura and Manenamia. This raises the question of whether there were pooling units or any units in Auyana named Auyana and, if not, whether this meant that the original members of Auyana were unable to found viable segments.

Before considering this question, I will discuss the claims to the forest in other sovereignties made by those in the Sinkura and Manenamia pooling units. Members of Manenamia claimed they could go to the forest in the mountains above Arora #1 and make salt and lime there. Those in the Sinkura pooling unit said they could do the same in the forest above sovereignty S. As mentioned earlier, the making of salt and lime involved burning and leaching various leaves, converting the lime leaves into a paste which was fire baked, and distilling the water to get salt. The process took several days, and temporary shelters were erected in certain place within the forest. One facet of the claims made by those in the pooling units of Manenamia and Sinkura was that they could go to the same sovereignty to use their shelters and, more importantly, they could gather leaves from the forest there. I was told that the leaves used for this purpose were not abundant, and, particularly when a forest had been long used for this purpose as the Auyana forest had been, it would be to their advantage to go to the area above Arora #1, as it had a large expanse of virgin forest. However, no one could recall any instances when this claim had ever been exercised. People said that Auyana and Arora #1 were always on such bad terms that it was not safe to do so. However, those in Manenamia insisted that if they had not been on such bad terms, they would have gone there. This might indeed have been the case, for those in Sinkura did occasionally go to the large forest above sovereignty S to make salt and lime.

Let us now return to the question of whether any pooling units in Auyana were named Auyana. At the beginning of the discussion of Ta's pooling unit, I mentioned that there were initially two pooling units in Auyana. The one that I referred to as pooling unit #2 was called Sinkura, and the descendants of those men plus others they recruited formed the present pooling unit of Sinkura. The other pooling unit, referred to as pooling unit #1, was called Auyana. Auyana then divided into two pooling units, referred to above as pooling units #1A and #1B. Both were still called Auyana. Pooling unit #1B was driven out, and those from it who returned became part of the Sinkura pooling unit, although they were also referred to sometimes as Auyana. For example, people would say that earlier Auyana had been a pooling unit but then it split and some of them went "inside" Sinkura. Pooling unit #1A eventually developed into the Manenamia pooling unit. However, those within Manenamia who were from the original Auyana pooling unit were also referred to sometimes as Auyana. Whenever I presented the names Sinkura, Auyana, and Manenamia and asked who went under that name, I found that some of those in the Sinkura pooling unit and some of those in the Manenamia pooling unit were called Auyana. That is, those who claimed to be descendants of the original Auyana did not form a separate pooling unit, but only segments of pooling units comprised mostly of foreigners. However, they did claim special access to the forest above sovereignty R (see Map 5). They said that some from Auyana were among those who founded sovereignty R, and thus those who could call themselves Auyana (as a subdivision within the sovereignty of Auyana) could make salt and lime in sovereignty R's large expanse of virgin forest. This claim was exercised only twice that anyone can remember. But note that this was an exact reversal of the claim that those in Sinkura and Manenamia made. The latter claimed to have access to the forest of the sovereignty from which their founder came, whereas those in Auyana claimed to have access to the forest of a sovereignty which was founded by someone from among them. This implies that such claims seemed to depend not only on one's ancestry, but on who had the largest expanse of virgin forest to be exploited.

The history of the pooling units of Auyana also illustrates a point which so far has had little discussion: even *close* agnates might divide. When the original pooling unit #1 divided into pooling units #1A and #1B, this division was not simply along the lines of more remote common ancestry. Of four brothers, two went to pooling unit #1A and two went to pooling unit #1B. The two who went to #1B remained there and later moved out of Auyana along with the others in #1B, following several killings within Auyana.

So far, the contexts in which patri-ancestry has been discussed have either been those within a sovereignty or those which involved only segments of one sovereignty and another sovereignty. This is because the idiom of ancestry (patri- or otherwise) was not used to talk about the relationships between entire sovereignties. By this I mean that relationships of entire sovereignties to one another were not initially presented this way, nor (based on the public discussions I recorded) did members of Auyana talk about them in this manner to one another or to those in other sovereignties. Instead, a rhetoric of *implied* biological descent was used.

Members of Auyana initially told me the following story regarding those within the larger grouping of Opoimpina. Once there was a group living at a place called Opoimpimpa located at the western edge of what is now Auyana territory. This group called themselves Opoimpina. *Opoimpi* is a name,

*-mpa* is a locative suffix, and *-na* is a suffix meaning a plurality of actors. According to the story, the people called Opoimpi were the people who lived at the place called Opoimpi. The use of place names as names for social units was common. Those in Opoimpina split into two groups as a result of fighting among themselves. One of these groups moved to the north and was the one from which the present sovereignty of Anokapa (sovereignty K on Map 5) derived. Members of Auyana said that as this group moved to the north, they eventually developed close ties with those in Onkena, and the word Anokapa is an Onkena word and does not derive from a name for a place.

The other group from Opoimpina moved to a place called Auyampa located at about the center of the present territory of Auyana. They then took the name of Auyana for themselves. At this point, there were two sovereignties, one named Auyana, the other Anokapa, and both could also call themselves Opoimpina, as they had both come from Opoimpimpa. Anokapa did not grow in size, whereas Auyana did, and eventually those in Auyana split into the remainder of the sovereignties comprising what was, in 1962, the larger collectivity of Opoimpina.[9]

The collectivity was, of course, called Opoimpina, because its members had all come from those who were originally at Opoimpimpa. In 1962, Opoimpina was divided into two segments: Anokapa and Auyana (Auyana was comprised of all those sovereignties originating from those who had lived at Auyampa and who called themselves Auyana). Members of the sovereignty of Auyana said that they used this name because they remained at Auyampa, whereas the others moved away. They distinguished between "big name" Auyana, used to refer to the entire collectivity, and "little name" Auyana, used to refer to themselves as a sovereignty.

Those who moved away also took names mainly derived from specific places. The sovereignty named Amaira[10] (sovereignty R on Map 5) took its name from a place called Amaiyepa, as this was one of the places to which they first moved as they became a distinct sovereignty. Somewhat different was the sovereignty called Nankona, which took its name from a spot located within the territory of Auyana sovereignty. But it was said that those who eventually formed the distinct sovereignty of Nankona had mostly lived at Nankompa when they were still part of the original Auyana group.

Several sovereignties had more than one name, depending on how recently they claimed to have separated from others when they dispersed from the original group of Auyana. Those who claimed to have recently split from one another said they still had the same original name but also had another name. The names on Map 5 are those used to distinguish them.

---

[9] The exact order in which they split off was not agreed on. The disagreements involved competing claims of amity and enmity.

[10] *-ra* and *-na* were allomorphs.

While the above story clearly implies a common ancestry for all those in the present collectivity of Opoimpina, the sovereignties were not talked about in terms of common ancestry but in terms of having come from a group of people at a particular place. If people were asked whether all those in Opoimpina had one ancestor, the initial response was *always* that they did not and that each sovereignty had a different ancestor. I took this to mean that common ancestry was the hallmark of a sovereignty and hence different sovereignties were talked about as coming from a group at a place, not as coming from a common ancestor. If one pursued the question, members of Auyana would say that all those in the present collectivity of Opoimpina had one ancestor because those in the original group of Opoimpina had one ancestor. But this was simply following the logic of their own conception of a sovereignty and was not a rhetoric which had any significance for them. In a sense, this is simply another way of saying that they had shallow genealogies. That is, beyond three or four generations, common ancestry was at most implied and did not provide a framework for conceptualizing relationships.

I will now summarize the discussion so far of the uses of agnatic ancestry in Auyana.

1. Members of Auyana presented themselves and the subdivisions within Auyana as being biological agnates.

   a. In fact, most of them were not biological agnates.

   b. The fact that most of them were not biological agnates was not primarily due to adult men moving from one sovereignty to another and becoming members there. While there were many men who moved to Auyana, most comprised a transient population whose importance rested primarily in that they might die while there, whereupon members of Auyana would get their children.

   c. Therefore, the main source of men who were not biological agnates was the children of dead or divorced men. Such children were then raised and sponsored by Auyana. In this sense, sociological agnation was heavily relied on in forming the social units of Auyana and the subdivision within it. At the same time, only death or divorce would prevent men from raising and sponsoring their sons, and in this sense the members of Auyana attached great significance to biological agnation.

   d. Notwithstanding sociological agnation, I attempted to demonstrate through moving out and return rates that there was at least one context in which those who were not biological agnates might be discriminated against. This situation occurred when a person's bio Fa was from another sovereignty with which he kept up contact. I argued that there was no evidence that those whose bio Fa had been sponsored by someone in Auyana, and who were themselves sponsored by someone in Auyana, but whose bio Fa had been a member of another sovereignty, were treated any differently than those whose biological paternal ancestors had all been members of Auyana. I further argued that even for those whose bio Fa was from another sovereignty, there was no evidence to indicate that their wives were bought any less readily than the wife of anyone who was adopted. I suggested, therefore, that whatever discrimination there may have been against them because of their bio Fa membership depended on their establishing contact with their bio Fa sovereignty. Moving out rates indicated that establishing such contact might result in some discrimination, but the only clear case was when homicidal fighting broke out between their adopted sovereignty and their bio Fa sovereignty.

e. At the same time, I attempted to show that even those whose bio Fa had been a member of Auyana could put themselves in a tenuous position by keeping up contact with a close patri-segment which had moved to another sovereignty. However, the return rates indicated that this was not as bad a position to be in as that of those whose bio Fa was from another sovereignty where they maintained contact.

f. I then presented several reasons why a person might claim foreign agnatic ancestry:

(1) to develop special trade relationships;
(2) to develop special relationships with men and through women for exchanging wealth apart from trade;
(3) to build segments within a sovereignty;
(4) if a segment was formed, to claim special access to the forest belonging to another sovereignty.

g. I presented a single case history to demonstrate that those who were close biological agnates did not necessarily remain as members of the same social unit, even when this did not involve moving out of the sovereignty. Once again, it seemed that at the most, biological agnation was only one of several variables affecting membership in social units.

2. Members of Auyana did not conceptualize relationships between entire sovereignties in terms of common ancestry. Rather, they spoke in terms of the origin of those living at a place. In tracing common ancestry, they referred back only three to four generations and always in the social context of a sovereignty or individuals in one sovereignty and segments in another one.

Up to this point, the question of the importance of coresidence has been pursued implicitly rather than explicitly. In the discussion of sovereignty attributes, I mentioned that coresidence was necessary for membership. A person did not entirely relinquish his membership in one sovereignty and immediately take over membership in another sovereignty if he moved. Certain attributes changed rapidly and others took more time. A man did not garden in two sovereignties; gardening was relinquished in the former sovereignty as soon as it became clear that a man intended to stay at another sovereignty. Along with this, a man never acted as a member in two sovereignties or pooling units in terms of participating in prosecutions. If a man moved, he might not initially act in prosecutions carried out by those in the sovereignty which he had left. However, as the case of Kasari (see p.217) shows, a man might never be able to avoid completely being considered as part of a legal unit even though he no longer lived with that unit or in any other sense acted as a member. Pooling was also an activity which might be carried on with those in more than one sovereignty. The result of these considerations is that although in the long run coresidence was sufficient for membership, in the short run, a coresident could be in an extremely ambiguous situation. In a sense, he was like a man with no country. This, I think, explains why few stayed in Auyana although a great many moved there, and why the return rates of those who moved out of Auyana were so high, especially for types 1-4.

Glasse has stated:

> In Melanesia generally, I believe, it can be shown that kinship ultimately rests on the principle of reciprocity, a conclusion valid in many parts of the world. In New Guinea, those who behave towards one another in a positive reciprocal manner regard each other as kin, whether or not they are known or believed to be genealogically connected. By the same token, in New Guinea, distinctions of status based upon descent are of limited relevance to group recruitment. Once a man demonstrates his loyalty to a group by appropriate acts and participation in corporate affairs, he belongs to the group in a full sense. The other members care little whether he is an agnate, a cognate or even an unrelated man. They take pains neither to conceal his "foreign" origin or to discriminate against him because of it. This may be one reason why unilineal models have limited usefulness in explaining New Guinea Highlands data. [Glasse 1969:37]

I have quoted Glasse's statement in full because I believe the main thrust of what he says is correct, but the explicit statement confuses the central issue in a fashion which I feel is typically New Guinean (although not limited to New Guinea).

The central issue is the question of whether descent (defined as parent-child links) is (a) the criterion, (b) one of the criteria, or (c) not a criterion used in determining either personal networks or group membership. The confusion is that Glasse provides no definition of "kinship." If we take the term in its usual English usage to include at least the criterion of biological or sociological descent from a common ancestor, then Glasse's statement is literally contradictory. "In New Guinea, those who behave towards one another in a positive reciprocal manner regard each other as kin [i.e., related by common descent], whether or not they are known or believed to be genealogically connected [i.e., related by common descent]."

Another way to interpret his statement, which is characteristic of at least the Auyana situation, is that there exist two systems, a system of personal networks and a system of social units, both of which are presented by the actors to an outsider as though biological descent were a necessary and sufficient condition for inclusion in them. But this is not true for either, and the relevance of biological or sociological descent in either of the actual operating systems is an empirical question. Glasse's statement could then be translated in the following way: "In New Guinea, those who behave toward one another in a positive reciprocal manner will present themselves to someone who doesn't know otherwise as being biologically descended from a common ancestor, whether or not they are known to be biologically descended from a common ancestor." This statement was true for at least the system of social units in Auyana. When I asked about the parent-child links of the present members of the social units, I was told that the present members had male parents who were children of men who were children of a certain man. Initially, the male parents were presented as biological parents, later as sociological parents, and, in some cases, later as not being parents at all.

At the beginning of this chapter, I stated that the image of social units being comprised of biological agnates was a model with which members of Auyana began the social game, but I did not define what I meant by a "model." There are three dimensions to my use of the concept here. One is that of the image presented to outsiders. This has been discussed. Another dimension is that of the image presented to one another. In the earlier discussion, I cited some examples in passing in which members of Auyana did make the realities presented to one another conform to the image of social units comprised of biological agnates. For example, in the discussion of the formation of Pawe's line, I mentioned that younger men believed that certain past members were biological agnates, whereas one of the older men presented a much different history for them. Information about the biological origins of individuals was either forgotten or modified over time so that succeeding generations perceived past generations as eternal members. I do not know, however, the exact extent to which this happened, nor the process by which it happened.

Information changed over social space as well as over time. While individuals varied in their genealogical knowledge, both about their own and others' ancestry, my impression was that in general the smaller the social unit, the more the individuals knew about one another's genealogies. Members of a subpooling unit were more likely to know that members of another subpooling unit were not biological agnates than were members of different pooling units to know that about one another. Even though an outsider would know that individuals of a social unit were undoubtedly not all biological agnates, he would not necessarily know who was and was not, and when in doubt he would consider them to be biological agnates. I do not have many cases to document this impression, as mostly I dealt with people talking about their own ancestry, not the ancestry of others.

In addition to the ways people presented themselves to outsiders and to one another, the other dimension in my use of the concept of a "model" is the existence of pressure exerted on individuals to conform to certain images presented. In the preceding chapter I discussed situations in which pressure was exerted and people attempted to conform to an image. Glasse's statement that "foreign" origin made no difference was not true in Auyana. Coresidence was a necessary and, along with participation in social unit tasks, a sufficient condition for membership in a social unit. There was, however, a definite preference for biological agnates as coresidents. If they did not die or get divorced, men reared their own biological sons and recruited them to their social units. Adult men who moved into another sovereignty were sometimes in a disadvantageous position. On the other hand, foreign origins were sometimes advantageous as they gave the person outside connections that others did not have. And so on.

Humans do build images of contingencies in their construction of social realities and exert pressure on one another to conform to those images. The mistake of normative views of social reality has been to construe pressure as overwhelming: rules are to be obeyed or else the system cannot function, and therefore to understand the system we only need to know the rules and the exceptions can be ignored. Certainly this is the image that a bureaucratic state would like its members to hold, but to impose this view on all social realities simply echoes the imperialism of the bureaucratic states. Some social realities are more negotiable than others. Some have a high degree of conformity to the image the actors present, some a low degree. And some may even be continually negotiated in some areas (Wagner 1975). Our task is to describe and appreciate this variation as something to be explained and understood, not as something to be intellectually or physically legislated out of existence.

I believe that in Auyana the immediate cause of the nonconformity to the image of biological agnation for social units was social dislocation due to warfare. Before considering this idea, I will first present the system of personal networks which coexisted and overlapped with the system of social units. I will not attempt to document the exact ways in which descent was relevant in this system. The image of personal networks was one of common ancestry, and the reality was that certain behaviors were sufficient for a person to be labeled as a member of the network. But I will not examine the ways in which ancestry was used. My main concern is to demonstrate the behavioral features of the personal networks and the overlap between these networks and the social units.

I stated earlier that for every pooling there were various levels of responsibility, usually with one individual being what I called the "major sponsor." Events had both a group and an individual focus, and I will now discuss that dual nature. Then, I will return to the question of why the images and realities did not fit in Auyana.

FAMILY FRIENDS

No special terms existed for people who were strangers and with whom no interaction occurred; they were "just people." For people with whom there was hostile interaction a special term existed: *hamuro* (enemy). For people with whom there was friendly interaction, special terms were used for reference and address. For convenience, I will consider them only as terms of address in the remainder of this analysis. If a little interaction had taken place, roughly what I would call having met someone and talked with him a bit, the person could be addressed as "my *wasi* (human)." However, some of the people with whom one traded were closer than "my human." If someone in Auyana traded regularly with an individual in another group and stayed with him while they were trading, he would address the person as "my *mara*." The same was true of any situation in which one person was what I would call friendly with another, but not really a friend yet. As he became a friend, he would address the person by terms referring to subdivisions of *mara*.

Looked at from this perspective, the realm of *mara* could be considered simply as a behavioral realm in the same way the realm of social units was initially described. Doing this would overlook the same set of facts that I have described in the case of social units. When I asked members of Auyana what *mara* meant, the answer was either *imbolanaeme* or *imbolaisapiko*. *Naeme* meant blood in other contexts and *imbolanaeme* was translated into pidgin as "wan blut" (one blood). By the Auyana theory of conception, to say two people were one blood would imply they had one mother and say nothing about their father. When I asked what was meant by *imbolanaeme*, however, I was told it meant they had one mother and one father. Or it might be said that one man and one woman bore them. *Imbolanaeme* was described to me as meaning common biological ancestry traced through males and females. *Imbolaisapiko* was described in the same way. In pidgin it was translated as "wan tumbuna" (one ancestor), and when asking what that meant I was given a description of biological ancestry leading back to one couple.

As I collected more individual genealogies, I began to find that people who were initially presented as biological descendants of someone were later said to have been raised by that person, and some who were said to have been raised were only cosponsored, and so on. In other words, my experience learning about the realm of *mara* from genealogies was much like my experience learning about social units. Similarly, if I asked someone to list all the people included in his *mara*, he would name various people who were not given to me when I collected his genealogy. The realm of *mara* differed from the realm of social units in one respect. There were people whom a person would refer to as *mara* even though the person had never met them. These were people who were related to the person through parent-child links back to a common ancestor but whom the person had only heard about. People who were unknown to a person and who were *mara* to someone the person considered *mara*, but with whom the person did not share common ancestry, were not referred to as *mara*. While most *mara* were related to a person through common ancestry (biological or sociological) and certain behaviors, some were related only through common ancestry and some only behaviorally. If a person's family is considered to be those with whom he or she can establish a common ancestry through parent-child links, and friends are those with whom he or she can establish a common intention of mutual benefit, then in Auyana there was pressure for family to be friends and for friends to become members of a family. I will gloss *mara* as "family friends" to emphasize the dual nature of the realm.

There were various reasons why family were not always friends, but I do not have the data to establish the parameters of this relationship in the realm of *mara* as I do for the realm of social units. In the presentation of *mara* I will primarily demonstrate the connections between this realm and the social units, and I will give relatively little consideration to the situations in which family and friends did not correspond.

In this discussion, people who were married around the same time will be said to be in the same generation. The concept of "generations" was used by those in Auyana to distinguish family friends, and had two components. One of these was the consideration of the number of parent-child links from a common ancestor and the other was whether the two people were children around the same time and married around the same time. Usually these two dimensions coincided but sometimes they did not and two individuals who were in the same generation in terms of parent-child links might be distant in age. The point at which the difference in age was turned into a generational difference was negotiable, which is why I used the ambiguous phrase of "around the same time." Although ambiguous, there were limits. If one person was married before another was born then neither would consider them to be in the same generation. And if one was about to get married or had just gotten married when the other was around puberty (first menstruation for females and first stage of initiation for males) then they would both consider themselves to be in the same generation. Between these two extremes, whether they would consider themselves (and be considered by others) to be in the same generation depended partly on whether the older person actually looked after the younger or considered himself to be in the same generation as whoever did look after him and partly on what might be handiest in order to carry out certain exchanges of wealth and/or women.

I will refer to those in adjacent generations as being in the first older or first younger generation. Those who were in the first older generation with respect to those who were in the first older generation will be said to be in the second older generation. Another way of specifying the second older generation would be to say they were those whose children were married when the person was still a child. Older generations—third, fourth, etc.— can be specified in the same manner as the second older generation.

The criterion of sex was binary, agreed upon at birth, and was nonnegotiable. Strong women might act like men and weak men might act like women but for a person to become the opposite sex was only a fantasy, a fantasy which might be verbalized by an enemy in a fight but otherwise remained unstated.

I will begin by dividing the realm of family friends into two subsets, which I will call the end set and the exchange set. This division was not made explicitly by members of Auyana. The divisions within the end set were used with the closest and most distant family friends, whereas those in the exchange set were used with family friends in between the closest and most distant. Terms in the end set were used between members of a household and members of the same pooling unit and thus were the first terms a person used. At the same time they were the terms used when a stranger who did not share common ancestry became a friend and was incorporated into the realm of family friends. The distinctions within the end set were as follows:

1. Family friends in the same generation could address one another by one of four terms:

    a. *nano*—an older female
    b. *u*—a younger female
    c. *wa*—an older male
    d. *pa'*—a younger male.

2. Family friends in adjacent generations could address one another by one of the following terms:

    a. Those in the first older generation could be addressed by one of two terms:

        (1) *po*—a male
        (2) *no*—a female.

    b. Those in the first younger generation could be addressed by a single term, *ara'*, or they could be distinguished by sex:

        (1) *yamu*—a female
        (2) *ani*—a male.

3. Family friends two generations apart could address one another by one of the following terms:

    a. Those in the second older generation were distinguished by sex:

        (1) *napu*—a male
        (2) *rama*—a female.

    b. Those in the second generation could be addressed by a single term, *nauwai*.

4. Family friends more than two generations apart could be addressed by a single term, *isapi'*.

In practice, *isapi'* was never used as a term of address, even when it was applicable, which was practically never. Rather, the only context in which I heard it used was when referring to some dead ancestor. Usually this meant a context of talking about the common ancestry framework for a pooling unit or sovereignty. As would be expected given the agnatic "model" in Auyana, people usually did not know the *isapi'* of their mother's natal pooling unit (using mother to mean female parent, father to mean male parent, and brother and sister to mean male and female children of a person's mother and/or father, excluding the person).

*Isapi'* also meant "little finger." The image for sovereignties and their subdivisions was a "line" or "rope." Lines and ropes usually are of equal thickness throughout their length, and perhaps the line metaphor for social units assumed the indefinite continuity of a strong unit. *Isapi'*, then, were the distant ends of a line and at the same time the distant ends of a personal network of family friends. Like little fingers, they were not much used, and they were equivalent whether looking into the past or the future. Just as other fingers in the hand get more use than the little finger, so did individuals get more use the closer they were in time and space to one another. In any case, in the realm of family friends, more divisions were made for closer generations, with those in the same generation always making the most distinctions between one another.

But, considering only the end set, even those in the same generation did not make many distinctions between one another. The entire set was based on three criteria: generation, relative age within the same generation, and sex. Or, if relative age and generation are considered to be the same criterion with a cutoff point when a certain disparity in age was reached, then the entire set used only two criteria: relative age and sex.

I have not mentioned spouses of family friends, nor the family friends of spouses, because these individuals occupied a somewhat ambiguous position. Spouses of family friends in the generations above a person could be addressed by, and referred to by, the appropriate terms from the end set. Such also was the case for the reciprocal relationships, the family friends of a person's spouse in the generations below. In practice, these terms were not used unless the individuals involved lived around one another and/or the family friends involved were close to one another. For example, a man would address a woman married to a man in his pooling unit in the generation above him as *no*, but he would not address a woman married to a family friend in another sovereignty in the generation above him by this or any family friend term. My feeling was that the use of family friend terms for spouses of family friends in the first older generation, and their reciprocal use, was simply because the individuals involved were friendly or because they were friends of friends and honored this connection by addressing one another as friends.

People tried to avoid marriages between known family friends. By now it is apparent that what was "known" in Auyana was oftentimes debatable. For the moment I will take the absence of a denial of a parent-child link to mean the link was known. By this definition of known, there were no cases of intermarriage between people who were known to have a common biological ancestry. There were five cases of marriage between people who were known to have parent-child links to a common ancestor, but at least one of the links was not biological. Other than that, numerous marriages took place between members of different pooling units in the same sovereignty. Members of the same sovereignty were said to have a common ancestor, but the links were not demonstrable, whereas those in the same pooling unit were usually able to demonstrate links to a common ancestor if they were descendants. In the two instances of marriage between members of the same pooling unit, either the husband or wife was the child of a man who moved into the pooling unit as a young man.

More marriages took place between pooling units in the same sovereignty than with any given pooling unit in another sovereignty. But the total number of marriages outside Auyana was greater than those within Auyana, and in the former cases the initial marriage was usually to someone unknown to the prospective spouse, although they may have heard of each other. Yet the willingness of these two strangers to live together and raise children provided the main channel for the flow of wealth and a means of consolidating friendships between pooling units and sovereignties. Hence, the family friends of a person's spouse had a special relationship to him or her. As noted above, those in the first younger generation could be addressed by terms from the end set, perhaps because they were children and not of any immediate importance except as excuses for gifts. In any case, the family friends of a person's spouse in the same and first older generations were *fewi*, and were their reciprocal counterparts. I would gloss this realm as "married strangers" except that the two strangers who were actually married to one another did not refer to themselves as *fewi* (nor as family friends). So, rather than married strangers, I have decided to gloss the realm of *fewi* as "spouse strangers." The realm included only those in the same or adjacent generations. It was partially subdivided in the following way:

1. Spouse strangers in the same generations included:
   a. Ego to a female family friend's spouse or a male to his wife's family friends: *yo*
   b. Ego to a male family friend's spouse or a female to her husband's family friends: *waye*.
2. Spouse strangers in adjacent generations included:
   a. Ego to those in the first older generation:
      (1) Ego's spouse's male family friends: *warendo*
      (2) Ego's spouse's female family friends: *rara*
   b. Ego to those in the first younger generation:
      (1) Ego to a female family friend's spouse: *sa*
      (2) Ego to a male family friend's spouse: *napu'*.

There were other spouse strangers whom I have not included in this list because they prefigure the exchange-set divisions within family friends which have not yet been considered. Spouses of two family friends of the same sex in the same, but not adjacent, generation were also spouse strangers. Spouses of family friends of the opposite sex had no special term of reference or address for one another. This distinction between pairs of family friends of the same sex and those of the opposite sex in the same generation was one of the major criteria used in the exchange set of terms for family friends. I believe this was because the arrangements for exchanges of wealth and women were both cause and effect of the identities set aside by the terms in the exchange set. But before considering some of the exchanges made, I will make explicit the different divisions, both among spouse strangers and family friends.

There were three possible combinations of two family friends taken two at a time. The order here is irrelevant and sex is the only dimension used:

1. Spouses of two male family friends, including "co-wives," addressed one another as *ro*.
2. Spouses of two female family friends addressed one another as *wane*.
3. Spouses of two family friends of opposite sex had no special terms for one another.

Not only were the spouses of these three types of pairs distinguished from one another, but so were the children, generating the divisions constituting the exchange set of family friends. First, consider those in the same generation:

1. Children of two male family friends in the same generation addressed one another by terms from the end set.
2. Children of two female family friends in the same generation addressed one another as *anauda*.
3. Children of two family friends of opposite sex in the same generation addressed one another as *noka*.

Next, consider those in adjacent generations:

1. A person addressed his or her parents, and family friends of each parent who were the same sex as the parent, by the appropriate terms from the end set—i.e., *no* for females and *po* for males.
2. A person addressed each parent's family friends who were the opposite sex of the parent as:
   a. *mamu*—a female
   b. *nao*—a male.

Consider those in the first younger generation:

1. Family friends of the same sex in the same generation addressed one another's children by the appropriate terms from the end set.
2. Family friends of opposite sex in the same generation addressed one another's children as *napae*. They could also refer to one another's children by the appropriate terms from the end set.

Taking the three pairs of family friends in the same generation, I would suggest that a pair of males was the prototype for the pooling unit, a pair of females was the prototype for those who were from the same pooling unit but became members of different pooling units, and a pair of opposite sex was the prototype for the exchange of women and wealth between pooling units. Metaphorically speaking, this exchange was the main channel for converting strangers into family friends. Initially, strangers were converted into spouse strangers through marriage. Through gifts of wealth at the birth and maturation of the children resulting from this marriage, those who were spouse strangers became friends, although not family friends, and their children became family friends.

As mentioned above, spouses were not spouse strangers, nor were they family friends. Rather, they referred to, and sometimes addressed, one another by a reciprocal term, with the term for the wife being a diminutive form ("little spouse"). Spouses can be seen as the two elements joining two networks. The spouses had special terms for each other, each term referring to the other's family-friend network as spouse strangers. The members of each spouse's family-friend network had no special terms for the members of the other, they were neither spouse strangers nor family friends to one another. Rather, they were linked only through the marriage between two of their members.

As I initially understood marriage and the gifts bestowed at certain points in the life cycle of children resulting from the marriage, the groom's pooling unit gave wealth to the bride's pooling unit. That is, wealth flowed only in one direction, from the groom's pooling unit to the bride's. One way of balancing such a flow would have been to have had exchange marriages, and this I was told was the case. Eventually I came to find that there were many exceptions as well as other balancing mechanisms which I will discuss later (cf. Cook 1969). For now, I will consider just the one-way flow, beginning with a marriage.

The wealth given in exchange for a woman always included valued items, cooked pig, and, except in rare instances, food. The groom's male parent, or sometimes older brother, was one of the major sponsors, and usually someone in the groom's subpooling unit who was close to the groom's male parent acted as a cosponsor. Others in the groom's pooling unit helped, and in addition family friends of the cosponsors would usually help. If it was to be a large bride wealth, other members of the groom's pooling unit would also ask for help from some of their family friends. Help provided by family friends was always given to individuals, not to the entire pooling unit, unless the helpers were biological agnates who were living with and acting as members of another pooling unit. When I say the help was given to individuals, I mean that individual family friends were responsible for returning the help given, not the entire pooling unit or anyone else in the pooling unit. One effect of this arrangement was to make it possible to have a large range in the number of people involved in a single pooling. Another effect was to relieve people from having to keep track of the help given by anyone other than those in their pooling unit and their own family friends. Of course, it might be to a person's advantage to keep track of this information, but it was not necessary. Another effect was to enable any pooling to be viewed as both an individual and group affair, not only in terms of debts for help but also in terms of the giving of the pooled wealth. For, the major sponsor (or cosponsors) could claim that they gave the wealth for a boy's wife—meaning they could demand more help from that young man in the future than could others in his pooling unit. Or the sons of a man might demand help from another man, claiming that their father gave the wealth for his wife.

Just as any pooling was a group, subgroup, and individual affair depending on the context, so was the distribution of wealth given to a pooling unit. One or two individuals, whom I will call major recipients, were responsible for actually going and getting the wealth and dividing it among those in their pooling unit, and they could take the largest portions for themselves and give large portions to those in their subpooling unit. In addition, they could also give portions to their family friends outside the pooling unit who had helped them, and in this way repay some of their debts. In most distributions of wealth, this was done, but not in the distribution of bride wealth. Portions of bride wealth were given only to those in the bride's pooling unit and, in this sense, the distribution of a bride wealth was one of the means to define pooling group membership, except that the bride's male parent and the males who had been raised by and were being raised by her male parent could not take any part of her bride wealth. The bride's female parent and her female siblings who were not yet married could eat some of the food and pig, but were not given any of the valued items from the bride wealth. This could be interpreted to mean that a man, his wife, and children were set apart as a single set with differentiation within the set depending on sex. However, the female members of a family were never given any of the valued items received by a pooling unit. For example, if a woman's husband died and she had no sons and did not remarry but continued to live with her ex-husband's pooling unit, she might raise pigs for men in the pooling unit and she would be given food and portions of pig whenever some was received by the pooling unit, but she would not be given any valued items from any wealth received.

The wives of the bride's brothers were treated in the same way as the bride's mother (and unmarried sisters): they were given portions of food and pig but not valued items. My interpretation is that the failure of the bride's mother to receive any valued items from her daughter's bride wealth was not because she was in the bride's family, but because she was a woman and her husband was receiving no valued items. This interpretation receives some support from the fact that no form existed in Auyana for what I would call a "family," that is, a man, his wife, and children. There were family-friend terms used by children which might best be glossed as "dad" and "mom," and there were also terms of reference which could be glossed as "the children of one man" and "the children of one woman." The distinction between children of one man and children of one woman became important where a man had several wives with children. In such cases, the children of one woman might not get any of a sibling's bride wealth, but the children of co-wives might, depending on other claimants.

Given the above schema, a man's children were a definite economic drain—a drain which might be repaired later with support, but still a drain. In fact, they were even more of a drain than indicated, for when a woman was sent to her husband, her pooling unit gave gifts at least to her mother's natal pooling unit and usually to several others as well. In addition, when she was sent to live with her husband, valued items were sent with her which could be used to set up her household: net bags, arrows, adzes, one small live pig, some sugar cane stalks to plant, and some cooked pig. The bride's father was a major sponsor if he was still socially active.

Within the schema described above, a man and his pooling unit gave wealth to his wife's natal pooling unit in celebration of, and in exchange for, the birth and maturation of his wife's children. A man was explicitly prevented from being the major recipient of gifts involving his sister or daughter. Therefore he could only become the major recipient of gifts through some other woman from his pooling unit.

The primary means by which this was done was through "marking" another man's daughter at her birth by either being a cosponsor of the gift given to the girl's mother's natal pooling unit or by giving a separate gift. If a girl was not marked at birth, a person could later assume control of her bride wealth by giving a large gift to the girl's father as compensation for not having helped with the gift when the girl was born. One retained control of bride wealth then by being a cosponsor for all the gifts given at different points in the girl's cycle, especially when she first menstruated.

Several considerations entered into who marked whose daughters. A man preferred to exchange daughters with a man who was initiated at the same time he was. There was a special term of reference (not address) for those who were initiated together made up of the terms for older and younger male family friends in the same generation: *parawa* ("age-mates"). As mentioned earlier, pooling units and subgroups within a pooling unit could be referred to by a term which can be glossed as "a bunch of age-mates." But in the context of controlling bride wealth, a man did not want to cooperate with those in, say, his subpooling unit or some other closer subgroup as much as with someone who was a friend and initiated at the same time as himself, regardless of the friend's subgroup.

Deaths, unequal reproduction, fluctuations in wealth, and likes and dislikes arising from past interactions sometimes made it impossible to do what was preferred, resulting in various arrangements of varying degrees of satisfaction.

After a girl was married, the man who was the major recipient of her bride wealth did not continue to be the major recipient of the gifts given at the maturation of her children. Rather, a younger man, usually someone in the same generation as the girl—in the first younger generation from the man who was the major recipient for her bride wealth—became the major recipient. This maintained a generational equivalence between the major sponsor of the gifts at the maturation of a child and the major recipient. It also provided the channel for passing on the flow of wealth begun by a man. However, there was no simple rule governing this succession. A man's son had the first claims to be the major recipients of the gifts given at the maturation of the children of a woman for whom their father had been the major recipient of her bride wealth, especially if the woman's bride wealth had been used in getting their bride. However, they might not want to or might not be married. If one of them was close to being married, someone might take over being a major recipient until he was married and then hand it over to him. But someone might also claim to have been cosponsored and helped by the boy's father and might want to become a major recipient, arguing that the man's sons could take over the gifts coming in from some other woman closer to their age after they were married. Even if there were agreement within the pooling unit about who should be a major recipient for the gifts, the girl and her husband might not agree. Personal likes and considerations of relative wealth and strength might lead them to want to give the gifts to someone other than the person those in the girl's natal pooling unit agreed should be the major recipient. Thus, considerable negotiation transpired both over "marking" daughters and over passing on the flow of wealth through a woman. Sometimes fights broke out within a pooling unit over these issues.

One way of resolving conflicting claims was for a woman's husband to give more than one gift to his wife's natal pooling unit and/or have different major recipients for different children. In particular, if a woman had a brother with whom she was on good terms, she would press to have him be the major recipient for at least one of her children (rarely the first child). If not, a woman would press to have some man with whom she was friendly become a major recipient, regardless of whether he was a son or possible heir of the man who was the major recipient of her bride wealth. The main thing was that a woman wanted to stay friendly with those with whom she had been friendly before she married, and while her husband nominally controlled the distribution of gifts, in practice a woman could make her wishes felt.

As a woman grew older, all her children would be married. After this, the only gifts given to her natal pooling unit would be at the deaths of her male children and at her own death. In this schema, the flow of gifts centering on a particular woman began with her birth, but did not usually end with her death. The latter was the case only when she outlived her sons. Otherwise, the flow of wealth ended when her married sons died. This cycle then extended usually over two generations. The realm of family friends was also basically a two-generational system, in the sense that beyond two generations there was a reciprocal residual category which was never used in addressing someone and which entered into everyday social life only when conceptualizing relationships between or within pooling units. Considering the cycle outlined above, those in the same generation were those who were in competition with one another to become the major recipients of a woman's bride wealth. The distinction of older and younger within the same

generation was a means of delimiting competition within the same generation. Those around the same age would be those upon whom a man was most
dependent for aid once he was an adult but with whom he was in the most
severe competition to control the flow of gifts of wealth.

It was said that an older brother demanded some obedience from a younger brother in return for which the older brother, like the father was to look
after his younger brother. Still, a younger brother could be exploited by his
older brother's insistence on monopolizing the wealth that came in through
women for whom their father had been a major sponsor and the major recipient of their bride wealth. In such cases, there had to be some limit which the
younger brother could claim had been exceeded by the older brother, in
order for the younger brother to get support from others for his position. For
instance, a man could say that his older brother should take his older sister
and let him take his younger sister, instead of the older brother taking them
both. And a clever younger brother could make his older brother appear to
be a stingy bully. The truth, in such cases, was difficult to ascertain.

Determining the value and proper distribution of a person's estate was not
easy in Auyana. Quarrels between brothers could develop, and sometimes a
person was physically threatened if he did not distribute his wealth in certain
ways. But other times a brother would act like a close friend and help in any
way he could. My impression is that most of the myths in Auyana pertaining
to brothers involved them in some way tricking and/or harming one another.
Relationships with fathers, older brothers, and all older males in a person's
pooling unit were characterized by a term which was translated into pidgin
as "hevi" ("heavy"), with relationships with an older brother being lighter
than those with a person's father.

Whenever I asked a man the general question of "What makes trouble?"
the stock answer was "women and pigs." For not only did sons get to be the
recipients of gifts secured by their father, they also had to take over his obligations, one of which was to give a gift of wealth to his wife's (their
mother's—unless he was polygamous) natal pooling unit when she died. If
she lived to be reasonably old, her husband would oftentimes die before she
did, and if he did not, he would be getting old by the time she died and
would not be very active in giving and receiving gifts. Therefore, her sons
would usually be cosponsors of the gift. The sons of the man in her natal
pooling unit who had been closest to her and had been a major recipient of
gifts given for her children would be the major recipients, with their father
and his closest helpers in the pooling unit being given a large share of the gift
but not controlling its distribution.

As mentioned above, when a man died, a gift of wealth was given to his
mother's natal pooling unit. This was also the case when an unmarried
woman died. But when a married woman died, only those in her own natal
pooling unit received a gift of wealth, those in her mother's natal pooling
unit usually received nothing. In any case, the major recipients in a man's

mother's natal pooling unit were the same ones as were major recipients at his mother's death. In summary, then, a woman's bride wealth was controlled by a man. One of his sons controlled the gifts given at the maturation of her children. This same son and his sons controlled the gift given at her death, and his sons controlled the gifts given at the death of her sons. The cycle was a two-generation one with a cross-sex pair as the intermediate generation.

Returning to the characterizations of the three pairs distinguished earlier, the pooling unit can be considered to be made up of the descendants of pairs of males who used the distinctions in the end set. These distinctions were also used with those outside the pooling unit who helped a person or his male parent in pooling and who were not involved in obligatory gift giving through women. While the entire pooling unit was held responsible for making a gift, the major sponsor and others could call on help from outside the pooling unit and these helpers were put in the same family-friend category as the members of the pooling unit who helped. In this way, helpers could be called upon bilaterally while maintaining a core of responsible agnates.

Women from a pooling unit—that is, women for whom the members of a pooling unit received bride wealth and gifts at the birth and maturation of their children—were referred to by members of the pooling unit by the terms from the end set if they were in a younger or the same generation. If they were in an older generation they were probably married and moved out of the pooling unit before ego was born or when ego was still a small child. Thus, from ego's point of view they were outsiders who used to be insiders, and the conversion meant that wealth came into ego's pooling unit at certain times, ultimately involving ego and sometimes ego's sons as at least recipients, if not major recipients. This conversion cycle of a woman and wealth was at least consistent with the exchange set of family-friend terms, which not only distinguished the cross-sex link in the same generation but also set aside particular individuals involved in the following generations. A husband used spouse-stranger terms for those in his wife's natal pooling unit and a wife used spouse-stranger terms for those in her husband's pooling unit, but other members of the two pooling units did not use spouse-stranger terms towards one another. The children of this union used the end set for members of their father's pooling unit and the exchange set for members of their mother's natal pooling unit. But no other members of the two pooling units used family-friend terms for one another. Thus, two groups were joined in exchanging a woman and her children for wealth, but once so joined, they did not all become spouse strangers to one another nor did their children become family friends. Rather, the personal network which was generated acted as a link between the two groups, a link based on the marriage and fertility of a *particular* woman. This was recognized in the terms her husband and her children used for those in her natal pooling unit which others in her husband's pooling unit did not use.

However, the use of the same terms for the children of a cross-sex link does not seem consistent with the one-way flow of wealth. Of course, if there were exchange marriages of a pair of brothers and sisters then the one-way flow would become an exchange. Or even if there were exchange marriages between two pooling units, regardless whether of brother-sister pairs, a balanced flow would result. As mentioned earlier, an attempt was made to arrange exchanges, although other considerations oftentimes made this impossible. However, another source of equivalence existed which has not yet been mentioned. This was that a man would give small gifts to his sisters and to the woman from his pooling unit through whom he received gifts at the major life-crisis events of his own children. These gifts were not large enough to be divided among an entire pooling unit. Rather, they were divided among the recipient's family and a few families who gave her and her husband the most help. Hence, there was not an equivalence in the amount of wealth transferred, only in the fact that a transfer occurred both ways.

If a woman had a lot of kids, the gifts given were mutually satisfactory, and the two pooling units and/or sovereignties remained friendly, then as she and the major recipient of the gifts for her children got old, an arrangement was usually made that not only would a gift be given to the major recipient's pooling unit when she died (i.e., to her natal pooling unit), a gift would be given by the major recipient's pooling unit to her husband's pooling unit when the major recipient died. In this way, a woman and the major recipient for gifts through her remained friends and became equivalent as they grew older. In cases where this happened the children of this pair would usually be friendly and would make the same arrangement for one another's deaths.

This switch from a one-way to a reciprocal flow coincided with a switch in the general behavioral posture of the participants over the generations. Relationships with spouse strangers were characterized as "very heavy" and entailed various avoidances. Spouse strangers could not mention one another's names. They had to always be friendly with one another. They were not to joke with one another, especially mockingly. Restraint, particularly the avoidance of anger, characterized the relationships. On the other hand, relationships between children of family friends of the opposite sex were characterized as just the opposite. They were the lightest relationships a person had. *Noka* were said to be genuinely friendly with one another, to be at ease with one another, to practically never get angry with one another—in general, they displayed a lot of friendly comraderie. I interpret this to mean that tension over whether a woman would stay married and be fertile on the one hand and whether her husband would be a generous man on the other hand generated a situation in which spouse strangers could easily get angry with one another. Because they were strangers, it would be easy for each to blame the other party. But if things went well then the tension eased and the children were the benefactors of the goodwill established and had no obligations with respect to one another which were hard to meet or in some way oppressive. If a brother and sister did right by one another, the affection they felt as children might mature and be passed on to their children. The chances of this happening were helped by having someone other than a woman's father or brother be the major recipient of her bride wealth. For this person would also arrange her marriage, and if she were forced to marry someone or someplace she disliked, her resentment over this would not be directed at her brother. Thus, the brother could enter into transactions later with her and her husband after it seemed likely things were going to be smooth.

This leaves the relationship of the children of two women in the same generation from the same pooling unit to be discussed. These children had no obligatory gifts to one another, nor did they necessarily help one another much to give gifts to one another. However, their relationship was characterized as being light and friendly. It could be that they had a special term for one another simply because they were a residual category. However, there was somewhat more to it than that. In the first place, children of two women from the same pooling unit were in an equivalent position with respect to their mothers' natal pooling unit, and while the children did not necessarily give gifts to one another, their mothers might. Women around the same age from the same pooling unit gathered together whenever the daughter of one of them was being sent to her husband and were given gifts by the mother of the bride-to-be. Such gifts were optional in the sense that any potential recipient would not be angry if she was not given a gift unless someone she considered less close than she to the bride's mother was given something. Relationships between such women were said to be usually quite friendly and supportive, and this general feeling was said to characterize the relationships of their children to one another (providing they knew one another).

One thing remaining to be considered is the use of terms in the exchange set outside the context of exchanges between two pooling units. For, as defined, exchange terms applied to any pair of family friends and their children, regardless of what pooling unit they were in. For example, following the definition of *noka* given earlier, a man would use *noka* to refer to the children of those women his father referred to as *noka* (that is, children of a cross-sex pair). In practice, this was true only if the woman and his father entered into a relationship where his father was given a gift or gifts at points in the maturation of her children. In other words, if his father treated her as though she were a woman from his pooling unit, then he would address her children as *noka*. Put another way, those in the same generation as a person who belonged to the person's mother's mother's natal pooling unit would address the person as *noka* only if exchanges took place between their parents. Or, if one person wanted to give the other a gift at, say, his mother's death, he might then address him as *noka*. Otherwise, if these individuals knew one another, they would use the terms from the end set. Similarly, the children of two women who were family friends who in turn were the children of two family friends—say, two women—could address one another as *unanda*. However, only if the two women were married into the same pooling unit or, sometimes, into the same sovereignty or chose to act as though they were from the same pooling unit (e.g., invite one another to their daughter's marriage) would their children address one another as *unanda*. But, if the two women were married into different sovereignties and/or had nothing to do with one another, their children, if they knew one another, would address one another by terms from the end set.

Although the network of family friends was infinitely extensible in each category, the terms in the exchange set were used only when some exchange (or the possibility of an exchange) was involved. Otherwise, although the exchange set could be used to distinguish the person, it would not be, and instead one of the terms from the end set would be used. Similarly, although spouse-stranger terms could be used for all the family friends of a spouse, they never were. Rather, they were used only with respect to those who actually helped pool, if a wife, or received part of the gifts given by a person for his children, if a husband. As this would imply, spouse-stranger terms were most widely extended to those in the same generation. Because the first younger generation would not be involved as adults until later, they were not even spouse strangers at all. I will return to the question of marriages and alliances after considering male-female relationships.

The use of spouse-stranger terms and the restraint demanded between spouse strangers were also related to the tension surrounding marriages and the adjustment of a bride to her new home. Looked at from a woman's point of view, marriage could be a catastrophe. In the first place, she had to leave home and usually home was a good place. Although a woman usually demanded of an adolescent daughter that she help her in the garden, in preparing food, and in taking care of the children, this did not take up most of the daughter's time, and she usually had a fair amount of free time to visit with other girls, arrange liaisons with boys, and pursue her own interests. After marriage, these leisure activities stopped and her workload increased, no matter whom or where she married. Marriage meant she had to start working a lot more and playing less. This was even more pronounced for men as they did practically nothing before marriage except play. In fact, it was said that some men never stopped: warfare was their play and their wives took care of everything else. But a woman had much less opportunity to play after marriage, although if she was beautiful, smart, sexual, and fertile the option was greatly increased. If she was ugly, dumb, afraid of sex, and sterile, life after marriage was just work and she might not even be able to stay married.

Leaving home meant a woman had to learn to live in a new home among people who were to varying degrees strangers. If she married someone in another pooling unit in her sovereignty she would at least be living among people she knew. A similar situation occurred if she married someone in a friendly sovereignty, as it was likely that other women from her sovereignty would have married there also. Women, then, applied pressure to be married to close, friendly groups. But of course this was not always possible. A woman might end up married to someone in a place where there were no other women from her sovereignty and where the people were not particularly friendly with those in her natal sovereignty—a stranger in a strange land.

No matter where a woman married, there was always the problem of whom she married. To some extent her husband would still be under the control of his parents, who would treat her as though she were their child expecting her to do as they bade her. This was said to be especially true of her husband's mother. Some women made life truly miserable for their son's wife until their son was able to become independent of his parents. Even if a girl's husband's parents were kind people, their son might not be. He might be mean, lazy, and scared of sex. Or he might be some kind of sex maniac. Or he might be extremely violent, a genuine killer who would think little of shooting his wife in the leg if she disobeyed him. Or he might be a beautiful person, friendly, sexual, supportive of those who were his friends, and unafraid in confrontations with his enemies.

He was least likely to be someone the girl knew before marriage and wanted to marry. Members of Auyana recognized states of existence which corresponded to the Western European notion of "love," but these were never used as the basis of marriage. In fact, one such state was considered to be a dangerous condition requiring special measures to release the participants. This was when a woman was said to have captured the thoughts of a man. In America, the feeling that "I can't get you off my mind" is taken as a sure sign of romance and is to be cultivated. In Auyana, it was taken as a sure sign that a woman had performed a special ritual which enabled her to possess a man. This was a dangerous condition for the man who had to be released from it by special procedures. If she was going to be his first wife, the others in the pooling unit simply refused to support him and this would stop him. If he was already married, he might be able to get enough support to go ahead and give the wealth for her. But this was just too bad for him, and he was thought of as a fool. Of course, Americans also recognize in song that "I'm just a fool in love"—but then they say it is great.

Members of Auyana also recognized a condition in which a man and a woman were like brother and sister except that they were sexually attracted to each other. That is, they seemed to understand and support one another perfectly. Sometimes this condition was almost immediately recognized by the two people ("love at first sight"), but more often it developed over time. In any case, while it was considered a desirable condition, it never served as the basis of a person's initial marriage, simply because those arranging the marriage only considered it one of the variables to be taken into account.

Tension existed both between a woman and those in her pooling unit re-

sponsible for arranging her marriage and between a new bride and her husband and his family friends. As mentioned earlier, tension was eliminated
from a woman's immediate family through the restriction on her brothers
and father from taking any of the bride wealth given for her. In fact, her
brothers and father were likely to support her wishes if anyone would. Their
support might only consist of telling others where she wanted to be married
(or did not want to be married) or they might refuse to be cosponsors for the
gifts given when she was sent to her husband and for her dowry. The latter
would put them in severe opposition to those in their pooling unit and seldom happened (only twice in the fifty-two cases for which I gathered extensive data). Her brothers and father were also those most likely to support her
if she had trouble with her new husband, especially if he beat her unjustifi-
ably. Again, the support could range all the way from protesting to threatening to kill her husband. But to kill a sister's husband was as far from being a
spouse stranger as possible. The essence of the behavior demanded between
spouse strangers was restraint, especially restraint from anger. Similarly, a
woman's resentment for her husband's family friends' treatment of her, especially their ordering her around, was also to be masked, as was their anger
at her for being a lazy slut. Even if she was not a lazy slut, if she came from a
sovereignty that became enemies with her husband's sovereignty, people
might be angry at her just because she was from there, but again this was to
be masked. Hence, the concept of spouse strangers and the behavior demanded of them had an individual as well as a group focus, with the two foci
being interrelated through the necessity for a marriage to be stable and fertile in order for there to be any group transactions.

As the above would imply, male-female hostility was expected, although
not necessarily desired, and at certain occasions was demanded. When a
woman was menstruating, if a man had sexual intercourse with her he would
get sick. Men claimed that unmarried girls sometimes like to trick boys by
offering to have intercourse with them when they were menstruating. Married women could do the same but supposedly usually did not. Rather, as
mentioned earlier, they could make a man sick by taking something close to
him and burying it in the menstrual house. It was also said that if a man had
intercourse too often he would also become weak and was liable to be killed
in battle. Having intercourse with a woman who had intercourse with a lot of
men was also said to be dangerous, as such women could make a man sick
(there was at least gonorrhea indigenously). The verb used to describe sexual
intercourse was the one used to describe shooting someone with an arrow or
in a soul assassination attempt, and if the woman had an orgasm, she was said
to have been killed. Then there was the story of the man whose wife did not
like having intercourse as much as he did, yet she could not get him to stop.
Finally, she put a piece of bamboo in her vagina and when he entered her,
he sliced his penis in half. It embarrassed him so badly he snuck into the
forest and climbed a tree hoping no one would find him until the bleeding

stopped. But some men trailed him and found him. They thought it was funny but patched him up and beat his wife for him. For the most part, however, men believed that no matter for how long or how many times you had intercourse with a woman, she always wanted more. Adultery rarely resulted in a woman being killed, although it did cause fights in which men got killed. On the one hand men and women had to have one another and on the other they only caused each other trouble.

In the discussion of pooling units, I mentioned several occasions that demanded male-female hostility. When a girl was being sent to her husband, skits were put on by the women for women only, mocking the demands men made on women. When a girl first menstruated, she was beaten with stinging nettles by the initiated but unmarried males in her pooling unit. At male initiations, when the boys were brought back from the stream to be put in the men's house a "battle" ensued with the women, who tried to prevent them from returning. Also, the myth about the origin of the flutes and bullroarers was that originally women had them and then men stole them, and since then women have thought flutes and bullroarers were spirits. When a beloved man died, little girls in his pooling unit had their fingers cut off, and adult women cut off part of their own earlobes.

As would be expected, there were a number of associations with each gender. The lists I have compiled were based on information given to me by males; I do not know whether women would have agreed with these lists.

| *Female associations* | *Male associations* |
|---|---|
| cold (except when menstruating) | hot |
| starters and supporters | killers |
| undemanding | demanding |
| gardens | forest |
| tame | wild |
| domestic food and animals | wild animals and plants |
| dependent | independent |
| unimpressive | flamboyant |
| did not deal in nonordinary forces | dealt with nonordinary forces |

I think it is accurate to summarize the female-male dichotomy by saying that women monopolized the creative forces whereas men monopolized the destructive forces. Although, ideally, destructive forces were used only in protection of a man's creative mate, in practice, destruction was sometimes directly opposed to creation, and sometimes protection was lost through the co-option of destruction by creation (e.g., some men would rather plant yams than kill). Although individual men and women could move toward the opposite direction, no man ever bore a child—although some died trying— and no woman ever entered a war—although some lived trying (Langness 1964b).

Before turning to a consideration of warfare and its relationship to marriages and the flow of wealth, I will discuss marriage and the flow of wealth in detail. First, consider the nature of marriage itself. In some senses, the exchange of a woman for wealth was a trade. As mentioned earlier, except for trial marriages, the woman and the wealth were usually exchanged on the same day, and only wealth—no food—was sent with the bride as her "dowry." But the wealth sent to the bride's pooling unit included food and in this sense was like a gift. Perhaps, however, a distinguishing characteristic of a gift, or of what I have been calling gifts, was that they were statements of anticipated future transactions. When a bride came from a distant place with which there would probably not be any more transaction, no food was included in the bride wealth given for her. Given this interpretation, the gifts of wealth relating to children were in trade for the children and at the same time were gifts promising further transactions.

If gifts were traded for children in the sense that bride wealth was traded for women, then there should have been no pressure for those receiving a gift to give anything in return, for they had already given what they promised: a fertile woman with healthy children. But those receiving the gift did not give the children, nor did the woman alone give them or raise them. Another interpretation then might be that the husband was giving wealth for the children because he would get the benefit of their energy, whereas the woman's pooling unit would get very little of the children's energy. Still, this interpretation implies that there would be no pressure to return the gifts, when in fact such pressure did exist and could be most clearly seen when the two groups were somewhat distant with no more than one or two marriages between them. In such situations, gifts of wealth at the maturation of a woman's children were reciprocated by the recipients, who would give an equivalent gift sometime not long after receiving their gift. In a sense, children were used as an excuse for the two groups to exchange wealth. Having exchange marriages made it possible for all gifts to also be markers of the maturation of a new member of the group.

This view of marriage suggests that members of Auyana definitely made long-term contracts with marriages but not with all marriages. The long-term contracts were between social units, with the major responsibility for the maintenance of the flow resting on individuals, who would ask family friends from outside their pooling unit to help them. Contracts were not always maintained, however, and when one was not, other individuals and groups would be chosen to replace the woman's natal pooling unit. This choice would affect both social units and some children's future personal networks. It would have no effect on the personal networks of the adult males carrying on the transactions, although it might result in the loss of a woman's ties with her natal pooling unit and their replacement by ties to the new pooling unit.

The interaction between group and individual concerns was revealed also in the distribution at life-crisis events. Gifts were given not only to a woman's natal pooling unit but also to various others. These were given by the major sponsor and were usually to his past family friends or to men with whom he was becoming or attempting to become family friends. Unlike the gifts to a woman's natal pooling unit, these gifts were said to be returned at an equivalent event involving one of the recipient's children. Although a considerable time might pass between a gift and its return, this did not mean that there was a long-term contract for continued gift-giving as in the case of gifts given to a woman's natal pooling unit. These were one-time contracts which could be renewed but which might also be dropped without bad feeling once completed. They could also develop into a relationship where each man helped the other with poolings. In this way, two men might be in different pooling units but still help at the poolings of the other's unit without taking on any of the other attributes of a member of the unit.

One effect of these open-ended contracts was to allow individuals to keep up relationships with those *mara* they wanted to and to develop new *mara* as this became useful. The effect on groups was through individuals and their personal networks. The distributions to individuals in a sovereignty and to pooling units in the sovereignty showed a high correlation. In this sense, group contracts and personal contracts usually reinforced one another. But they were separate and responsibility for them was separate. The flow of wealth had both an individual and a group aspect, and the networks maintained by this flow were separate but interlocked. Neither the "descent" nor "alliance" models were applicable to Auyana; rather, there was an interaction between the two (cf. Strathern 1969, Cook 1969).

"The flow of wealth" is a rather cryptic way of saying that gifts provided a means of storing pig, which is another way of saying that in a semi-tropical climate with no storage facilities, pigs had to be eaten when they were killed. By distributing portions of a pig to others, the owner in a sense built up "credits" for himself and his pooling unit to receive portions of pig in the future. Of course, pigs were sometimes distributed just among those in a pooling unit, but to do this all the time would have had the same effect as if the members of the pooling unit were to always marry one another—i.e., isolation. To be isolated was a dangerous position, for it meant that you could not rally allies to defend yourself, you had no option for wives, and you had no outside channels for valued items which could not be produced locally (or only at a high cost). Warfare and the necessity for allies is the variable that interests me the most, and I will now turn to an intensive consideration of warfare, followed by a quantitative analysis of marriages and the distribution of wealth in relationship to friend/enemy patterns.

# 5. Warfare

There has been a general unwillingness in the social sciences to attribute much importance to violence in human affairs (Coser 1956). In line with this unwillingness, detailed analyses of armed combat and its consequences are rare in anthropological literature (Turney-High 1949; Fried et al. 1968). This is true even for areas where fighting was a prominent part of existence. Although fighting in the Highlands of New Guinea has often been described as "intense," no authors have provided systematic quantitative data on the intensity, and only two authors (Ryan 1959; Langness 1964b) have suggested that intensive warfare may have been the basic cause of shifting group membership in the Highlands. In this chapter, I will provide a quantified analysis in order (1) to establish the degrees of enmity between different sovereignties so as to compare these findings with rates of marriage and the distribution of wealth, (2) to determine the extent to which armed combat resulted in movements of people, decimation of social units, or other dislocations of the social order. The second point has been partially dealt with in the earlier analysis of social units. There, I tried to demonstrate that warfare led to a higher rate of moving out of members with *foreign* origins and/or connections. In the following discussion, I will consider to what extent warfare resulted in moving out, regardless of origins or connections.

I will not attempt a systematic analysis of the causes of warfare in Auyana. Rather, I will only present what members of Auyana claimed to have been the cause for each fight. By a small sovereignty, I mean one of less than a thousand members. I will not attempt to give a quantitative definition of severe and frequent fighting as there is practically no comparative data on which to base one (cf. Fried et al. 1968, Turney-High 1949). Instead, I will define it as a situation where there were few, if any, periods during which homicidal fighting was thought by the participants to be unlikely. That is, while homicidal fighting did not necessarily have a high probability of occuring, there was the constant possibility it might occur.

I assume that knowledge of loyalties and fighting skills was crucial where numbers were small and a single fighter could make the difference between victory and catastrophe. On the basis of this assumption, I further assume that the male children of a sovereignty were preferred as recruits, because their abilities and loyalties were established and known since childhood. Note, however, that this alone does not mean recruitment to the *subdivisions* of a sovereignty would be agnatic. If sovereignties were *not* endogamous, then this would be the case. However, if they were endogamous then subdivisions of a sovereignty might be matrilineally organized and still meet the stipulation that male children of present members of the sovereignty were preferred recruits.

The next assumption I make is that sovereignties were also residential units, as a dispersed membership would make defense extremely difficult, especially when the population was small. By this argument, even if sovereignties were comprised mainly of biological agnates this would not mean that coresidence was unimportant.

Granting the above propositions, the next question is why the preference for male children did not result in the sovereignty's having a completely agnatic membership. I believe this can be explained in terms of the necessity for members to be coresidents and the presence of a lot of movement. In a period of severe fighting, biological descent would *appear* to be unimportant, and coresidence the main criterion used. Intensive warfare between sovereignties of any size resulted in a lot of movement. In large sovereignties, this movement may only have been within the territory of the sovereignty. But in small sovereignties which did not control enormous expanses of land, warfare could not be escaped by means of movement within the territory, and hence movement into another sovereignty was an alternative more frequently used. I have said that there were a number of social units which moved to Auyana as a result of warfare, and some of the children adopted by members of Auyana were offspring of members of these refugee social units. In the preceding pages, I have attempted to demonstrate that suspected loyalties during homicidal fighting resulted in much *individual* movement. While I have not attempted to examine the other causes of individual movements, I think the considerably lower rate of movement in the Young (i.e., post-contact) category (see Table 8) is evidence that intensive warfare was a major cause of movement.

In the second place, intensive warfare in small sovereignties may not only have caused a lot of movement, it may have generated a greater willingness to accept people who wanted to move in. My argument for this assertion is that the movement caused by warfare made it difficult to know whether any given child would be raised within a sovereignty or whether any given adult would remain in a sovereignty. Hence, potential new members were welcomed as insurance. Small-sized groups also placed a premium on numbers, as small differences in absolute numbers assumed a relatively large importance. While the Auyana data confirm the hypothesis of greater willingness to accept people, in that in pre-contact times members of Auyana did recruit widely and seemed willing to take all those who wanted to join, a further test would be to examine whether in the post-contact period they were less willing to recruit members from other sovereignties. This test would require a survey of surrounding groups to find people who tried to move into Auyana but were rebuffed. Alternatively, those in Auyana who tried to move to another group but were rebuffed could be calculated. I do not have such information, and it would be extremely difficult to get, as it would require a person's public admission that he wanted to leave. Further, I do not have, nor would it be possible to get, comparable data for the pre-contact period. As a result of these difficulties, the hypothesis of greater willingness to accept people is at this point neither confirmed nor denied.

If intensive warfare operated as postulated above, then one might expect it to have other consequences as well. I believe that the pattern of marriages and certain aspects of the distribution of wealth are two such consequences.

TECHNIQUES AND STRATEGIES

The first instances of armed combat I will consider are those between members of different sovereignties. These could range from individual men attacking one another to several sovereignties attacking one another. I will first discuss some of the weapons and strategies used when the fighting involved at least most of those in two sovereignties.

The major weapon used in armed combat between different sovereignties was the bow and arrow. I mentioned earlier that members of Auyana distinguished between arrow fighting and stick fighting. The sticks which might be used were black palm clubs. These were called *wanda* and stick fighting was sometimes referred to as *wanda time*. However, palm clubs were never used in fighting outside the sovereignty.

Black palm spears about five to six feet long were also available and were sometimes carried into battle. But no man ever went into a battle with just a spear, and eight out of thirteen men I asked denied that they *ever* took a spear into battle. They said that if it became hand-to-hand fighting they would unstring their bows and use them as spears (the bows were black palm and sharpened at the ends). In the histories I collected, hand-to-hand fighting was rare and almost all the armed combat consisted of shooting arrows at one another from as close as two to three feet to as far as one hundred yards or so.

Fire-hardened hardwood shields about four to five feet high and two to three feet wide were also used. They were often decorated with geometric designs made of colored clays with a feather plume fastened to the top in such a way as to bob and wave in rhythm with the warrior's movements. The attitude toward shields was ambivalent. On the one hand, men would talk quite affectionately about their shields and say the shields were like an older brother in that they protected the men from their enemies. On the other hand, they complained that the shields were heavy and hindered movement. In addition it was a mark of bravery and skill to go into a fight without a shield. As would be expected, there were men who claimed not to use a shield. However, others would claim that this was merely braggadocio and that most men took a shield into battle if it was not an ambush raid. At the same time there was agreement that some men never used a shield. I would guess that it was probably the case that at least half the men would have shields in any planned confrontation. Men did not carry their shields with them unless they knew they were going to a battle.

There were three kinds of arrow fighting. In the first type, two sides would get into an argument which would eventually turn into an arrow fight. This type of arrow fight had no special name. The second type of arrow fight was called *uwara'*.[1] I will translate this as "challenge fighting." In this type of fighting, one side would prepare themselves to fight and would come to some point where their adversaries could see, hear, and count them. They would then shout challenges to come and fight. These usually entailed various taunts and insults, such as dancing and singing, to show their adversaries how unafraid they were and to make sure they would not be ignored. If the challenge were accepted, the adversaries would come to a point where they were easily visible and engage in the same sort of name-calling and taunting. Gradually, the two groups would move toward one another, still making insults, singing, and dancing. At some point one would fire at the other and then the fighting would begin.

The third type of arrow fighting was called *mai*. I will translate this as "ambush." There were several types of ambushes, depending upon the circumstances in which the ambush took place. In one type, the ambushers would go out just before dawn and station themselves close to the men's house of their adversary. As the men came out in the morning, the ambushers would attempt to shoot them. This type of ambush was thought to be particularly effective because the men were usually just getting up and were slow and drowsy. In addition, there was the possibility of shooting several of them.

Another variety of ambush involved surprise attacks on isolated individuals in the morning or late afternoon. This could be accomplished by sneaking up to the village in the hopes that someone might be there and not in their gardens. It could also be done by either hiding along the trails to the gardens or going to the gardens and attempting to get someone while he was working.

In either type ambush, the intention might be to complete the ambush and flee as rapidly as possible or to follow it up with a general confrontation.

[1] The grouping named Uwara' (Tairora) was given this name by Auyana because it was said its members were always engaged in this type of fighting.

When the intention was to strike and flee, a specific strategy was used. The ambushers divided themselves into four segments (each segment had a special term). One segment of three to five of the best fighters would attempt the killing. The next segment consisted of those stationed along the trail which the killers would use when they fled. Their task was to cover for the killers as they fled. It was hoped that those who had been ambushed would know these men were stationed somewhere along the trail and would be more cautious in their pursuit. A third segment consisted of those stationed further along the escape route. Their task was to fight a delaying action for the killers and the others stationed along the trail. The last segment consisted of men placed along those trails which intersected with the escape route. Their job was to fight off those attempting to come along these trails in order to intercept the killers. This was considered a very dangerous job, as usually only a few defenders would be stationed at any one trail and they might encounter large groups of adversaries. Moreover, they had no ready trail along which they could flee. These defenders generally consisted of the best fighters other than those who did the actual killing. Membership in all these groups was self-determined.

A third variety of ambush was executed as men responded to a challenge. When a group issued a challenge, they would observe the point at which their adversaries gathered and what trails they moved along to get to that point. If the challengers judged that their adversaries were not being cautious about moving along these trails, they might attempt an ambush. A few men would hide beside the trails while the remainder issued a challenge to fight. This was a particularly risky type of ambush, as the ambushers might easily be cut off from their own group. It was therefore infrequently attempted and, hence, it was said to have a good chance of working simply because the adversaries would be surprised.

It was said that one did not ambush those with whom one wanted to remain friends. Ambushes were viewed as being intended solely to kill without warning. For those with whom one wanted to retain some level of friendship, challenge fighting at least gave them warning.

Once a general confrontation occurred, whether following an ambush or a challenge, the action which took place varied from complete confusion with every man for himself—a rare occurrence—to coordinated maneuvers. The most basic maneuver was to maintain an unbroken skirmish line behind which men might be resting and occasionally firing. The basic strategy was to prevent men from becoming isolated and to provide an area close to the battle to which men could retire and rest for a while before returning to the fight. The main intent of the counter-strategies was to isolate individuals or small segments of men from the main body. It was denied that any one man or combination of men determined which of these strategies was to be used. It was said that while people would generally listen to a man who was a renowned warrior, they would not always listen to him, and men did not keep checking with him for directions. Rather, the execution of one of these strategies depended upon the willingness of someone to suggest and undertake it and his ability to get enough others to join him.

The simplest isolating strategy was for some men to attempt to sneak around to the side or behind the enemy skirmish line and pick off any unsuspecting individuals who might think they were safe behind their own lines. This was very dangerous for the ambushers, as they were also separated from their own line and thus had to be able to get away quickly. One tactic used to help them flee was the one mentioned above—to station some men along the trail which the ambushers would use for their retreat.

Another strategy was based upon the generalization that during the course of a fight which lasted days, both sides would entirely withdraw from fighting and rest for a while. When this occurred, a few men would attempt to sneak close to where the enemy were resting and hope to catch a man or a few men separated from the rest and not alert.

One strategy was much more risky. This was to send several men secretly behind the enemy line. These men would hide by the trails along which it was thought the enemy would retreat. Once the ambushers were stationed, a signal such as waving a branch was given and others in their group would make a concerted attack, attempting to drive the enemy group back into the ambush. They hoped to drive the enemy beyond the point where the ambushers were stationed. If this failed, the ambushers were completely separated from their own group with no one stationed along the trails to engage in delaying tactics as they attempted to flee.

I mentioned earlier that those who wanted to maintain some degree of friendship did not ambush one another. This applied as well during a general confrontation. If people were engaged in challenge fighting with those they thought were probably not willing to become complete enemies, they were not very worried about ambushers during the fight. But, of course, no one could be sure when a group might change its intentions, and consequently there was always the danger of an ambush during a general confrontation. When the confrontation was between those who were avowed enemies, men from both sides were always trying to set up ambushes. These men would sometimes encounter one another and this was generally thought to be amusing. Apparently undercover men are not particularly liked anywhere.

There was said to be no way by which a man could surrender. A person could plead not to be shot, but whether he was or not depended upon the relationship between the person and the would-be shooter and situational factors. Captives were practically never taken. In the fighting histories I collected, captives were taken only twice. One of these was the case of Komo discussed on page 217. In the other case, those in sovereignty K were fighting with those in sovereignty O. Sovereignty K asked Auyana for help. Auyana agreed but then secretly made an arrangement with sovereignty O that if Auyana would turn on sovereignty K, then sovereignty O would give Auyana some wealth (Auyana had past grudges against sovereignty K). Once the warriors from Auyana got inside the hamlet in sovereignty K, they turned on the residents and shot several people. One famous warrior shot so many he ran out of arrows. He then unstrung his bow and began spearing women. But he saw one woman he liked, and grabbed her and took her back with him. When I questioned others in Auyana about this, they said that this was never done because the woman probably would not stay and because men were supposed to be thinking of killing during a fight, not grabbing women. They also said that if this man had not been a man with a name and an Auyana "post," he could not have done this.

As mentioned in the discussion of sovereignty attributes, women, children, and infirm men would go to some area overlooking the battlefield. From there they could shout insults at the enemy and help spot ambushes. They also set up a station for the wounded and a resting place where a warrior might catch his wind and impress others with his blood-covered arrows (some men were accused of shooting already dead men and then bragging to the women about what fierce warriors they were and showing them their blood-covered arrows to prove it). Also, as was mentioned in the discussion of sovereignty attributes, women and children were not often shot. In particular, they were not shot when they were on the sidelines watching a confrontation. When they were shot, it was during an ambush.

Given that every sovereignty had a number of groups with whom they were not concerned to maintain friendly relationships, ambush was a frequently used tactic. Members of Auyana said that the following protections against ambush had been devised, although not necessarily solely for that reason.

First, the men's house was said to be for protection. They agreed that they could be easily surrounded there, and there was also the possibility that the men's house could be burned, trapping them inside. However, in line with their general strategy of warfare, they argued that if they were all together they had a better chance of escaping than if they were isolated from one another. In addition, two strategies were used to minimize the risks. One of these was to build a small house beside the men's house in which a few men would sleep. It was hoped that they might hear any would-be attackers or be able to set up a cross-fire if the men's house were ambushed. The other strategy was to build an escape hatch in the men's house. A section of the wall was built without any posts or frame. Instead, it had only bark covering it and could easily be kicked through if necessary. The escape hatch was designed in such a way that it was impossible to tell from the outside where it was. Enemy attackers, it was hoped, could thus be taken by surprise.

Second, all residential units were placed along ridge tops where they could command a view of the surrounding territory. As a result, the inhabitants would have some chance of spotting ambushers before they got too close.

Third, around each cluster of houses there was planted a dense stand of cane, forming a barrier which could only be penetrated with a great deal of noise, if at all. Only two or three paths were made through this cane into each hamlet. At the points where the paths entered the hamlets, a seven to eight foot wall of large branches jammed into the ground and lashed together was built. This wall, or palisade, might also be extended inside the cane around the hamlet, and sometimes a second wall would be built around the *outside* of the cane. A completely defended hamlet would have a palisade with a dense growth of cane inside it, and a second palisade inside the first. The obvious offensive tactic against such defenses is fire, but this was seldom successful unless there had been a long dry spell. Otherwise, a fire took too long to get started. Consequently, if a hamlet burned to the ground, it usually occurred when the enemy had entered the hamlet and set fire to the houses.

Fourth, during times when there was a high probability of an ambush, guards were posted at the edge of the cane. Others might sit on a high point outside the hamlet and would raise an alarm if they saw the enemy approaching.

Fifth, some men always accompanied women to the gardens, and either worked with them or stayed to guard them.

Sixth, men very rarely traveled anywhere alone, especially outside the sovereignty.

The attitude of men toward fighting varied. I do not know how much of what was said to me would have been said before the arrival of the government. I doubt that I would have been told then, as I was a few times, that fighting was *totally* bad and resulted in nothing but killing and more killing. I do not, however, think it was mere rhetoric when I was told life was better since the government had come because a man could now eat without looking over his shoulder and could leave his house in the morning to urinate without fear of being shot. All men admitted that they were afraid when they fought. In fact, they usually looked at me as though I were a mental defective for even asking. Men admitted having nightmares in which they became isolated from others in their group during a fight and could see no way back. I made no attempt to find out how many men had such nightmares, but three men who were known as good fighters said they did.

On the other hand, fighting was an enjoyable enterprise to some extent. To kill those who had killed one of your group made your "stomach good," and you were proud, for it showed others that you were not to be trifled with. This mixture of hatred, delight, and pride was made quite clear when I was collecting fighting histories. Some men would become animated and would act out how they or someone else had killed an enemy or escaped from a dangerous situation. They obviously delighted in telling how they did not just defend themselves but literally terrorized their enemies. They wanted me and other listeners to know that they were fierce men and were proud of it. I think this particularly impressed me because these same men were ones who otherwise went about their business fairly inconspicuously, as did all men in 1962-65. This made it rather obvious that warfare was the activity which had provided the focus for a lot of male exhibitionism in the past. This focus was gone by 1962 and so, for the most part, was male exhibitionism.

The most contempt was reserved for cowardly men. It was said of them that they would run for home when their adversaries first shouted insults at them. Contempt was also shown for those who were continually arguing for peace. They were usually referred to as "garden men," which had three connotations: (1) they were frequently in their garden when actual fighting broke out and only managed to arrive at the fight when it was nearing completion; (2) they were like women, as gardening was primarily a woman's task; (3) they were more concerned with food and pigs than they were with getting revenge and frightening others, as fighting would at least interrupt normal gardening and husbandry activities and might result in pigs being killed, gardens torn up, and houses burned. I suggest that considerable contempt was reserved for garden men because the above alternatives were precisely the ones which tempted all men to cease fighting.

It was said that pressure was exerted on boys to begin fighting sometime after they underwent the first stage of initiation. Boys were introduced to fighting by being primarily weapon bearers for the fighters. They were next encouraged to get close enough to the fighting to have to dodge arrows and to shoot men who were already dead or dying. This would help the boys get used to shooting people. By the time they were around fifteen, they were presumably pressured to become full warriors. At the very least, they went with the others and fought as part of the front skirmish line.

I have so far discussed fighting between sovereignties as though all the men on each side were equally intent on shooting the men on the other side. However, this was not the case. Members of Auyana said that men refrained from killing three classes of people in another sovereignty. First, a man did not kill those in his wife's natal pooling unit, especially those in her subpooling unit. The reciprocal of this was that those in a pooling unit would not kill the husband of a woman from that pooling unit. It was said that these men refrained from killing one another for several reasons. First, they were men who exchanged wealth with one another. While whole pooling units were involved in giving, some man had to be the major sponsor. As a result, a pooling unit might not receive any wealth at the life-crisis events of a woman's children if her husband was unable to initiate and organize the event. Second, a woman would get mad if her husband killed those in her natal pooling unit, especially if he killed someone in her natal subpooling unit. Third, it was said that others would ridicule a man who killed any of these.

The second class of people a man did not kill were those with whom he could trace common ancestry to someone in the second generation above him. When questioned specifically, this turned out to mean those in his mother's natal subpooling unit, or the reciprocal (those who were children of women from his own subpooling unit), or those who were children of his mother's sister. There were again several reasons given for refraining from killing one another. These men were ones who exchanged wealth with one another and might pool with one another. They also were those whose parents had presumably been friendly with one another, and others would ridicule them for killing these people.

The third class of people a man did not kill were those with whom he was particularly close but who did not fit into any of the above categories. Such men refrained from killing one another because they were friends and helped one another and one did not shoot a close friend.

In addition to not killing one another, men in these three classes might also act as channels for secret information. In other words, they might betray their own groups. For example, Ka had developed a relationship with a man in Kawaina with whom he could deal as though he were Ka's wife's brother. Kawaina was a long-standing enemy of Auyana. During one period of fighting between the two sovereignties over a presumed soul assassination, this man came over to Ka and warned him that the next day Auyana was going to be ambushed at a certain spot as they responded to a challenge to fight. The next day the Auyana forces responded to the challenge by going to the fight on a different trail from that they had been using, and managed to avoid the ambush. It was, of course, impossible to tell exactly how much and what kind of information was transmitted in this way. However, in the cases I collected, the information was not of the sort that would endanger the informer's own group. Rather, it enabled the recipients of the information to avoid some sort of trap or surprise. Apart from the fact that it would have been very difficult to stop the transmission of such information (intermediaries could always be used), there may have been a reason for allowing it: it reduced the likelihood of severe casualties in a group. In effect, the price one paid for managing to avoid a number of surprises was that the surprises one had planned might not work either. I suggest that those in Auyana were willing to pay such a price, at least up to a point. Cases such as the one given above of Ka and the men in Kawaina were rare. Kawaina was a long-standing enemy and Ka was the only person in Auyana who carried on any transactions with those in Kawaina. Ka was a "post." It could be that it was only his standing as a post which enabled him to get away with this. Otherwise, men carried on very few transactions with those in long-standing enemy groups, and I elicited no cases of secret information being transmitted between members of such groups other than the Ka case. Hence, it could be argued that as groups became severe enemies, they became willing to run the risk of annihilation in order to have the chance of annihilating the others and would be angry at men suspected of transmitting secret information.

Although it was impossible to get any quantitative estimation of the passing of secret information to groups who were *not* long-standing enemies, my impression from the way they talked about it is that it occurred frequently. In any case, it was possible to get some idea of whether men killed men whom, supposedly, one did not kill. I made no attempt to determine the frequency with which men in these categories shot at, but did not kill, one another (that is, I did not itemize wounds or near misses). However, I did attempt to determine the relationship between a killer and those he killed. I say "attempt" because this was not an unambiguous process, as the exact relationship between a man and someone he killed was not always agreed upon by those still living. It was possible, though, to cross-check this against the genealogical information I obtained, and I could reasonably determine whether the person was in the killer's wife's natal unit or was someone with whom he had close common ancestry. But I could not determine whether indeed a man was a close friend of someone in another sovereignty before one killed the other. The other source of ambiguity was that in most cases a man was killed by several men. He might have been shot by three or four men before he actually collapsed and, after collapsing, he might have continued to crawl around or twitch and might have been shot by several others. Each of these men might later claim to have killed him. In compiling my data, I took to be the killers only those who initially shot the victim.

Given the above ambiguities, for the twenty-five years of fighting for which I collected information I recorded the following:

1. One man killed his wife's father, one killed a man in his wife's natal pooling unit, and one killed the husband of a woman from his own pooling unit.

2. No men killed those with whom they had close common ancestry. However, three men did initially shoot such a person, who was then shot by others and died. Two of these three men were still alive; each said he shot the victim before realizing his identity. Once the victim was wounded, others were able to hit him several times.

3. No one killed a man who was not in either of the above categories but was a close friend.

This indicates that men in these categories did give one another special exemptions during fights. They treated one another in the same manner members of Auyana said those within the sovereignty treated one another— i.e., they might fight with arrows but they did not shoot to kill. It follows that if two sovereignties had many intermarriages between their members and carried on numerous transactions, then the fighting between them would be muted simply through individuals granting exemptions to individuals on the other side. One consequence was that a sovereignty could remain friendly with another without there being any public deliberation to arrive at a consensus.

A Twenty-Five-Year History

The period for which I obtained a history of fighting between members of Auyana and those in other sovereignties begins with the birth of my oldest interpreter, which I estimate to have been in 1924. This date was chosen because several of the men alive in 1962-65 had participated in the fights at the beginning of this period, although only as initiated or young married men. Further, I have an extensive autobiography for my oldest interpreter and therefore have a number of ways by which I can estimate the year in which he was born and his age at any given fight. As fighting ended wih the arrival of the Australians, this history runs from 1924 to late 1949, roughly a twenty-five-year period.

I first got together several men from one of the pooling units and asked them to describe for me every instance in which someone in Auyana had been involved in a fight (armed combat) with someone from another sovereignty. I then did the same with several men from the other pooling unit in Auyana. This gave me a skeletal outline. Whenever possible, I would get together with several men who had participated in a given fight and get a detailed account of the fight. If this was not possible, I would get separate detailed accounts of every fight from at least two men who had participated in it. If there were no discrepancies, I would not check with someone else. If there were discrepancies, I would try to check each discrepancy with at least one other person. As I gathered detailed accounts of the fights in the skeletal outline, various other fights not originally mentioned in that outline were uncovered. In addition, as part of the LeVine and Campbell questionnaire for each large collectivity, I asked whether anyone in Auyana had ever fought against anyone in that collectivity. I believe I learned about almost every fight during this period and if I did miss any they were those in which only a few individuals were involved.

I will use the word "war" to refer to the situation following armed combat between members of different sovereignties in which several fights occurred relatively close to one another and each group assumed the other still intended to attack them and both were planning attacks on each other. Any armed combat was potentially the beginning of a war. While some forms of armed combat (e.g., ambushes in which a person was killed) were certain to precipitate a war and some (e.g., two men briefly fighting over one man's pig getting into the other's garden) were quite unlikely to precipitate further fighting, others (e.g., a fight over a case of adultery in which someone was seriously wounded) generated a period of uncertainty which could last for an indefinite time. Hence, it might be difficult to determine when a war had begun, if indeed it had begun at all. Further, it might be unclear whether it had ended or not. In the discussion of sovereignty attribute number six, I mentioned that following a fight those in different sovereignties might "give hands" to one another. In cases where the sovereignties had been on good terms prior to the fighting and there were no homicides during the fighting, this was done by gathering at a place on some prearranged date. Each side presented killed pigs to the other and they then cooked and ate them together. If the two groups had not been on good terms and the fighting had involved homicide, then both sides came to a prearranged spot fully armed. They then moved towards each other dancing and singing (much as they did when moving to fight in response to a challenge). If someone did not get carried away and begin shooting, the two groups eventually came face to face. One man on each side handed over a cooked sweet potato to someone on the other side. The recipient immediately shouted that he had been given food. The dancing and singing stopped and both groups then presented killed pigs to one another. But they did not cook them together. Each group retired to their territory and cooked and ate their pigs there.

When the two groups "gave hands," both assumed that it was unlikely there would be any further fighting and that the war was ended. However, groups who had been fighting did not always "give hands," and in these cases it was not clear when the war had ended; the likelihood of future hostilities gradually declined over a period of time if there were no further fighting.

The duration of a war could be calculated from the number of days of fighting and the number of days between fights. It was more difficult to estimate the amount of time elapsed between wars. I mostly relied upon estimates people made of the size of my interpreter at the time. Using this to calculate years and knowing the amount of time taken by any single series of fights, I constructed a chronology which I would guess to be accurate within one-half a year.

Another source of ambiguity was estimating the number of men involved in a fight. Members of Auyana would often say that "sovereignty X came to fight . . ." when only some from sovereignty X came to fight. I consistently asked how many came from any sovereignty, thereby clarifying this point. Nevertheless, I may have made errors in estimating exactly how many came. Members of Auyana could make estimates of the total numbers, but I found these to be quite unreliable when more than ten were involved. The other means they used to estimate size was by referring to the number of men's houses involved in a fight. I have a record of the residence of Auyana members for the period 1925-49 and during this time there were from six to twenty-four initiated men in a single men's house with an average of about fifteen initiated men (of whom twelve were married men). This average multiplied by the Auyana estimates of the number of men's houses in the sovereignties gives figures which, allowing for some growth, are consistent with the government census figures of 1962 for these groups.

I have decided to use this average figure for the calculations of numbers involved in a fight. Table 29 contains the Auyana estimates of the number of men's houses in the sovereignties which figure most importantly in this fighting. The number of initiated men can be found by multiplying that figure by fifteen. When members of Auyana told me that "all" those from some sovereignty came, this of course did not mean that literally every initiated male came. When they said of themselves that "all" of them went to some fight, this meant that all except perhaps three or four men did so. Hence, I took the phrase "all" to mean somewhere around 90 percent of a group and calculated accordingly. When not all were involved, I used the Auyana estimates of the numbers of men's houses involved and multiplied by the average per house (fifteen) to get an estimate. When fewer than one men's house came, I used the participants' estimate of the number of men.

I would now like to present a condensed version of the last series of fights in which members of Auyana were involved, in order to give some reality to the prior discussion and the analysis which will follow. The designations used for the sovereignties are the ones used on Map 6. If fewer than one men's house was involved, I will use the following conventions: the phrase "some" will mean between five and ten men, the phrase "a few" will mean less than five men.

TABLE 29
SOVEREIGNTY SIZES

| Sovereignty | Number of Men's Houses at Beginning of Last Series of Fights |
|---|---|
| Auyana | 4 |
| A | 2-3 |
| O | 2 |
| Indona | 2-3 |
| N | 4 |
| W | 4 |
| K | 5-6 |
| R | 7-8 |
| S | 6-7 |
| V | 7-8 |
| Arora #1 | 5-6 |
| Arora #2 | 3 |
| Arora #3 | 2-3 |
| Arora #4 | 6-7 |
| Kawaina #1 | 7-8 |
| Kawaina #2 | 6-7 |

As discussed earlier, Auyana was divided into two pooling units at the time of white contact. I will continue to refer to these as pooling units #2 and #1A. At the beginning of this sequence of fighting, pooling unit #2 had twenty married men and four initiated adolescents and pooling unit #1A had twenty-nine married men and seven initiated adolescents.

This last sequence of fighting began for members of Auyana around the middle of 1949 when a man in A died, and those in A, suspecting that someone in S had killed him by sorcery, sent to Auyana for help in attacking S. For various reasons, there was disagreement among those in Auyana, but they finally all agreed to help. Auyana and A ambushed a S hamlet one morning. This resulted in a general confrontation which lasted for the remainder of the day. No one was killed, although there were several serious injuries to those in both S and A. Those in A wanted to continue fighting the next day, but most of those in Auyana's pooling unit #1A did not want to fight against S any more. The result was that the next day those in pooling unit #2 and a few from pooling unit #1A went with A to issue a challenge to those in S. S responded, and the two sides fought for the rest of the day with no deaths and a few injuries, none to Auyana members. Nothing more was done for a week. During this time, A solicited and received the aid of those in K as well as pooling unit #2, but not #1A. This alliance then challenged S to fight. They fought for another two days with no deaths. But while they were fighting the second day, those in Auyana who had not gone to help got involved in another altercation, which started when those in W attacked Indona. Auyana became involved by helping Indona.

Indona had been driven off their territory and had moved to Aunaya sometime around 1931. They had been living as a separate sovereignty on part of Auyana territory since that time. After moving to Auyana, they had helped Auyana in several fights and the two groups were quite friendly. Auyana and W had also been fairly friendly until 1941, when Auyana had gone to the aid of N against W and killed people from W. Indona helped in that fight and had killed a W man. Since 1941, there had been some pig thefts and suspected house burnings between W and Indona and between Auyana and W.

O was a group very friendly with Auyana but friendly also with W. Since the 1941 fight, they had been in a somewhat awkward position. Finally, in late 1948 or early 1949, they moved from living fairly close to Auyana hamlets to a part of the territory which bordered directly on the W hamlets. Members of Auyana took this to mean that some hostilities were likely, because, since O moved, there was no group between W and Indona, and those in W could ambush Indona without warning.

Returning to the second day of the battle in which those in pooling unit #2 were helping A against S, those in W ambushed an Indona hamlet in the morning. Three Indona people were wounded. One was a married woman who died later that day from the wound. Those in W did not remain for a general confrontation but retreated rapidly. As they left, they yelled that they had come only to kill members of Indona and were not angry at those from Auyana. Most of those in pooling unit #1A (the only members of Auyana there at the time) did nothing. However, three men who were in gardens close to the trail along which the W men were retreating decided to stage a "mock ambush" just to show them that if they intended to start a fight with Auyana, those in Auyana would fight. They hid along the trail, and as the last few members of W came by, they jumped out of hiding and drew back their arrows as if to shoot. Before the others could do anything, they released the strings without shooting the arrows and reassured the W men that they were just pretending. This not only was a device to demonstrate that they were willing to fight, it was a way of demonstrating what could have happened if they had been fighting and was, thus, a way of saying that the pretenders were not hostile. If they had been, then the others would have been killed.

The three Auyana men then asked the W men what they were doing. The latter assured them that they were only interested in killing some members of Indona and did not want to fight with Auyana. After more talk, the W men went on their way.

When those in pooling unit #2 returned that day, they were told the news, and a big argument followed over what Auyana should do. The basic argument was over the intent of those in W and whether Auyana should help Indona against W or, by not fighting with W, attempt to befriend W again. It ended in a stalemate; the only decision made was to see what developed next.

The next morning, members of S ambushed an A hamlet, killed one A man, and fled. After mourning and burying the man, which took from three to four days, those in A again got the aid of K and pooling unit #2 and ambushed an S hamlet in the morning. This turned into a general confrontation which went on until those from A killed an S man. S then withdrew, as did the A forces and the fighting ended for that day.

Nothing happened for several days; then W challenged Indona to a fight. Indona responded, and some men from pooling unit #1A went to help. The Auyana men tried to go unnoticed by using Indona shields.[2] However, the W men spotted them and shouted to them, asking what they were doing. The Auyana men answered that they were fighting during the middle of the day and that it was easy to dodge arrows and those in W shouldn't worry about being shot. The two sides fought for the remainder of the day with no deaths or serious injuries.

Three or four days passed until W again challenged Indona to fight. Indona responded with the help of some men from pooling unit #1A who had moved to live with Indona several days before. They had moved because they anticipated further action by W and were going to give aid to Indona regardless of the involvement of others in Auyana. Several of these men received serious wounds very early in the fight (one was blinded for life), and when the others in #1A heard this, they decided to ambush the warriors from W as they returned from fighting. Instead of running to help those in Indona, the members of #1A stationed themselves along the trail which would be used by W as they left the fight. W and Indona ceased fighting in

[2] Not every sovereignty had distinctive markings. Indona shields were distinctive because they were similar to the Tau (Fore) shields.

the middle of the afternoon, and as the last body of W men came along the trail, the Auyana ambushers attacked and wounded four of them. As the W men ran off, the Auyana men shouted at them, "We are Auyana and you shot us and now how does it feel?" That evening, word of this encounter was sent to the others in Auyana and to those in A, as it was expected that this action would result in retaliation by W. But before any retaliation occurred, those in pooling unit #2 again went to help A against S. The morning after the fight between Indona and W, S ambushed an A hamlet and those in pooling unit #1A convinced those in #2 that they would have to withdraw from helping A, as it was likely that W would soon attack Auyana. Fighting continued between A and S, and A enlisted K's help. The belief that W would attack turned out to be correct; about two days after pooling unit #2 helped A, W appeared with N to challenge Auyana to fight. As mentioned earlier in 1941 Auyana had gone to help N against W. N had been slaughtered by W during this fight and had moved to live at Auyana for a while. In addition, several N boys had been raised and sponsored by Auyana men, and N and Auyana had had many intermarriages. Despite this, the members of N thought that a man who died in 1947 while living at Auyana had been killed by soul assassination by Auyana. They claimed that some of those in Auyana had been bribed by those in R to do it. Whatever the cause of the mistrust between the two groups, it was enough that six boys whose bio Fa was from N and who had been raised and sponsored by Auyana men (all in pooling unit #2A), had moved to live at N when the trouble between Indona and W first erupted.

Both Auyana and Indona responded to the challenge from W and N, and the two sides fought for the day with no deaths and one wounded W man. Nothing happened for three days. Then W and N attempted to ambush an Auyana hamlet in the morning. This move meant that the fighting had escalated to clear intent to kill. An Auyana guard shot the W scout through the chest, killing him almost instantly. The Auyana man then shouted, "You didn't come to nurse at the breast, but to kill us. Drink this milk, then." Other Auyana men gathered to fight. However, the W and N forces took the dead man and left without any further fighting.

Meanwhile, A and S were still fighting, and the day after the above incident occurred, members of A convinced some men from pooling unit #2 to go with them on an attack against S. During the attack, one of the Auyana men was shot by S and died. All those in Auyana were angry when they heard this, but those in pooling unit #1A were particularly angry at A, for they had never supported helping A against S and now they were placed in the position of having to choose between ignoring that S had killed an Auyana man or fighting both S and W simultaneously. Their solution to this dilemma was to attack A. The afternoon when members of A returned with the dead man, most of those in pooling unit #1A stormed over to A. Those in pooling unit #2, the dead man's pooling unit, were also at A, but were not in on the prosecution against A. Rather, they tried to act as mediators between A and those in pooling unit #1A. Pooling unit #1A first demanded that those in A give several pigs to Auyana, as the Auyana man would not be dead if those in A had not kept asking him to help them. Those in A refused. Those in pooling unit #1A then shot at several A pigs, which started a general fight between A and those in pooling unit #1A. Pooling unit #2's attempts at mediation had obviously failed, so they simply took the dead man and returned to Auyana. The fight did not last long before both sides withdrew. However, the next day, as those in Auyana were mourning the dead man, A and K arrived together. At first the members of Auyana thought they had come to mourn the dead man. However, those in A said that the Auyana men turned out to be *apa'wasi* (wild men), because they had attacked those in A who were their friends, and so they were going to have to fight. General fighting broke out with all in Auyana on one side and A and K on the other side. It did not last very long, however, before others convinced them all to quit. Those in A and Auyana then agreed to drop the matter, and those in A and K attended the funeral. At the same time, A and K pledged to help Auyana against W if necessary.

The day after the Auyana man had been buried, W appeared with a large number of allies and challenged Auyana and Indona to fight. In the W alliance were all of N, all of O, and five to six men's houses from Kawaina #1 and #2. Auyana called for A, who relayed this to K, and both came to help Auyana and Indona. The two sides fought for the day with no deaths, but two Kawaina men were seriously wounded. The next day, the W alliance did not appear. Members of Auyana decided to attempt to avenge the death of their man killed by S and got A and K to go with them to see if they could ambush any unsuspecting men from S. The ambushing party came across a group of S men in the late morning. Men from Auyana shot one and men from Auyana and K shot another, killing them both. As they were retreating, the members of S staged a counterambush and killed two K men.

Nothing happened for several days. Then, W, N, and O, but not Kawaina, challenged Auyana and Indona to fight. This time, only A came to the latter's aid, as K was organizing to fight S. The two sides engaged in challenge fighting for three days with no deaths. Members of Auyana were living in hamlets which were fairly widely scattered, and the ones closest to W decided to move closer to the other Auyana hamlets, away from W. They moved following the third day of challenge fighting and erected temporary shelters the next day. The following day, a party of S men ambushed them and killed a married woman. The same day, those in W and N burned down the Auyana houses they had left, shot any pigs which were left, and tore up their gardens. The next day, members of Auyana sent two women from S who were married to Auyana men to tell S that Auyana wanted no further fighting with them as they had each killed two people. Those in S sent back word that they would not fight further as long as those in Auyana did not give help to either A or K against them.

Two days passed and then W and N (but not O) again attempted to ambush an Auyana hamlet and were again discovered by an Auyana guard. One W man was wounded seriously and the would-be ambushers withdrew. Auyana then bribed those in K to kill some members of W. Before the fighting with Indona and Auyana had begun, W had helped S against K. At the same time, it was known that some hostility existed between S and W. The ruse to be used by K was to play upon this bad feeling. Those in K were to ask those in W to come help fight S, for which W would be given wealth. When the men from W came, the members of K were to turn on them and kill any they could. About a week after the ambush against Auyana, the members of K did just that, killing two W men.

Nothing happened for about a week and then W, N, O, Kawaina #2, and two men's houses from a Uwara' (Tairora) sovereignty (Uwara' #2) ambushed a newly-built Auyana hamlet. The ambushers were able to get inside the palisades, but before they could do much damage others from Auyana and from A arrived to help, and the ambushers disengaged from fighting and retreated to the foot of the ridge. As the W alliance was resting at the foot of the ridge, Indona and K arrived to give help to Auyana. Four Auyana men decided to sneak down while their opponents were resting and see if they could ambush some careless person. One of the four men got ahead of the others, and while he was waiting for them to catch up with him, an O man appeared. Instead of shooting the O man, the Auyana man got his attention and asked him to go back and send out an N man so that the Auyana men could shoot him. The O man agreed, and the Auyana man subsequently heard him argue with the others in his party, but none of them were willing to act as guards. In the meantime, the other three Auyana men had arrived and decided to remain in hiding, although it seemed unlikely that anyone would come close to them. Finally, as both sides were preparing to begin fighting again, three men wandered fairly close to where the Auyana men were hidden. The latter decided to shoot the three men, as it would probably be their only opportunity for an ambush. Their attack, which wounded one of the three men slightly in the chest, caused the remainder of the W forces to counterattack. General fighting began again, and continued for the rest of the day. No one was killed and there were no serious injuries.

The next day, the W alliance, with the addition of a men's house from an Onkena sovereignty (Onkena #2), challenged Auyana and Indona to fight. Before the men from Auyana and Indona could gather, the W alliance attacked. Those from Onkena #2 killed one Auyana man and wounded another seriously. The W alliance also overran a hamlet and attempted to set fire to the houses. They were driven off before they were able to do so, but they did set fire to the cane surrounding the hamlet. Having killed a man and caused some damage, the W alliance withdrew to the foot of a ridge. By this time, all of Auyana and Indona had gathered at the top of the ridge and all of A had come to help them. As the two sides were waiting, several Auyana men attempted an ambush. As one of them was nearing the W forces, he noticed above him an N man with a name (i.e., with a fierce reputation) who was attemtping to sneak up on the Auyana forces. Someone from within the Auyana forces also discovered him and began shooting at him. The N man did not know there was anyone behind him and so was intent only on retreating. As he got close to the Auyana ambusher, the latter shot him in the chest, causing him to fall. The Auyana ambusher attempted to shoot him again, but missed. Before the ambusher could shoot any more, some of those in the W alliance came to save the fallen N man. Those in the Auyana forces also came running, and general fighting broke out again and lasted for the remainder of the day with no further deaths.

There was no further fighting for several days while the dead Auyana man was mourned and buried. About two days after the burial, W, N, and two men's houses of Kawaina #1 again ambushed the newly built Auyana hamlet. This time they were able to tear down part of the palisade and burn some of the houses before enough help arrived to drive them back. However, two of their men were killed in the process. An older Auyana "post" and his son, who had a reputation as a killer, were both living in the ambushed hamlet. During the fighting, they tried to remain unseen in order to make those in the W forces think that they were not in the hamlet. They hoped the W forces would be less cautious and that it might be possible to kill someone in the W forces who also had a reputation. Finally, a man from Kawaina #1 with a reputation appeared, and the young Auyana killer surprised him from behind and killed him. The killer than shouted to the W forces, "You don't need to look for Si's name. You have come and burned my houses and it would be no good if you were to say, 'I thought Si was a killer; where is he?' I'm here." The older Auyana post still remained off to the side, and not long after this incident he surprised and killed an N man. The post then shouted to the W forces, "It would be no good if the name of Ta were lost and you searched and searched for it. I am the post at this place and I look after all those here and I'm still here." Shortly after the killing of the N man, others from Auyana and some from A arrived to help. This, combined with the two deaths, forced the W alliance to withdraw.

The newly built hamlet was abandoned the next day, both because several houses had been burned and because the occupants were afraid they would be the object of further reprisals. Most of the families moved to live with those in the two other Auyana hamlets. However, three families moved to live in Arora #1 and three moved to live in A. About a week after the families had abandoned the new hamlet, both pooling units in Auyana decided to initiate some boys. It was thought that W would retaliate and would probably be attempting to organize larger forces. This meant that future fighting would be serious, and it was thought better to kill some pigs, now rather than have them killed during the fighting.

A week after the initiations, a group of Indona men went to Tau (Fore) sovereignty #1 to receive some wealth. As the Indona men returned, they were ambushed by a group from W with the help of three to four men's houses of Kawaina #1. One Indona man was killed immediately by a W warrior, and another died the next day from a wound suffered during the attack. The ambushers fled after the attack and and there was no further fighting that day.

After the Indona men had been buried, Auyana and Indona decided not to attempt any immediate retaliation. They planned to wait for a few weeks and then attempt to ambush someone; that is, they would do what had just been done to them. Two or three weeks later, an ambush was set up along a trail often used by W men when they went hunting. Three W men were ambushed in the afternoon as they returned from the forest; one was killed by an Auyana man.

Again, those in W did nothing for several weeks. Then an O man who was married to a woman from Auyana sneaked over one night and told some Auyana men that W was attempting to get together a large alliance to kill several men from Auyana and Indona. Auyana and Indona then attempted to form a large alliance and got promises of help from A, K, some in an Onkena sovereignty (Onkena #1), some in Arora #1, and all of Tau #1.

About two days after the O man's warning, W, N, O, and Kawaina #2 attempted to ambush one of the Auyana hamlets. The W forces were almost at the hamlet before they were discovered, as the Auyana men had become confused over who was to be guarding which trail, and consequently one trail had been left unguarded. For some reason, the hamlet was not overrun nor was anyone seriously wounded before the rest of Auyana and Indona were able to drive back the attackers. The two sides then fought for the remainder of the day with no deaths on either side. That evening, Auyana and Indona sent word to those who had promised them help. A, Tau #1, two men's houses of Onkena #1, and three men's houses of Arora #1 gathered the next morning to help them. K, however, had once again been in a fight with S and did not come. After the Auyana forces had gathered, they challenged the W forces to fight. The two sides fought for that day with no deaths on either side. The Arora #1 men then went home. The next day, the two sides again engaged in challenge fighting. Just after the fighting began, four Auyana men crept behind the W forces and hid along the trail which had been used by the W forces in the hopes of ambushing those coming late to the fight or leaving it early. After they were positioned, one decided to hide on the other side of the trail. As he started to cross, three Kawaina #1 men came into sight. The Auyana man thought they might not recognize him, so he pretended to be picking a sliver from his foot. The Kawaina #1 took him to be a W man and asked him which way the fight was. He directed them and they started to leave. As the last one went by him, the Auyana man jumped him from behind, knocking him down. The other Auyana men fired at the other two and made a lot of noise to make them think there was a large force of ambushers. The man that had been knocked down was shot several times and killed; the others fled before they were wounded. The ambushed men returned to the main battle and told the others. Kawaina #1 then withdrew from the fighting and took their dead man home. The rest of the W forces continued fighting for the remainder of the day with no further deaths on either side.

The next morning, two women from Auyana who were married to W men appeared at Auyana, saying that some W men wanted to talk with them. A secret meeting was arranged for the next day. The W men appeared at the meeting with several pigs and some valued items which they gave to the Auyana men, saying they wanted Auyana to help them kill some N men. The W men said that even though N was allied with them, those in N were still angry at W for the large number of N people killed by W in an earlier fight and had killed two W men by soul assassination during the fighting against Auyana. Consequently, the W men wanted to kill some N men. The reason for the secret meeting with Auyana was to arrange a means of betraying N. The plan offered was for W to ask N to help them fight Auyana. If large numbers from N appeared, then W would secretly send word to Auyana designating the trail along which they would come to challenge Auyana. Auyana was to ambush the N men as they came along this trail and the W men would also turn on them; thus many could be killed. The Auyana men took the pigs and valued items and agreed to the plan. However, about two days after the secret meeting, W, N, and Kawaina #1 came on a moonlit night and began destroying Auyana gardens. Auyana and Indona men rushed to drive them off and during the brief fighting which occurred, a W man was killed. It was not known whether he had been killed by someone from Indona or Auyana or both.

Two days later, while the W man was still being mourned, the members of N packed their possessions and moved to live with Uwara' #2 (which had given some earlier help in the fighting). Members of Auyana said this was because those in N had heard rumors that W was going to betray them and were afraid to remain on their own territory. The day after N moved out, W and O appeared and challenged Auyana to fight. As some A men were coming to help Auyana, they were ambushed and one of them was killed by W. Following this, both sides withdrew.

A couple of days after the A man had been buried, the members of N returned to their homes, bringing all the men from Uwara' #2 and Kawaina #2. These joined with W and O and the next day challenged Auyana to fight. Auyana and Indona were joined by A and three men's houses of S. The latter came despite the recent homicides involving them and Auyana. The Auyana forces decided to split into two groups and attack the W forces from both sides. As one of these groups was going towards the W alliance, the two men in the lead as scouts came across some cane jammed in the trail. This meant there was an ambush ahead.[3]

---

[3] Members of Auyana later heard that the man who had put the cane in the trail was one of the renowned warriors in W, who had close ties with several men in Auyana.

Because the two scouts were both young men trying to gain a reputation as warriors, they knocked the cane aside so that others would not see it and turn back. There was indeed an ambush, and the two scouts, plus some other men in the lead, were cut off from the main Auyana group and were completely surrounded by the W forces. However, except for one man, they were able to fight their way out of the ambush. This man, while attempting to break through when they were first set upon, was shot several times. Although he died later in the day from these wounds, he was able to continue running when several from the W forces took after him. He and his pursuers suddenly came upon a body of Auyana men, who shot the nearest pursuer, a man from Uwara' #2, killing him instantly. The other pursuers did not see what had happened because they were around a curve of the trail. As a result, they were taken completely by surprise when they came around the curve, and two w men were killed, one by Auyana men and the other by a man from A. Despite the killings, both sides continued to fight for the remainder of the day. As the W forces retired, someone from W shouted out that the fight had not ended as they had killed only one Auyana man, whereas three of their men had been killed.

The next day the first Australian patrol came into the area, and there has been no further fighting.

The total duration of this was was about four and one-half months. The total deaths were eighteen married men and two married women. The largest number fighting at any given time was about 520 men. However, this never lasted for more than a few days. As will become obvious from the later summary of fighting from 1924 to 1949, the above sequence is not the most common type of fighting. Most of the fighting did not involve such large numbers on both sides, nor such large numbers of deaths, and did not last as long. However, it is typical of the kind of fighting that was engaged in periodically by members of Auyana during this period and represents an eventuality for which people had to be prepared.

Tables 30 and 31 summarize some aspects of the fighting between members of Auyana and those in other sovereignties from 1924 to 1949. Section I in each table contains the instances where members of Auyana were the main disputants. Section II contains instances where members of Auyana helped against a sovereignty when the latter was the main disputant, or where members of a sovereignty helped against Auyana when Auyana was a main disputant (with one qualification noted below). Section III contains the instances where Auyana helped others or others helped Auyana. Table 30 contains those sovereignties with whom there was much interaction, be it friendly or hostile. Table 31 contains those with whom there was little interaction.

First, I will consider the rows in Table 30 (columns in Table 31) to make clear the nature of the instances classified in each row and to establish the magnitude of the fighting engaged in by members of Auyana during this period.

## TABLE 30
### FIGHTS BETWEEN SOVEREIGNTIES: MUCH INTERACTION

| Sovereignties | Class I | | | Class II | | Class III | Class IV | | | Arora #1 | Arora #4 | Tau #1 | Kawaina #1 | Kawaina #2 | Total |
|---|---|---|---|---|---|---|---|---|---|---|---|---|---|---|---|
| | A | O | In-dona | N | W | R | R | S | V | | | | | | |
| S E C T I O N  I  #1 Main disputant with help | 1 | | | 1 | 3 | 2 | 1 | 2 | 1 | 2 | | 2 | 1 | 1 | 17 |
| #2 Auyana deaths from #1 | | | | | 3 | 1 | 2 | 3 | 4 | 1 | | 2 | 4 | 1 | 21 |
| #3 Other deaths from #1 | | | | 1 | 3 | 1 | 2 | 4 | 7 | 5 | | 5 | 6 | 4 | 38 |
| #4 Main disputant with no help | 4 | 3 | 2 | 1 | | | | | | | | | | | 10 |
| #5 Deaths from #4 | | | | | | | | | | | | | | | |
| #6 Skirmishes | | 1 | 4 | 2 | 2 | 1 | 1 | 1 | 1 | 1 | | | | | 14 |
| #7 Auyana deaths from #6 | | | | | | | | | | | | | | | |
| #8 Other deaths from #6 | | | 1 | 1 | | 1 | | | | | | | | | 3 |
| #9 Auyana helps someone a long time | | | | | 1 | | 1 | 1 | | 1 | | 1 | | | 5 |
| #10 Auyana deaths from #9 | | | | | | | | | | | | | | | |
| #11 Other deaths from #9 | | | | | | | | | | | | 3 | | | 3 |
| #12 Auyana helps against them a long time | | | 1 | 1 | 1 | | 1 | 1 | | 2 | 3 | 3 | | | 13 |

| | | | 1 | 2 | 3 | 4 | 5 | 6 | 7 | 8 | 9 | 10 | 11 | 12 | 13 | Total |
|---|---|---|---|---|---|---|---|---|---|---|---|---|---|---|---|---|
| | #13 | Auyana deaths from #12 | | | | | | | | | | | | | | |
| S E C T I O N | #14 | Other deaths from #12 | | | | | | | | 1 | | 3 | 3 | | | 7 |
| | #15 | They help against Auyana a long time | 1 | | | 1 | | | | | 1 | | 2 | 1 | 1 | 7 |
| | #16 | Auyana deaths from #15 | | | | 1 | | | | | | | | | | 1 |
| | #17 | Other deaths from #15 | | | | | | | | | | 2 | | | | 2 |
| II | #18 | They help against Auyana a short time | | | | | 1 | | | | | 1 | | | 1 | 3 |
| | #19 | Auyana deaths from #18 | | | | | | | | | | | | | | |
| | #20 | Other deaths from #18 | | | | | | | | | | | | | | |
| | #21 | Auyana helps a long time | 4 | | | | | | | | | 1 | | | | 5 |
| | #22 | Auyana deaths from #21 | | | | | | | | | | | | | | |
| S E C T I O N | #23 | Auyana helps a short time | 2 | 2 | 1 | 1 | 1 | 1 | 2 | 1 | 1 | 2 | | | | 14 |
| | #24 | Auyana deaths from #23 | | | 3 | 1 | | 1 | | | | | | | | |
| III | #25 | They help Auyana a long time | 5 | 3 | | 1 | 1 | | | | | | 3 | | | 13 |
| | #26 | They help Auyana a short time | 2 | 1 | | 2 | 3 | 2 | 1 | 1 | 2 | 2 | | | | 16 |

TABLE 31
FIGHTS BETWEEN SOVEREIGNTIES: LITTLE INTERACTION

| Sovereignties | #1 | #2 | #3 | #4 | #5 | #6 | #7 | #8 |
|---|---|---|---|---|---|---|---|---|
| Tau #2 | | | | | | | | |
| Onkena #1 | | | | | | | | |
| Uwara' #1 | | | | | | | | |
| Anepa' #1 | | | | | | | | |
| Tau #3 | | | | | | | | |
| Isurupa | | | | | | | | |
| Uwara' #N | | | | | | | | |
| Tau #N | | | | | | | | |
| Arora #2 | | | | | | 1 | | |
| Arora #3 | | | | | | | | |
| Onkena #2 | | | | | | | | |
| Anepa' #3 | | | | | | 1 | | 1 |
| Anepa' #2 | | | | | | | | |
| Anepa' #4 | | | | | | | | |
| Akarawe | | | | | | | | |
| Tau #4 | | | | | | | | |
| Uwara' #2 | | | | | | | | |
| Total | | | | | | 2 | | 1 |

TABLE 31 (cont'd.)

| Sovereignties | #9 | #10 | #11 | #12 | #13 | #14 | #15 | #16 | #17 |
|---|---|---|---|---|---|---|---|---|---|
| Tau #2 | | | | | | | | | |
| Onkena #1 | | | | | | | | | |
| Uwara' #1 | | | | | | | | | |
| Anepa' #1 | | | | | | | | | |
| Tau #3 | | | | | | | | | |
| Isurupa | | | | 1 | | | | | |
| Uwara' #N | | | | 2 | | | 2 | | |
| Tau #N | | | | 2 | | | | | |
| Arora #2 | | | | | | | 2 | | |
| Arora #3 | | | | 1 | | | 1 | | |
| Onkena #2 | | | | | | | | | |
| Anepa' #3 | | | | | | | | | |
| Anepa' #2 | | | | 1 | | 1 | | | |
| Anepa' #4 | | | | 1 | | 1 | | | |
| Akarawe | | | | 2 | | 1 | | | |
| Tau #4 | | | | 1 | | 3 | | | |
| Uwara' #2 | | | | | | | 1 | | 1 |
| Total | | | | 11 | | 6 | 6 | | 1 |

Row 1 (main disputant with help) includes those instances where Auyana and the other sovereignty were the main disputants and at least one of them got help from another sovereignty. These were generally the most protracted fights and, as the homicide figures make clear, the most deadly.

TABLE 31 (cont'd.)

| Sovereignties | #18 | #19 | #20 | #21 | #22 | #23 | #24 | #25 | #26 |
|---|---|---|---|---|---|---|---|---|---|
| Tau #2 | | | | 1 | | | | 1 | 1 |
| Onkena #1 | | | | | | 4 | | 1 | 4 |
| Uwara' #1 | | | | | | 1 | | | 2 |
| Anepa' #1 | | | | | | 1 | | | 2 |
| Tau #3 | | | | | | 1 | | | |
| Isurupa | 1 | | | | | | | | |
| Uwara' #N | | | | | | | | | |
| Tau #N | | | | | | | | | |
| Arora #2 | | | | | | 1 | | | |
| Arora #3 | | | | | | 1 | | | 1 |
| Onkena #2 | | 1 | | | | | | | |
| Anepa' #3 | | | | | | 1 | | 1 | 1 |
| Anepa' #2 | | | | | | | | | 1 |
| Anepa' #4 | | | | | | | | | |
| Akarawe | | | | | | | | | |
| Tau #4 | | | | | | 1 | | 1 | |
| Uwara' #2 | | | | | | | | | |
| Total | 1 | 1 | | 1 | | 11 | | 4 | 12 |

Although the total number of instances in row 1 is seventeen, six of these fights were carried on simultaneously. For example, in the previous account, Auyana was a main disputant (with help on at least one side) against S, A, and W. Hence, the total number of wars was only eleven. One of the eleven wars lasted only one day and another only four days. The remaining nine lasted several weeks, with an average of about three months. In each case, "all" the initiated male members of Auyana participated, to the extent that no segments within Auyana refused to become involved in the fighting. As will be seen, these instances in row 1 are the only ones in which this was true.

Of the fifty-nine homicides in rows 2 and 3, fifty-three were initiated males, three were married women, two were little girls—daughters of two of the married women that were killed—and one was a little boy.

Row 4 (main disputant with no help) contains those instances wherein (1) members of Auyana and the other sovereignty were the main disputants, (2) more than just a few persons became involved on both sides, and (3) neither side received any help from anyone in another sovereignty.

As row 5 (deaths from #4) indicates, the fights in row 4 were not long, deadly ones. The longest one lasted only two days. Further, in only four of the ten fights were "all" those in both sovereignties involved. In the other six cases, segments of about pooling unit size, although not comprised exclusively of those in a single pooling unit, were involved on one or both sides. This means it was here and in row 6 that the exceptions to the sovereignty attribute of all coming to help anyone against someone outside the sovereignty occurred.

Row 6 (skirmishes) is the same as row 4 except that only a few were involved on either side. The interesting thing is that there were four deaths during these skirmishes that did not result in further fighting. Three of those who died were married men and one a married woman. Nonetheless, neither sovereignty was willing to fight in these instances, and instead both made immediate and successful efforts to prevent any further fighting. Even homicide did not always result in immediate fighting, although in all cases it resulted in later accusations of murder by soul assassination.

A summary of Section I shows that members of Auyana were main disputants against forty-one other sovereignties during 1924-49. In these situations twenty-one members of Auyana were killed and forty-one members of other sovereignties were killed by Auyana. If each instance in rows 4 and 6 is counted as lasting one day, then the total time spent fighting by some member of Auyana against someone in another sovereignty for these two rows was twenty-four days and the total for row 1 was about twenty-seven months.

Section II, row 9 (Auyana helps someone a long time) includes those cases where some members of Auyana helped another sovereignty for more than just a few days but Auyana did not become a main disputant. When this aid did result in Auyana becoming a main disputant, then these cases were classified as instances of row 1. For example, in the above war account, Auyana started out helping Indona, but rather quickly became a main disputant. This case was not classified in row 9, but was entered in row 1. There are a total of four such cases in row 1. When some members of Auyana gave aid for only a few days, then these were classified as instances in row 12. A case of this in the above war account would be when Tau #1 helped Auyana for a few days and then returned. A contrasting case that was classified in row 9 is that of pooling unit #2 helping A against S several times. In three of the five cases in row 9, all of those in Auyana were involved in helping. In each of the other two cases, only one of the pooling units plus a few men from the other pooling unit were involved. There were no cases where just a few individuals gave aid to another sovereignty for a long time. All of the five cases involved aid over a period of several weeks with the average being about a month and a half.

All three deaths in rows 10 and 11 were initiated males. The low number of deaths in these cases attests to the difference between being a main disputant and a helper, even when the latter gave aid over a long period of time in a serious fight. Members of Auyana said that helpers were not as mad as the main disputants, which was why helpers did not kill very many—helpers did not want to become involved as main disputants. They also said that the reason helpers rarely got killed was that those on the other side were mad at the main disputants and wanted to kill them. Evidence that this was probably the main reason can be found in the number of homicides (rows 13 and 14) resulting from occasions when some members of Auyana gave aid for only a few days to another sovereignty (row 12). Here there were still no Auyana deaths, but members of Auyana killed thirteen of the main disputants on the other side.[4]

One interesting thing is that I could find no cases where members of Auyana, going to help someone, killed anyone other than the main disputant on the other side. As this would indicate, if helpers did get killed it was by the main disputant on the other side (cf. rows 16, 17, 19, and 20).

The cases in row 12 show a much larger range than those in row 9 in the number from Auyana who went to help. In eleven of the twenty-five cases, all the members of Auyana went to help. In ten of the twenty-five instances, between one-half and one-fourth of them went to help, and in the remaining four instances, only a few men went to help. It is in cases of short-term aid that one finds only a few men from a sovereignty going to help another sovereignty.

Row 15 is analogous to row 9 except that in row 15 Auyana was the main disputant and members of the other group were helpers *against* Auyana. Row 18 is similarly related to row 12. The deaths in rows 16, 17, 19, and 20 were all initiated males, and while main disputants may have killed helpers on the other side, the number of men killed in this manner was quite small compared to the number who were killed when their group was the main disputant (cf. section I).

Sections I and II are primarily concerned with who fought against whom, whereas section III attempts to summarize who helped whom. Row 21 is row 9 viewed from the other side. That is, row 9 establishes whom Auyana fought against for a long time while helping someone, and row 21 deals with who it was Auyana was helping. Row 23 is similarly related to row 12. Rows 25 and 26 deal with instances in which those from other sovereignties helped Auyana with the same stipulation as was made for row 9 (that the aid did not result in the helpers' becoming main disputants). Rows 22 and 24 are similarly related to rows 10 and 13 respectively and are a reminder of the low mortality associated with giving aid. The main conclusion indicated by section III is that there were not large forces fighting one another for long periods of time. Rather, there were periodic gatherings of large numbers, and then most of the helpers would return home after a few days. Several examples of large forces clashing for short periods of time occur in the above war account, but that account is unusual in the numbers of consistent helpers that both Auyana and W had.

EFFECTS OF WARFARE

Having summarized the history of fighting between members of Auyana and those in other sovereignties, I find it difficult to comment on the relative intensity, or severity, of the fighting among these groups. To compare them

[4] Eleven of the thirteen deaths were initiated males, one was a married woman, and one was an adolescent girl.

precisely with modern nation-states would require calculating man-hours. However, a rough estimate can be obtained by comparing the amount of time the United States was at war from 1900 to 1969 with the total number of days any members of Auyana were fighting or warring. For Auyana, the bulk of this time comes from row 1 and row 9 of Table 30. These two yield about thirty-four months. Row 4 gives about half a month, row 6 about half a month, and row 12 about a month. This then gives a total of about three years for Auyana or about one-eighth of the total twenty-five years. For the United States from 1900 to 1969, roughly twelve years were spent in a state of declared war (or "police actions") or about one-sixth to one-seventh of the total time.[5] It would not appear, then, that the members of Auyana spent a greater proportion of time in a state of war than the United States. However, a characteristic of Auyana fighting was that periods of hostility were much shorter and more frequent than for the United States. In Auyana, some sort of severe fighting occurred at least once a year during the twenty-five years. One could argue then that the members of Auyana had to be constantly prepared for severe fighting, whereas members of the United States did not.

Twenty-one members of Auyana were killed as a result of fighting between Auyana and other sovereignties during a twenty-five-year period, or about .84 per year. If we assume an average population of about two hundred during this period, the mortality rate from warfare was .0042 or 4.2 per thousand. If we assume a population average of about 150 million for the United States from 1940 to 1970, then if the United States were to have equivalent warfare losses it would mean a loss of 630,000 per year due to battle deaths. In fact, the number of American battle deaths during World War II, the Korean War, and the Vietnam War (as of November 1, 1969) totaled only 358,792 (World Almanac, 1970:37, 62). Even if deaths only indirectly attributable to the fighting were added, this would add only 140,000 more, making a total of 500,792 deaths, still lower than the number which would be lost in a single year if the United States had a warfare mortality rate equivalent to Auyana.

Of course, there have been bloodier periods in American history, notably the Civil War. But even there the loss rate was lower than for Auyana. In 1861, the United States had a population of about 31 million (World Almanac, 1970:62). If American losses had been at the Auyana rate, they would have been about 130,000 per year. If the Civil War is taken as lasting four years, the combined Union and Confederate populations should have lost 520,000 to equal the Auyana rate. Even if it is taken to have lasted only two to three years, the deaths would have to have been 260,000 to 390,000 to equal the Auyana rate. Clearly, even the bloodiest period in United States history did not come near the Auyana rate.

[5] Compiled from the 1970 World Almanac for both world wars, the Korean War, and the Vietnam War until 1969.

This is not to say that industrial nations have not equaled or exceeded the Auyana rate for at least short periods of time. The Russian population in 1941 was relatively nonindustrialized compared to the United States and Russian deaths in World War II were relatively high compared to Europe or, especially, the United States. The Russian population is estimated to have been about 192 million (*World Almanac, 1945*:134). The Russians are estimated to have had 7,500,000 battle deaths during World War II (*World Almanac, 1970*:38). If they had suffered losses at the Auyana rate they would have lost about 800,000 per year. If we take World War II as having lasted four years for the Russians, they would have lost about 3,200,000 during World War II had they had a rate equivalent to Auyana. Their actual loss rate, then, was about double the Auyana loss rate for this period. However, over a longer period their rate obviously averages out much lower, and one can point to periods in Auyana history when the members of Auyana too were killed at a much higher rate than their average.

I have not been able to find figures on completely nonurbanized populations to compare with those on Auyana. However, there are indications that Auyana was not unique in its warfare mortality rate (Chagnon 1968:24n). Perhaps then the supposed enormity of war casualties in urbanized populations is part myth, as is the belief in "ritual killings" in tribal populations.

While the relative death rates may in themselves be significant, an equally important consideration is the social dislocation resulting from these deaths. I think it is in this area that one can argue that warfare had a more drastic impact on Auyana (and other groups like it) than it does on most modern nation-states. I will not attempt to prove this point here, but I would like to examine some of the direct consequences of warfare for members of Auyana and surrounding groups.

First, I will consider a situation that seldom occurred but had a dramatic effect: when deaths due to warfare were concentrated within one pooling unit over a short period of time. This happened to pooling unit #2 around 1925. A war begun in 1925 lasted for about four and one-half months. At the beginning of this war, there were twenty-two married men in pooling unit #2. During the war, six of these men were killed. As a result of these deaths and fighting within Auyana during the war, eight more men moved out of Auyana and stayed out. This left eight married men in pooling unit #2 at the end of the war. Eight men is closer to the size of a subpooling unit, and these men were able to maintain themselves as a separate pooling unit only by eventually allying with those in pooling unit #1B. What had been a good-sized strong pooling unit became reduced to at best a subpooling unit in about four to five months. However, such circumstances did not occur often, and there was no other group within Auyana which suffered quite such drastic losses in such a short period of time during the twenty-five years for which I have data. Nonetheless members of Auyana remembered quite well this one case and sometimes cited it when I asked whether any groups were ever exterminated as a result of warfare. While it was unusual for any segment to be as hard hit as was pooling unit #2, it was not unheard of, nor was it talked about as being so rare as to be irrelevant.

Another sort of dislocation was when whole groups, or large segments of groups, moved to live on another territory. Other than the case mentioned above for pooling unit #2, this never happened to Auyana during the twenty-five years from 1924 to 1949, and members of Auyana claimed that it had not happened to them previously. However, it did happen to other groups during this period. I will consider only those who moved onto Auyana territory. The first case is that of Tau #2. The members of this sovereignty actually moved over to Auyana about four years prior to 1924, but they are included here because they were residing with Auyana for most of the twenty-five-year period (they moved back to their original place about 1940). Members of Auyana claimed that Tau #2 originally moved because its members were being decimated in a fight with other Tau groups. "All" the members moved to Auyana and lived most of the time on territory that had belonged to Kawaina #2 before the latter group was driven off by Auyana approximately ten to fifteen years before 1924. Tau #2 maintained itself as a separate soveriegnty and, as Table 30 shows, did not give much aid to Auyana in fighting or vice versa.

The other case of long-term coresidence with Auyana was that of Indona. Due to a losing fight with Tau #1, "all" the members of Indona moved to live with Auyana in about 1931 and remained there until the Australians arrived in 1949. During this time, they maintained themselves as a separate sovereignty living mostly on the periphery of Auyana territory closest to sovereignty O. As Table 29 shows, they gave considerable help to Auyana, and vice versa, during their residence with Auyana. Three other groups lived more than a year at Auyana. One of these consisted of about three men's houses of Anepa' #3 who moved to Auyana in about 1928 and moved back to their original territory in about 1932. While at Auyana they maintained themselves as a separate sovereignty and did not give much aid to Auyana or vice versa (cf. Table 31). Another group consisted of about four men's houses of Onkena #1 who move to Auyana in about 1925 and moved back to their original territory in about 1928. While at Auyana they maintained themselves as a separate sovereignty and gave some small aid to Auyana (cf. Table 31). The third group consisted of all those in Tau #4. Due to a losing fight with Tau #1, the same group which drove out Indona, they moved to Auyana in about 1939 and were driven out by Auyana because of suspected soul assassinations in about 1942. During their stay at Auyana they also maintained themselves as a separate sovereignty and give little aid to Auyana or vice versa (cf. Table 31).

In summary, there were five sovereignties, or large segments of sovereignties, that lived at Auyana for more than a year during this twenty-five-year period. In addition to these there were seven cases of sovereignties, or large segments of sovereignties, that lived at Auyana for several weeks to several months. All were said to have been driven out by warfare. While I have no records for other sovereignties within Opoimpina, the number of possible sovereignties which could move is not sufficient that there could have been this high a rate of moving into each of them. As I have indicated before, I believe Auyana was in an expansionist phase during these twenty-five years, and the rate of moving into Auyana was probably unusually high. However, it does give some idea of the movement that resulted from warfare.

In each of the above cases, the dislocated group eventually moved back to its original territory. However, the members of Auyana claimed to know of one case where this did not happen. This involved a sovereignty that had previously lived in the southern part of where Kawaina #2 was living in 1962. Members of Auyana claimed that perhaps a generation or so in the past, the members of this sovereignty were driven out and a large segment of them first moved to Arora #1. From there they eventually moved to form about one-half of what is now Arora #4. While they were able to maintain themselves as a distinct group, they were not able to return to their original territory and apparently have never operated as an independent sovereignty since leaving.

I believe it can be reasonably concluded from the above that members of Auyana were aware there was a fair chance of having to move from one's original territory for at least several years, and lived with the possibility that they might never be able to return to their original territory. This was revealed in another way also. While collecting the twenty-five-year history of fighting, I was told several times that Auyana had never had to move and had held strongly onto their land. This was obviously a point of pride with them, not simply a routine statement.

When Auyana men were asked what caused serious fights, they would answer "pigs and women." In Table 32, I have tabulated the asserted cause of each fight between Auyana and other sovereignties during the twenty-five-year period. As the table shows, deaths, women, and pigs caused fights with about equal frequency. The role of women and pigs was even more important than this indicates, as the deaths resulting in fights were themselves almost always a result of a past history of disputes over women and/or pigs.

In addition to confirming that "pigs and women" were the major proximate cause of fighting, the table has an interesting implication. Land shortage has often been assumed to underlie intensive fighting (Vayda 1961, Brown and Brookfield 1959: 43); yet members of Auyana did not attribute a single fight between them and others to a quarrel over land. They considered themselves to have plenty of land, and they never gave unavailability of land as a reason for moving to another sovereignty or for fighting between sovereignties. To pursue this argument would require demonstrating that their perception that they had plenty of land was an accurate one (Carneiro

## TABLE 32
### Causes of Fights between Auyana and Other Sovereignties

| | Causes | Disputants | | | | |
|---|---|---|---|---|---|---|
| | | Main disputant with help | Main disputant with no help | Skirmishes | Subtotal | Total |
| Death | Homicide | 5 | | | 5 | 13 |
| | Sorcery | 8 | | | 8 | |
| | Marriage arrangements | 2 | | | 2 | |
| Women | Adultery | | 3 | 1 | 4 | |
| | Runaway wife | | 2 | 3 | 5 | 12 |
| | Rape | | | 1 | 1 | |
| | Pig theft | 1 | 5 | 7 | 13 | 13 |
| | Other | 1 | | 3 | 4 | 4 |
| | Total | 17 | 10 | 15 | 42 | 42 |

1956). I have only the indirect evidence that large areas of land which had been in use at one time had not been used for over a generation.

However, even if it is assumed that in general there was plenty of land, this does not rule out the possibility that there may have been a shortage of particular types of land, e.g., used land which had not yet been converted into grass climax (Robbins 1962). Again, I have only indirect evidence on this question. There have been many disputes between members of Auyana over land. On the other hand, even granting that this means there was a shortage of some type of land, it is hard to see how moving would resolve this shortage unless people were able to move somewhere where there was no such shortage. The members of Auyana, however, claimed that all groups had land disputes of the same nature as theirs. Further, such disputes rarely directly resulted in a person's moving and shifting group membership. In the rare cases where someone did move immediately after a dispute over land, it was said that the person moved because of the fighting during the dispute, not because he could get no land. This may have been a rationalization, but I am inclined to think it was not. Consequently, I think that shortages of particular types of land may have at most exacerbated tensions *within* a sovereignty, and only in this sense did such shortages affect movement.

However, Watson (1965b, 1965c) has suggested another type of land shortage which may be operating in the Highlands in situations where there appears to be plenty of cultivatible land. He suggests that many present populations have only fairly recently begun intensive horticulture resulting from the introduction of the sweet potato. He argues this may have resulted in a "population explosion," which in turn resulted in communities' becoming not only sedentary but larger, and living closer to one another. This process meant that not only did the living space available to each group become smaller than it had been in the past, there was also a constant readjustment of boundaries. The resultant tension and fighting may have been exacerbated by the greater emphasis on pigs and larger pig herds, as this necessitated larger areas of land in which pigs could forage without being stolen by neighbors. While an interesting suggestion, Watson's thesis is one for which I have no direct or indirect evidence. Lacking this evidence, and evidence on the shortage of cultivated land, I am unable to determine the exact role of land in Auyana fighting and movement. Further research is needed. For example, it would be useful to compare Auyana with neighboring groups such as Tairora, which is in many ways highly similar but has different man/land ratios (Pataki 1966).

So far nothing has been said concerning fighting *within* Auyana. Table 33 summarizes my records of this fighting during the 1934-49 period. However, the extent to which this table accurately represents the amount of fighting between members of Auyana during this period is difficult to estimate. Members of Auyana were quite reluctant to talk to me about fighting among themselves. This is, of course, not surprising. To discuss fights was to acknowledge that they were remembered. It may even have meant that a grudge was still being held, and the discussion might provoke someone who would otherwise have been willing to forget. Given those difficulties, I finally decided to inquire about this subject with two men with whom I was fairly close and who seemed willing to talk to me about it in private. As a result, I have no systematic checks on each incident they described to me. Some of these incidents came up in other contexts, but very few. This alone would not be too bad, as the main thing affected would probably be the assignment of responsibility to someone for starting the fight. However, both these men were from pooling unit #1A, and they admitted that they were not aware of all the fights that had taken place between those in pooling unit #2. Consequently, while I am reasonably confident that Table 33 contains the fights between those in different pooling units, the fights within pooling unit #1A, and homicides resulting from *any* fighting within Auyana, there were in addition an unknown number of fights between those within pooling unit #2 which are not included in the table.

TABLE 33
PRE-CONTACT FIGHTS WITHIN AUYANA:1934-49

| Disputants | Number of Fights | Instances in Which Either Had Helpers | Number of Deaths | Number of Arrow Fights |
|---|---|---|---|---|
| Father and son | 8 | 1 | 0 | 3 |
| Brothers | 16 | 2 | 0 | 5 |
| Within subpooling unit | 11 | 8 | 0 | 7 |
| Within pooling unit | 18 | 10 | 0 | 12 |
| Within sovereignty | 7 | 5 | 3 | 5 |

As Table 33 shows, fighting between those in different pooling units was much less frequent than fighting within pooling units. At the same time, the only homicides occurred in fights between pooling units. Two of the dead were initiated but unmarried adolescent males, and one of them was a seven-to-eight-year-old boy. The first two occurred during a fight in about 1925 which was discussed earlier (page 73). The seven-to-eight-year-old boy was killed in about 1935. He was a member of pooling unit #2 and was killed by a member of pooling unit #1A. As related to me by the two members of pooling unit #1A, an older married brother of the boy came across an initiated but unmarried brother of the killer attempting to steal a pig. The boy's older brother, who owned the pig, shot the thief in the thigh. The thief staggered up to the hamlet where he collapsed. His brother thought he had died and grabbed a bow and ran after the owner before anyone could stop him. Before he found the owner, he came upon the owner's seven-to-eight-year-old brother and shot him in the thigh or lower groin. The boy died later in the day and this precipitated two days of fighting between the two pooling units. The two members of pooling unit #1A said that their man had acted rashly, but they could not let him be killed by those in pooling unit #2 and so they helped him.

As the column labeled "Instances in which either had helpers" indicates, individuals might not get any help from others in their subdivision. Excluding the fights between brothers and between fathers and sons, of the other twenty-three cases, in which some help was given, only twelve were participated in by all of those in the subdivision. This indicates that members of Auyana were much less willing to become involved in fights *within* Auyana than they were in fights between Auyana and other sovereignties. At the same time, there was only one case where a man ever helped those in another subdivision against those in his own subdivision. Interestingly enough, this man later moved out of Auyana and had not returned in 1962. However, whether this was due to his helping others against his own subdivision or to his general pugnacity (he was involved in several fights) was impossible to tell.

Obviously, fighting within the sovereignty rarely had the intensity of that between members of different sovereignties. At the same time, it could cause whole segments to move out at least temporarily, although only one such case occurred in Auyana during the twenty-five-year period. Seen from the point of view of homicides, those in pooling unit #2 and pooling unit #1A were on worse terms with each other than were Auyana and sovereignty A or O (see Table 30).

Table 34 contains the figures for the asserted causes of the fights *within* Auyana. Disputes over the allocation of garden land were the single largest source of fights. "Pigs and women" were frequent causes, but not as frequent as fighting between sovereignties (see Table 32). This suggests that, as mentioned earlier, certain types of land may have been scarce, but the competition for such land was usually between those within a sovereignty.

In conclusion, fighting constituted a significant disruptive force in the life of Auyana and posed a more or less constant threat of social, if not physical, annihilation. This disruption (real or potential) was due not just to the intensity of the fighting but to the small size of the groups involved. Accidental concentrations of deaths or temporary concentrations of strength could result in a social group's ceasing to function. Given the importance of groups, the threat posed by fighting at least suggests that the allocations of marriages and wealth would have been influenced by fighting. In the remainder of my analysis, I will attempt to determine what correlations, if any, exist between these phenomena in Auyana. I will do this by comparing the marriages and some of the allocations of wealth during the period from 1924 to 1949 with the degree of hostility between Auyana and other groups.

TABLE 34
CAUSES OF FIGHTING WITHIN AUYANA

| Causes | | Disputants | | | | | | |
|---|---|---|---|---|---|---|---|---|
| | | Fa-Son | Brother | Sub-pooling | Pooling | Sover-eignty | Sub-total | Total |
| Women | Adultery | | | 1 | 2 | 1 | 4 | 7 |
| | Marriages | 1 | | | 2 | | 3 | |
| Pigs | Pig theft | | | 1 | 4 | 2 | 7 | 11 |
| | Pig in gardens | | | 1 | 2 | 1 | 4 | |
| Garden land division | | 2 | 7 | 4 | 2 | | 15 | 15 |
| Wealth | Wealth division | | | 1 | 3 | | 4 | 7 |
| | Wealth theft | | | | 2 | 1 | 3 | |
| Failure to help | | 2 | 5 | 2 | | | 9 | 9 |
| Other | | 3 | 4 | 1 | 1 | 2 | 11 | 11 |
| Total | | 8 | 16 | 11 | 18 | 7 | 60 | 60 |

The first consideration, then, is to establish some ranking of the relative friendliness between Auyana and other sovereignties. To do this, I have used a combination of the data compiled from the history of fighting and the answers concerning friendliness/hostility derived from the LeVine and Campbell questionnaire. Table 31 includes those with whom members of Auyana had few transactions relating to fighting. All of these except for Arora #2 and #3 spoke a different language than Auyana. While it would be possible to isolate those within Table 31 with whom members of Auyana claimed to be more friendly, this is not necessary for the analysis here. The more important considerations involve the sovereignties in Table 30. Class I in Table 30 (A, O, and Indona) contains those who were friends of Auyana at the beginning of the twenty-five-year period and were still considered friends in 1949. As can be seen, they were the ones who gave the most help to Auyana (and vice versa), and with the exception of the one Indona homicide, there were no homicides between them and Auyana. This did not mean that they did not get into fights with Auyana. As row 4 indicates, several fights took place. But in only one case, A, did either they or Auyana get any help from another sovereignty. Further, as rows 9, 12, 15, and 18 show, except in two cases they did not help anyone against Auyana, nor did Auyana help anyone against them. In addition, these are the three sovereignties that gave Auyana the most aid during the twenty-five-year period and vice versa.

Class II in Table 30 contains two sovereignties that members of Auyana said were their friends until near the end of the twenty-five-year period. As Section III in Table 30 indicates, this did not mean the two sovereignties gave a lot of aid to Auyana, nor vice versa. Rather it meant that they managed to avoid getting into homicidal fights with Auyana and that they gave some help to Auyana but not much help to enemies of Auyana. However, as discussed earlier, in 1941 Auyana aided N against W and killed several in W. Again in 1949, Auyana and W were involved in protracted homicidal fights. It was also in 1949 that N and Auyana first became engaged in protracted homicidal fighting with each other.

Class III contains K sovereignty, which members of Auyana said was sometimes a friend and sometimes an enemy during the twenty-five-year period. At the beginning of this period, there had already been homicidal fighting between K and Auyana, and, as row 1 of Table 30 indicates, homicidal fighting occurred between them once during the twenty-five-year period. However, the number of deaths was low, and K helped Auyana in subsequent fights.

Class IV contains those who were more or less enemies of Auyana during the twenty-five years. The first three (R, S, and V) were sovereignties with whom members of Auyana said they were friendly until homicidal fighting involving all three of them versus Auyana and others occurred in 1925. All except three of the casualties involving these sovereignties given in rows 2 and 3 occurred during this war. It was a particularly virulent war and members of Auyana said that while they made friends to some extent with those in R after this fight, those in S and V (especially V) remained more or less enemies. Arora #1, and Arora #4, Kawaina #1, and Kawaina #2 were said by members of Auyana to have been the enemies of their grandfathers, their fathers, and themselves. Homicidal fighting between these sovereignties and Auyana began so long ago that no one in 1962 could remember when the beginning was. Despite this, there were a few instances of aid between Arora #1 and Auyana, and members of Auyana said that this sovereignty was not as irreconcilable an enemy as the other three. This was partly because one pooling unit in Auyana had been founded by men whose bio Fa were from Arora #1. Tau #1 is included with these four because during the twenty-five-year period it was one of Auyana's greatest enemies (largely through Auyana's affiliating with Indona), although prior to this time it had not been an enemy (or a friend). Although Tau #1 and Auyana were enemies, near the end of the period they managed to befriend one another somewhat, and the instances of war aid between them (rows 23 and 26) occurred subsequently.

# 6. Marriages and Wealth

Table 35 contains a tabulation of the initial marriages between members of Auyana and others during the twenty-five years prior to contact. Each marriage between members of Auyana was counted as two marriages (i.e., one marriage of the woman and one marriage of the man) in order to make this category equivalent to marriages between members of Auyana and those outside Auyana. Further, the columns labeled "Auyana Female" and "Other Female" refer to pooling units #2 and #1A respectively when the marriages were between members of Auyana. Meaningful totals for the columns "Auyana Female" and "Other Female" cannot be obtained from adding the figures in each column, as there were thirteen Auyana males and fourteen Auyana females involved in marriges within Auyana. If the marriages within Auyana are ignored, male members of Auyana married forty-seven females from outside Auyana, and thirty-nine Auyana females married into other sovereignties. This imbalance was largely due to the fact that members of Auyana were able to adopt more boys than girls from outside Auyana. This obviously meant that an exchange of one Auyana woman for a woman from another sovereignty was impossible. However, this disparity was more marked for some sovereignties than others, with the most striking imbalances being for sovereignties W and S. Unfortunately, I was unable to gather any evidence on whether these imbalances resulted in any hostility as one might expect from the statement by members of Auyana that exchange marriages were desirable (see page 84, also Strathern 1969). But it is interesting to note that sovereignty W was one that began the twenty-five-year period as a friend of Auyana and ended it as an enemy. Further, of the thirteen marriages between Auyana and W, all but two occurred before about 1935. Between 1935 and 1941 there was one marriage, and between 1941 and 1949 there was one marriage not long before the 1949 fight between Auyana and W. The relatively high number of marriages between Auyana and W were thus concentrated in a relatively short period of time.

## TABLE 35
### PRE-CONTACT MARRIAGES: 1924-49

| Sovereignties | | Marriages | | Other Female | Auyana Female |
|---|---|---|---|---|---|
| | | Percentage | Number | | |
| | Auyana | 25 | 28 | 8 | 6 |
| Class I | A | 7 | 8 | 3 | 5 |
| | O | 13 | 15 | 9 | 6 |
| | Indona | 8 | 9 | 5 | 4 |
| Class II | N | 9 | 10 | 4 | 6 |
| | W | 13 | 9 | 11 | 4 |
| Class III | K | 5 | 6 | 2 | 4 |
| Class IV | R | 6 | 7 | 4 | 3 |
| | S | 4 | 5 | 1 | 4 |
| | V | 1 | 1 | 1 | |
| | Arora #1 | 1 | 1 | | 1 |
| | Arora #4 | 1 | 1 | 1 | |
| | Tau #1 | 1 | 1 | 1 | |
| | Kawaina | | | | |
| Table 31 | Tau #4 | 1 | 1 | 1 | |
| | Onkena #1 | 3 | 4 | 2 | 2 |
| | Arora #2 | 1 | 1 | 1 | |
| | Arora #3 | 1 | 1 | 1 | |
| | Total | 100 | 108 | 55 | 45 |

Regardless of whether the imbalance in the number of marriages of females was one of the variables resulting in homicidal fighting between Auyana and W, the few years just prior to the first homicidal fighting saw no marriages between Auyana and W. In the first eight years after the first homicidal fight, only one marriage between them took place. As Table 36 shows, there was only one marriage between W and Auyana between 1949 and 1962. While the case of W indicates that a high rate of marriage was not sufficient to prevent homicidal fighting, it appears that periods of homicidal fighting, including the prior period during which relationships were steadily worsening, were sufficient to prevent a high rate of marriage. This conclusion would seem to be confirmed by other cases as well. The other member of Class II in Table 30, N, had only three marriages with Auyana between 1937 and 1949, when the first homicidal fighting occurred between them. Table 36 shows that between 1949 and 1962 there were no marriages between N and Auyana.

However, as those in classes III and IV indicate, while the rate of marriage may be low following homicidal fighting, it need not remain at practically zero (as in the case of W and N). The homicidal fighting between Auyana and K during the period of 1924-49 occurred in 1944. Five of the six marriages between K and Auyana occurred before 1944. There was one marriage in the

TABLE 36
POST-CONTACT MARRIAGES: 1949-62

| Sovereignties | | Marriages | | Other | Auyana |
|---|---|---|---|---|---|
| | | Percentage | Number | Female | Female |
| | Auyana | 38 | 28 | 3 | 12 |
| Class I | A | 11 | 8 | 4 | 4 |
| | O | 19 | 14 | 6 | 8 |
| | Indona | 8 | 6 | 5 | 1 |
| Class II | N | | | | |
| | W | 1 | 1 | 1 | |
| Class III | K | 8 | 6 | 1 | 5 |
| Class IV | R | 4 | 3 | 1 | 2 |
| | S | 1 | 1 | 1 | |
| | V | | | | |
| | Arora #1 | 3 | 2 | | 2 |
| | Arora #4 | | | | |
| | Tau #1 | 1 | 1 | 1 | |
| | Kawaina | | | | |
| Tabe 31 | Tau #2 | 1 | 1 | 1 | |
| | Onkena #1 | 1 | 1 | | 1 |
| | Arora #2 | 1 | 1 | | 1 |
| | Arora #3 | 1 | 1 | | 1 |
| | Other | 1 | 1 | | 1 |
| | Total | 99 | 75 | 24 | 38 |

period between 1944 and 1949 and, as Table 36 shows, there were several marriages between 1949 and 1962. The homicidal fighting between R and Auyana occurred in about 1925. There were no marriages between R and Auyana until about 1938. The seven cases in Table 35 all occurred between 1938 and 1949. Between 1949 and 1962 there were a few marriages between R and Auyana. Hence, although there were no marriages between Auyana and R for about thirteen years following the first homicidal fighting between them, eventually they began marrying one another.

Kawaina #1 and #2 are the only sovereignties in Table 30 with whom there was not at least one marriage during the period 1924-49. However, this raises the question of why there were any marriages at all between Auyana and those in class IV or with those from Table 31 (rows 15-18). The Auyana marriages with Tau #4 and with Onkena #1 all occurred while the latter were refugees in Auyana territory. But this was not true of the others from Table 31 and those from class IV.

Members of Auyana said of these marriages that they were attempts to make friends with these sovereignties. As this indicates, members of Auyana were reluctant to cease completely any rewarding transactions with those living close to them, whether they were enemies or not. They said that the

reason there were not more marriages was because before this could hap-
pend the two groups would start fighting and become enemies again. Interestingly, this was the only context in which the desire to make friends was
cited as a reason for marriage. I was told that they married those in class I
because they were friends and they wanted wives for their sons. The marriages were not described as being attempts to maintain some sort of alliance. Rather, they were described as being a result of already being allied.
When asked in general why they chose spouses from so many places, they
said it was because if they married all their women to men from one place,
then if those in another place killed a pig they would not get any.

I would assume, then, that in their minds marriages were closely related
to fighting alliances only when such an alliance did not previously exist and
they were attempting to build one, or when it had been at least temporarily
destroyed by homicidal fighting. Once alliances seemed to be established,
various other considerations apparently would become more important in
contracting future marriages. It follows that while there might have been a
rough correspondence between friendship (including fighting alliances) and
marriages, there would not have been a direct correlation. Table 35 does
show that there was a *rough* correspondence. The two main exceptions were
the low marriage rates between Auyana and A and between Auyana and Indona. These rates also remained relatively low between 1949 and 1962 (see
Table 36). While there was some relationship between marriages and alliances, it was not a simple one. The discussion in Glasse and Meggitt (1969)
suggests that this relationship was complicated in other New Guinea societies also.

What other variables may have been operating in Auyana remains unclear
to me. An obvious suggestion would be the size of the other sovereignties.
As Table 28 shows, O was smaller than both A and Indona. However, there
was a high rate of marriage between Auyana and O, as well as within Auyana
for the 1924-49 and 1949-62 periods, which seem to directly contradict the
assumption that relative size was important. It might be argued that high
rates of marriage over a period of time resulted in common ancestry for many
of those in both sovereignties; and a pressure against marrying those with
common ancestry would result in having to find spouses elsewhere. Again,
the high rates within Auyana and between Auyana and O over the period
since 1924 would seem to contradict this as a relevant variable.


WEALTH

I will now turn to a consideration of the distribution of wealth in relationship to fighting and alliances. There are two aspects to the allocation of
wealth to be considered: (1) the percentage of wealth allocated to activities
directly connected with fighting, and (2) the relationship between wealth
that was not so allocated and the degree of friendliness.

I will be primarily concerned with pigs, as an item of wealth, because pigs were one of the most important forms of wealth and because it was possible to obtain records on them. I will not further consider the allocation of land for gardens, nor the borrowing, lending, or giving of gifts which did not involve pigs, unless they occurred in connection with some specific event. In addition, I will not consider one type of transaction involving pigs: the giving of a live pig to another person to raise, as this also took place almost entirely *within* the sovereignty and is irrelevant to the relationship *between* sovereignties.

I will now list those activities other than fighting and recurrent *rites de passage* that involved wealth and about which I collected data.

When a person was sick, pigs might be introduced at two points. One of these was when a lot of people came to visit the sick person if he was seriously ill. A small pig might be killed, cut into pieces, cooked with vegetables, and given to the visitors. The other was when a pig was killed and given to the curers. No valued items were distributed during an illness.

*Aso'a* was a term for a transaction that was highly similar to trade except for the parties involved. It referred to any time a woman gave a pig and no food to those in her natal pooling unit and they pooled and gave her various valued items. The transaction was usually completed within a day or so.

Pigs might be killed and eaten outside the context of any specific event, including exchanges. There was no special term for this. I will refer to it as individual pig distribution. Generally, it involved one man deciding to kill one or more pigs and distribute cooked portions to various people. Sometimes, another man might do this simultaneously. The most pigs I recorded as being killed at one time for this purpose was three.

A man might also decide to kill a pig and present the *entire* pig to another person outside the context of any specific event. The latter would then cook the pig and distribute it amongst various individuals. The Auyana term for this transaction was "just giving"; I will refer to such transactions as individual pig *gifts*.

*Usi* was a male renewal ceremony which has not so far been discussed. Although this was not an event performed exclusively by any social unit, it generally included most of those in a sovereignty and thus was perhaps the only event other than fighting that involved the sovereignty as a group. *Usi* has not been performed since the arrival of the Australians. I was told that it was a ceremony designed to make the men handsome and strong, and that it had been performed five times in the period from about 1929 to 1949. I was unable to determine exactly what led to the performance of a *usi*, but one of the main variables seems to have been the presence of unitiated but unmarried males who would soon be married and who had never participated in a *usi*. In any case, although most of the men in Auyana were involved in four of the five cases mentioned above, in one of them only one pooling unit plus a few from the other pooling unit were involved. It was not necessary that all those in a sovereignty participate, although it was common.

On the day a *usi* began, all the initiated males gathered at a place near a stream. There the boys who had not been in a *usi* before and who were thought to be growing too slowly had cane leaves jammed in their nose and swallowed cane as at initiations. The rationale for these actions was the same as an initiation: it would rid them of the "bad" substances within them. Other men might voluntarily swallow cane, have someone jam cane leaves in their nose, or make small incisions in their glans penis as a means of cleansing themselves. Following this, the men returned to a hamlet and went inside a men's house where they remained for three to four days. During this time, most men went out only to eliminate. A few of them went out to gather leaves from the forest, as one of the primary features of a *usi* was the consumption of a large variety of leaves from wild trees and plants. They did not drink any water, because this would make them "cold" and weak. They also spent a lot of time near a large fire in order to sweat out debilitating substances and become "hot" and strong. The *usi* was concluded when the men donned their finery and emerged from the men's house to sing and dance for a while. Following this, there were two distributions of pig. One of these was to social units, usually war allies who brought them water to drink after they emerged. The other distribution, conducted simultaneously, involved giving smaller portions of pig to married women from the pooling unit. Each man mixed his sweat with leaves and cooked the mixture with the pig given to the women close to him—usually his sisters and any women with whom he was friendly and through whom he was a major recipient of gifts. I was never certain about the entire meaning of this act, but it was mainly an act of trust. To give one's sweat to someone was to make it possible for that person to perform the most deadly form of soul assassination on you, or to give the sweat to someone who would.

Dances were another activity organized not on the basis of a social unit. The following simplified description is based on case histories and on my observation of several dances in 1962. The impetus to hold a dance came from a single man or a small number of men within a sovereignty who had pigs they were willing to kill and give away. If they could get enough others in the sovereignty to help prepare the dancing area and provide vegetables to be cooked and fed to the dancers, then a dance would be held. As this implies, help was not based primarily on membership in the same social unit. Rather, living at the same hamlet or a nearby hamlet seemed to be the most important consideration. Thus, dances were sponsored mainly by a hamlet or several close hamlets within a sovereignty, with some members of other hamlets in the sovereignty also giving help.

Any stretch of relatively flat ground within or near a hamlet could serve as a dancing area. A lean-to was built in a circle around the edge of the area. Dances began after dark and lasted until daybreak, and those who had come to watch sat or slept under the lean-to. While the lean-to was being built, word was spread that a dance was to be held. As the shelter neared completion, the hosts would set a specific night for the dance.

Attendance at a dance depended on several factors, the most important being friendship with the hosts. If at least a sizable contingent from a normally close, friendly sovereignty did not come to a dance, the hosts would take this to mean those in that sovereignty were angry at them. On the other extreme were enemies or those in quite distant sovereignties. There were only two conditions under which members of these sovereignties would attend a dance. First, a special invitation might be sent to them by the hosts. Such invitations were extended when the hosts were attempting to initiate some friendly transactions or wanted to give special recognition to a distant sovereignty. The second condition by which those from such sovereignties might come was when an individual had some sort of special relationship with some of the hosts. Generally, this meant he was married to or was the descendant of a woman from that sovereignty. However, it might only mean that he carried on various transactions with some of the hosts. In any case, when an individual had such a relationship he might come to a dance without an invitation. Those who were not invited and who were members of sovereignties that were not clearly friends with the host or who did not, as individuals have some sort of special relationship with the hosts might be met with bad feelings if they came uninvited, and fights might result. I could find no cases of this occurring, but I was told of an instance where a fight almost erupted. Therefore, deciding whether to go to a dance was apparently not a trivial matter, but I was unable to determine what factors other than the above operated in making the decision.

Once at a dance, the dancers formed into distinct clusters, each cluster moving around the dancing arena, dancing, singing, and pounding drums shaped like hourglasses. Clusters were composed mainly of those from a single sovereignty, with the males in a bunch at the front. But if only one or a few men came from a certain sovereignty, then they would join the cluster of those from a friendly sovereignty. Males wore feather headdresses and dancing frames with feathers on them. Adolescent females who were being exhibited to attract a husband might also wear much the same. Other females simply wore a bustlelike affair of leaves attached to their skirt just above the buttocks.

Sometime during the night, the dancers would usually be given cooked vegetables, occasionally mixed with a pig cut into small pieces. In the morning, as the dancers left, there might be another distribution of pig and vegetables. In this case, large portions of pig were given to certain social units or individuals. A portion might vary from a third of a pig to a whole pig, and a total of between one and four pigs might be given. Social units receiving pigs were either allies, those who had been allies but with whom there had been some recent trouble, or (more frequently) those in a distant sovereignty.

Generally, a segment would take it upon themselves to make such a gift. While no public convocation was held to decide whether to do this, others in the sovereignty could exercise veto power. Those who wanted to make such a gift would make it known sometime before the preparation of the dance arena was actually begun. Those who opposed the gift might then talk directly to those proposing it or simply complain to others and word eventually would get back to them. If it appeared that there was sizable opposition, the project would be dropped. In a sense, then, such gifts were given in the name of the entire sovereignty even though only a few individuals in the sovereignty were actually involved in arranging it and in killing the pigs. This was not true of the portions presented to single individuals. In the latter case, whoever killed a pig might give it to whomever he wanted, and others in the sovereignty did not interfere in any way with his gift. Nor did they receive any credit for it either.

The cargo cult meeting was the remaining event at which pigs were distributed. As mentioned earlier, the cult began in the 1930s and continued through 1962-65. Pigs killed for this purpose were generally cooked and given to the cult leader, who then distributed them among all those gathered at a cult meeting (much as dancers received food).

The above events plus fighting and repeated rites of passage were the only ones at which pigs were killed and given to others. For convenience, I have referred to repeated rites of passage as "life-crisis events." In order to get some idea of the relative amounts of pig used for each type of event, I collected from thirty-nine of the men in Auyana a record of the pigs they had killed or given to someone.[1] I first asked each man to list the pigs he had killed, when he had killed them, and other relevant details. Several months later, each man was again interviewed concerning his pigs. However, this time he was not asked to list all the pigs he had killed, but was rather asked to state the number of pigs he had killed at each event. For trade, illness, *aso'a*, individual pig distribution, and individual pig gifts, I made no attempt to find out whether others would agree or disagree with the records obtained from an individual man. Hence, for these events, the only checks I have are (1) that the record was obtained through an interpreter whose presence may have reduced deliberate or inadvertent exaggeration, and (2) the consistency of the two interviews. However, for dances, *usi*, fighting, and life-crisis events, I was able to obtain some check on the individual accounts. For each of these events, I attempted to get a record of how many pigs were donated or given to an Auyana pooling and who gave them, beginning about 1929 and running through 1962. I had wanted to collect this information for the same time period as the fighting history, beginning about 1924. However, there were only a couple of men alive in 1962 who had been active in poolings at that time and their recollection of the events was somewhat vague, so I limited my survey to events beginning about 1929. For each event, I got information from the major sponsor, if alive, or from someone close to the major

---

[1] I collected data from six other men, but I know this information is incomplete and hence I have not included it.

sponsor if he was dead. In addtion, I checked these accounts with some of the older men in the pooling unit of the major sponsor.

Table 37 contains the figures for the number of pigs killed by the men alive in 1962, with the dividing line between pre-contact and post-contact being the first Australian patrol in 1949. Table 38 contains the figures for the numbers of pigs killed at group events (except the cargo cult) beginning around 1929, and Table 39 compares the figures for group events in the two previous tables. As can be seen, the percentages in the two tables are very close to one another.

TABLE 37
PIGS KILLED BY MEN ALIVE IN 1962

|  | Pre-Contact | | Post-Contact | |
|---|---|---|---|---|
|  | Number | Percentage | Number | Percentage |
| Trade | 24 | 5 | 27 | 3 |
| Illness | 30 | 6 | 48 | 6 |
| Aso'a | 6 | 1 | 9 | 1 |
| Individual pig distribution | 51 | 10 | 151 | 18 |
| Individual pig gift | 39 | 8 | 110 | 13 |
| Cargo cult | 15 | 3 | 22 | 3 |
| Dances | 30 | 6 | 13 | 1 |
| Usi | 9 | 2 | -- | -- |
| Life-crisis events* | 253 | 50 | 442 | 53 |
| Fighting | 53 | 10 | 11 | 1 |
| Total | 510 | 101† | 833 | 99 |

*Life-crisis events include only repeated *rites de passage*.
†Percentages do not always add up to 100, as they are rounded off to the nearest percentage.

TABLE 38
PIGS KILLED AT GROUP EVENTS

|  | Pre-Contact | | Post-Contact | |
|---|---|---|---|---|
|  | Number | Percentage | Number | Percentage |
| Dances | 92 | 8 | 25 | 3 |
| Usi | 25 | 2 | -- | -- |
| Life-crisis events | 843 | 74 | 786 | 95 |
| Fighting | 182 | 16 | 18 | 2 |
| Total | 1142 | 100 | 829 | 100 |

For both the pre-contact and post-contact periods, life-crisis events were by far the single most important occasions of pig-giving. Of particular importance in terms of the general question of the relationship between fighting and the distribution of wealth is the relatively small percentage (10 percent) of pigs killed in connection with fights in the pre-contact period. If there were some significant relationship between the distribution of wealth and fights, it would not be through wealth being distributed in *direct* connection with fights.

TABLE 39
COMPARISON OF TABLES 37 AND 38 FOR GROUP EVENTS

| | Pre-Contact | | | | Post-Contact | | | |
|---|---|---|---|---|---|---|---|---|
| | Table 37 | | Table 38 | | Table 37 | | Table 38 | |
| | Number | Percentage | Number | Percentage | Number | Percentage | Number | Percentage |
| Dances | 30 | 9 | 92 | 8 | 13 | 3 | 25 | 3 |
| *Usi* | 9 | 3 | 25 | 2 | -- | -- | -- | -- |
| Life-crisis events | 253 | 73 | 843 | 74 | 442 | 95 | 786 | 95 |
| Fighting | 53 | 15 | 182 | 16 | 11 | 2 | 18 | 2 |
| Total | 345 | 100 | 1142 | 100 | 466 | 100 | 829 | 100 |

Trade, illness, *aso'a*, and the cargo cult are all small percentages in Table 37 and have remained about the same in the post-contact period (with some decrease in the number involved in trade). Dances and *usi* on the other hand have dwindled to practically nothing in the post-contact period. Simultaneously, there has been a marked increase of both individual pig distribution and individual pig gifts in the post-contact period. My hypothesis to account for this increase and also the decrease in the percentage for dances and *usi* is that they were due to the decline in the severity and frequency of fighting.

I am assuming that in the pre-contact period, the male members of Auyana had to be almost constantly prepared to fight. I further assume that to remain in such a state of readiness required that at least two conditions be met: (1) males periodically engaged in activities designed to convince themselves and others that they were invincible or, at least, as powerful as anyone else around, and (2) males did not allow other interests to take precedence over fighting. I have no hypotheses as to exactly how these conditions were met under varying conditions. However, if the actors said that the conditions were met, I have assumed that they were. The hypothesis, then, is that if fighting became less severe and less frequent, then these preparatory activities would decrease in importance.

From the earlier description of *usi*, it is obvious that *usi* was such an activity, and *usi* not only declined in importance but ceased. Dances were viewed as at least partially directed toward demonstrating male invincibility. One of the stated aims of the ornamentation and dancing in clusters was to impress others with the strength and power of the dancers. As part of this, efforts were made to make as much noise as possible by singing and beating drums. It was said that if people could hear the noise a long way off then they would be impressed that there were enough dancers to sing so strongly and make that much noise. In addition, the dancing style used by men was the one used to taunt the other side during fights, and if a man did not want to take a drum to a dance, he would take his bow and arrows and twang the bow string to make noise, mock-shooting people while dancing. While the number of pigs killed at dances declined in the post-contract period, the frequency of dances did not appear to decline. This may be because dances were a multi-purpose activity, whereas *usi* seems to have been much more exclusively focused on male strength. In any case, the decrease in the number of pigs killed at dances partially confirms the hypothesis. Extending this reasoning further, it could be hypothesized that the disappearance of the men's house and the diminution of the male initiations were also related to the cessation of severe fighting.

However, even if the above hypotheses are accepted, they would not explain why there was a relative increase in individual pig distributions and individual pig gifts rather than, for example, distributions at life-crisis events. I would suggest that at least one of the main purposes of social units was that of mutual protection in fights, and consequently social units became less important in the post-contact period. Since life-crisis events were in one sense social-unit events, to increase the number of pigs killed at life-crisis events would be contrary to the declining importance of social units.

While the above arguments may suggest some points of articulation between fighting and other activities, the fact remains that even in the pre-contact period, the sum of pigs used at dances, *usi*, and fighting was still only 28 percent.

I will now return to the question of the relationship between the distribution of wealth and amity/enmity. My classification of the latter is the same as that used in the discussion of marrige patterns. As mentioned above, when I collected information on the number of pigs involved in pooling for the period from 1929 to 1962, I also got information on the donors. In addition I attempted to determine to whom the wealth was given. Except for the poolings and gifts in connection with fights, my information on both these subjects contains duplications and contradictions which I was unable to clarify, and hence the figures are to be taken as, at best, good estimates. Nonetheless, certain patterns clearly emerge.

For dances and *usi*, all the pigs involved were donated by members of Auyana. For poolings, in connection with fighting, all but 6 of the 182 pigs donated in the pre-contact period were donated by members of Auyana. Significant donations of pigs by someone from outside Auyana occurred only in connection with life-crisis events, and Table 40 contains the figures for the donors of pigs at life-crises events, and Table 41 contains the figures for the donors of pigs from outside Auyana at life-crisis events. For both pre-contact and post-contact periods, only about 10 percent of the pigs were from outside Auyana. As can be seen from Table 41, the source of this 10 percent was directly related to the degree of friendship between sovereignties, with the marked exception of Indona. Note also that the percentage given by those in class II (former friends that were becoming enemies at the end of the pre-

## TABLE 40
### Sources of Pigs Pooled at Life-Crisis Events

| Events | Pre-Contact | | | | Post-Contact | | | |
|---|---|---|---|---|---|---|---|---|
| | From Own Pooling Unit | From Auyana Pooling Unit | From Outside Auyana | Total | From Own Pooling Unit | From Auyana Pooling Unit | From Outside Auyana | Total |
| Birth | 23 | | | 23 | 43 | 7 | | 50 |
| Septum piercing | 33 | | | 33 | 21 | 2 | | 23 |
| First menstruation | 25 | 3 | | 28 | 26 | 1 | | 27 |
| Initiation | 100 | 57 | 15 | 172 | 104 | 57 | 10 | 171 |
| Bride wealth | 72 | 19 | 9 | 100 | 56 | 14 | 8 | 78 |
| *Apemba* | 26 | | | 26 | 21 | | | 21 |
| Changing clothes | 54 | 37 | 5 | 96 | 49 | 44 | 8 | 101 |
| Dowry | 23 | 7 | 7 | 37 | 28 | 7 | 5 | 40 |
| Death | 202 | 56 | 51 | 309 | 169 | 54 | 39 | 262 |
| Death repays | 17 | 2 | | 19 | 13 | | | 13 |
| Total | 575 | 181 | 87 | 843 | 530 | 186 | 70 | 786 |

contact period) dropped by more than half in the post-contact period and that this difference was made up by an increased percentage of pigs being given by A and O in class I.

TABLE 41
PIGS FROM OUTSIDE AUYANA AT POOLINGS

| Sovereignties | | Pre-Contact | | Post-Contact | |
|---|---|---|---|---|---|
| | | Percentage | Number | Percentage | Number |
| Class I | A | 24 | 21 | 41 | 29 |
| | O | 35 | 30 | 33 | 23 |
| | Indona | 8 | 7 | 7 | 5 |
| Class II | N | 10 | 9 | 4 | 3 |
| | W | 11 | 10 | 3 | 2 |
| Class III | K | 6 | 5 | 4 | 3 |
| Class IV | R | | | | |
| | S | | | | |
| | V | | | | |
| | Arora #1 | 2 | 2 | 1 | 1 |
| | Arora #4 | | | | |
| | Tau #1 | | | | |
| | Kawaina | | | | |
| Table 30 | Arora #2 | 3 | 3 | 3 | 2 |
| | Arora #3 | | | | |
| | Other | | | | |
| | Total | 99 | 87 | 96 | 68 |

I will now turn to the question of who received wealth at various events. Particularly, I want to examine whether there was a direct relationship between the amount of wealth given to those in another sovereignty and the degree of friendship with that sovereignty. I also want to examine to what extent wealth was concentrated in a few sovereignties or given to several sovereignties. To completely answer these questions would require information on the amount of wealth given *to* those in Auyana *by* others. However, I do not have this information and can only consider the amount of wealth given *by* those in Auyana *to* others.

The wealth given in trade will not be considered here, as trading involved more distant sovereignties with whom there was otherwise little interaction. Pigs that were killed when someone was ill were mostly consumed by those within Auyana or those from neighboring friendly sovereignties, as these were the groups from which most of the visitors came, and curers were almost always from the same sovereignty as the sick person. About three-quarters of the pigs distributed in "individual pig distribution" were divided among those in the pig owner's pooling unit, with most of the remaining one-quarter being given to someone within Auyana. About half those given as "individual pig gifts" were given to those in the pig owner's pooling unit, about one-fifth were given to others in Auyana, and the remaining 30 percent were distributed to those outside Auyana, in much the same percentages as those for outside donors of pigs to Auyana poolings (see Table 40).

The endeavors considered above were mostly individual affairs, and the overall distribution of pigs on these occasions involved a heavy concentration within Auyana and, for those given outside Auyana, a heavy concentration in relatively few friendly sovereignties.

Again, the four group-events wich I will consider are dances, *usi*, fighting, and life-crisis events. Table 42 contains the numbers of pigs given in the pre-contact period at these events. Relatively few pigs were used at *usi*. Of these, about one third were cut into portions and given to sisters or women acting as sisters and are not included in Table 42. The remainder were pretty evenly distributed over those in class I and class II, with some concentration in class I.

Eighty-six of the pigs killed in direct connection with fighting were given to another member or group within Auyana either to make peace or to celebrate a victory. Of the remainder, a little less than half were given to those in class I, with A receiving the most. Slightly less than a third were given to those in class IV and to the distant people listed in Table 31. The remaining one-sixth were evenly spread over the three sovereignties in classes II and III. Given that my definition of friendliness is based heavily on the amount of mutual aid in times of war, it is not surprising that there is almost a perfect correlation between degree of friendliness and the giving of pigs in connection with fighting. It simply means that those who came to help in fights were given pig almost every time they gave some help. Further, pigs were sometimes given in anticipation of war aid and were almost always given after two or three days of fighting at the most, especially if a large number came and gave help. Given that wars were times of high energy consumption, the donation of pigs in connection with fighting, and the staging of initiations and other life-crisis events at which pigs were killed and eaten, are consistent with the hypothesis that populations have self-regulatory mechanisms which enable them to maintain a dynamic homeostasis, and that various "rituals" may be functioning as these regulatory mechanisms (Rappaport 1968).

About one-fifth of the pigs killed at dances were cut into small pieces and given to all the dancers during the dance; these are not included in Table 42. Of those in Table 42, about one-quarter were given to those in class IV and to those listed in Table 31, and the remaining three-quarters were about evenly distributed to those in classes I-III.

The distribution of wealth at life-crisis events has to be further discussed before it is possible to consider the relationship between friendliness and the number of pigs given at these events. In the discussion of pooling unit attributes and family friends, I stated that I was initially told that at all life-crisis events except marriage, gifts were given to the natal pooling unit of the

TABLE 42
PRE-CONTACT PIG DISTRIBUTION

| | Dances (Number) | Usi (Number) | Fighting (Number) | Life-Crisis Events | | Total | |
|---|---|---|---|---|---|---|---|
| | | | | Number | Percentage | Number | Percentage |
| Auyana | | | 86 | 214 | 32 | 300 | 34 |
| A | 8 | 4 | 22 | 58 | 9 | 92 | 10 |
| O | 9 | 4 | 14 | 65 | 11 | 92 | 10 |
| Indona | 11 | 3 | 12 | 38 | 5 | 64 | 7 |
| N | 8 | 3 | 5 | 53 | 9 | 69 | 8 |
| W | 7 | 2 | 4 | 55 | 9 | 68 | 5 |
| K | 7 | 1 | 8 | 34 | 5 | 50 | 6 |
| R | 4 | | 2 | 25 | 4 | 31 | 4 |
| S | 2 | | 1 | 17 | 3 | 20 | 2 |
| V | 1 | | | 5 | 1 | 6 | 1 |
| Arora #1 | 2 | | 2 | 3 | 1 | 7 | 1 |
| Arora #4 | | | | 2 | 1 | 2 | 1 |
| Tau #1 | | | 4 | 3 | 1 | 7 | 1 |
| Kawaina | 1 | | | 4 | 1 | 5 | 1 |
| Arora #2 | 2 | | 1 | 11 | 2 | 14 | 2 |
| Arora #3 | 2 | | 1 | 5 | 1 | 8 | 1 |
| Other | 4 | | 20 | 24 | 4 | 48 | 5 |
| Total | 68 | 17 | 182 | 616 | 99 | 883 | 99 |

mother of the individual upon whom the event centered. I also mentioned that a married pair could develop a relationship with those in some pooling unit other than the woman's natal pooling unit whereby the couple would be treated as though they were in the woman's pooling unit, and the appropriate spouse-stranger and family-friend terms would be used by the couple and their children. This was one means by which distributions of wealth were freed from being strictly contingent upon prior marriages and fertility rates. Usually a married pair maintained their relationship with the wife's natal pooling unit when they developed a similar arrangement with another pooling unit, but occasionally they would drop the relationship and give nothing to the wife's natal pooling unit.

In addition to the development of relationships through which a pooling unit was treated as though it were a woman's natal pooling unit, at death gifts were demanded by certain types of family friends, and at most life-crisis events gifts were also given to friends and family friends, based upon mutual consent rather than consensual demand. The effect of giving gifts to family friends who had common ancestry was still to tie the distribution of wealth to prior marriages. However, family friends based on common ancestry were derived from marriages made one or two generations prior to the people actually distributing the wealth and represented a long history of continuing good will. If at some point this friendship was broken, people simply did not give gifts to these classes of individuals, and the lack of pressure to do so allowed more flexibility than for gifts demanded through a woman by her natal pooling unit. Further, it was possible to develop a relationship with someone as though the person were a certain type of family friend, regardless of whether gifts were given to those types of family friends through common ancestry.

I would like to present a case history of the giving of wealth to demonstrate the flexibility of gift-giving in Auyana. This case involves a girl, Fe, who was the eldest daughter of an important man in Auyana and was married in 1962. On the day she was sent to her husband, three pigs were killed and distributed. One pig belonged to Fe's father, another was her father's brother's, and the third was from a man in her father's subpooling unit. One pig was given to the girl's mother's natal pooling unit in sovereignty W. One-half of one pig was given to those in a pooling unit in sovereignty N, because the girls's mother's father had lived there for a while and was treated like a member of N. The other half of the pig was given to a pooling unit in Indona, because it was said that the biological father of the girl's mother was from Indona, and the girl's mother had been gotten when small by the man from W when the mother married him after the girl's biological father died. The remaining pig was divided into six portions: the head, four haunches, and the back strip. One portion was given to Fe's father's mother's natal pooling unit in sovereignty S (i.e., Fe's father's *noka*). Another portion was given to a pooling unit in sovereignty A, as it was claimed that Fe's father's mother's father had actually been born there and was raised in sovereignty S (i.e., they were also Fe's father's *noka*). Another portion was given to a woman from Fe's father's subpooling unit married to a man from sovereignty O. Another portion was given to a woman married to a man in a different Auyana pooling unit from Fe's father. This woman was said to be like a sister to Fe's father. Two portions were given to men said to be family friends of Fe's father, one of them from sovereignty O and one of them from sovereignty K.

This makes a total of nine gifts given to individuals or groups in eight different sovereignties at an event about which I was initially told that pigs were killed and given to the bride's mother's natal pooling unit. It was deliberate that so many different sovereignties were given gifts, and this was characteristic of any large-sized event.

The above arrangements meant that gift-giving at life-crisis events was not only much more flexible than initially presented to me, but also that portions of pig rather than whole pigs were oftentimes given, even to a woman's natal pooling unit. Hence, the numbers of pigs given to any group in Table 41 are only estimates based on statements about the amount of pig given and on the distributions I recorded while I was there. Still, it seems clear that the effect of the various negotiations was to make the distribution of pig correspond even more closely to the degree of friendship than did the distribution of marriages during the same period. Of the pigs given at the group events in the post-contact period, eighteen were given in connection with fighting, all except two being given to someone within Auyana. Fifteen pigs were given at dances and were distributed much as they were in the pre-contact period. None were given at a *usi*. The remainder were given in connection with life-crisis events, and Table 43 lists the total number of pigs given in the post-contact period.

When collecting information on pigs, I also attempted to record who donated valued items to the pooling. However, this proved to be extremely unreliable, and I will only enter my impressions. The main point to be made about valued items is that they could vary considerably in quality and quantity, whereas one pig was generally as valuable as the next. This meant that while the bulk of the valued items in a pooling were given by the major sponsors and those in their pooling unit, large numbers of individuals from outside Auyana could give small items to make up the remainder of the pooling. In this way, large numbers of individuals became involved in a single pooling, although in terms of the total amount given, the percentage was not much greater than that for the number of pigs donated from outside Auyana. Inasmuch as the items were small, people could give them even in situations where the donors were uncertain that they would ever be repaid. In this way, those from more distant or less friendly sovereignties could still maintain relations with one another, and large poolings would include donations from several individuals in several different sovereignties, some of them from fairly distant places.

TABLE 43
POST-CONTACT PIG DISTRIBUTION

|           |          | Number | Percentage |
|-----------|----------|--------|------------|
| Auyana    |          | 245    | 41         |
| Class I   | A        | 71     | 12         |
|           | O        | 82     | 14         |
|           | Indona   | 50     | 8          |
| Class II  | N        | 26     | 4          |
|           | W        | 22     | 4          |
| Class III | K        | 33     | 5          |
|           | R        | 24     | 4          |
|           | S        | 12     | 2          |
|           | U        | 2      | 1          |
|           | Arora #1 | 5      | 1          |
|           | Arora #4 | 4      | 1          |
|           | Tau #1   | 2      | 1          |
|           | Kawaina  | 2      | 1          |
|           | Arora #2 | 7      | 1          |
|           | Arora #3 | 4      | 1          |
|           | Other    | 13     | 2          |
|           | Total    | 604    | 103        |

# 7. Women, Wealth, and Warfare

In this chapter, I will discuss the relationship between intensive warfare, patterns of marriage, and the distribution of wealth. I will first develop general considerations concerning the distribution of material wealth and then apply these considerations to a situation in which there was intensive warfare between small groups.

Despite the debate between "substantivists" and "formalists" (Cook 1966, LeClair 1968), and the increasing number of detailed descriptions of the production and distribution of goods (Epstein 1962), it seems that we still know very little about the conditions under which certain rewards have priorities over others. In particular, we are relatively ignorant of the conditions under which maximizing the consumption of material wealth has lower priority than other goals. One hypothesis, stated in 1935 by Mauss and expanded more recently by Sahlins (1965), is that the primary threat with which members of "primitive" populations must cope is that of physical attack by other members. Although both Mauss and Sahlins consider this to be the case in certain types of societies, it may be more useful to consider it as applying to a certain type of *situation*—one in which there is no third party to whom disputants can or will take a dispute for adjudication. Disputes between nations and within families are good examples of this type of situation. While I believe that many of the propositions to be made in this chapter apply to the use of material wealth whenever this situation obtains between actors, I will be concerned here only with populations in which this situation obtains in almost all contexts. Beatrice Whiting refers to these populations as possessing "coordinate control," which she characterizes as "the absence of an individual or group of individuals with delegated authority to settle disputes and punish offenses and the presence of retaliation administered by peers as the major mechanism for social control" (Whiting 1950:82). I will assume, as did Mauss, that the "basic formula" governing the use of material wealth in coordinate control populations is, as Sahlins has put it, "If friends make gifts, gifts make friends" (Sahlins 1965:139). However, Sahlins adds little to Mauss's exposition of why this is the case. Mauss points to three conditions, other than the possibility of physical violence, that cause material wealth to be exchanged as gifts: (1) little specialization in the production of goods; (2) participation of individuals and groups, especially groups, in a variety of transactions with the same party; (3) lack of clear separation between persons and things (Mauss 1935).

Granting that a lack of specialization in the production of material wealth implies that the exchange of material wealth is not *primarily* an attempt to obtain other material wealth or services at a lower cost, and granting that such a lack of specialization makes the existence of "multipurpose" relationships possible, this does not explain why any material wealth at all is given to anyone. While intuitively there seems to be a relationship between Mauss's three conditions and an identification of persons and things, the cause underlying this relationships is unclear, especially since this identification is not restricted to small-scale populations, although it *may* be more widespread among them. I therefore would like to suggest a set of more or less commonsense assumptions from which it may be possible to derive the basic formula given above.

My first assumption is that the "balance of terror" is rarely a balance; that is, if two actors can or will deliver only costs to one another and no rewards, unless one can deliver a much larger amount of costs than the other, neither can have security from physical attack by the other. When neither actor delivers overwhelmingly large costs to the other, the corollary of this assumption is that giving rewards is a necessary (although not sufficient) condition for attaining a high degree of security from physical attack. Let us examine two methods by which the giving of rewards operates to contain physical violence. In one, there is specialization in the production of rewards; the actors are mutually dependent on obtaining the rewards, and this dependency may limit the use of physical violence. Coordinate control populations of course have little of this sort of dependence. In them, there is characteristically little specialization in the production of rewards, and many rewards can be (and to a large extent are) self-produced.

Even when rewards cannot be self-produced, and as a consequence actors are dependent on others for a given reward, there are many from whom the reward could be obtained with equal efficiency, assuming it is a single type of reward. I suggest that it is this aspect of the lack of specialization of production that results in the giving of material wealth as gifts. My argument for how this comes about is taken from Heider (1958). Heider argues that when P gives O a reward, and O perceives (1) the reward as not being given because P desires some specific reward in return, and (2) that P could as easily have given the reward to several others but did not, then two things result. First, O perceives P as desiring to benefit O. That is, O perceives P as "friendly" and becomes more predisposed to benefit P (Heider 1958:252 ff.). To relate this argument to the use of material wealth in coordinate control populations, it is necessary to make several further assumptions. I first assume that members of such populations are *primarily* (but not solely) interested in using their rewards to communicate *and* generate predispositions to benefit others rather than to attempt to generate means of exchanging specific rewards in order to maximize them. But even if this assumption is granted, the question of why material items are used this way still remains. Why is it that actors do not exclusively use other rewards as their gifts? To answer this, consider Heider's restriction that O perceive P as selecting O to receive the gift over others (i.e., P could have equally well given it to others but did not). If the reward given could be "cheaply produced" (e.g., words) and could be given to almost anyone, then no matter what P claimed, O would have very little assurance that he had been chosen over anyone else. The only reasonably certain means of gaining this assurance would be if the reward given by P were one which was in limited supply and could therefore only be given to a limited number. Material wealth used for rewards is almost always in limited supply and is hence well suited for this purpose. I will assume then that material wealth in limited supply is universally used in coordinate control populations for rewards. Further, I will assume it is the reward most used for this purpose.

If we accept Heider's argument and the above assumptions, the oft-cited "obligation" to make some return for those things that are freely given still remains to be examined. I assume the following pressures result in this obligation. First, there is the pressure to make friends with *someone*. I am assuming that in small-scale populations this is a strong pressure. Part of the perception, then, of an obligation to *return* a gift is simply the perception of the necessity of *making* gifts. There is also a pressure resulting from a desire to make friends with those who have the highest probability of becoming and remaining friends. I assume that one of the primary means of assessing this probability is whether they are willing to give gifts to you. I consider these pressures to be the most important in creating the obligation to return a gift. I, therefore, consider a "rule of reciprocity" and the concomitant—that a person who makes a gift may become angry if it is not returned—to be a secondary pressure arising as a result of the two pressures mentioned above.

The above reasoning does not imply that *all* material wealth will be used as gifts, but only that most of it will be used for this purpose. Stated simply, it is possible for members of coordinate control populations to carry on transactions which are oriented toward maximizing some specific reward and not generating generalized friendship. To do this, the actors need only make clear that a reward is being given because some specific reward is expected in return. Auyana transactions that I have labeled "trade" were of this sort, as were instances where men aided another sovereignty briefly during a war.

One objection to the above analysis might be that it is phrased in terms of individuals, whereas, in most of the populations being considered, groups, not individuals, engaged in gift-giving. The thrust of such an objection is that individuals within a group do not engage in gift-giving as individuals to those outside the group, nor do they engage in gift-giving to each other within the group. I will discuss individuals giving gifts to those in other groups later, as I believe this is due to conditions other than that of belonging to a coordinate control population. As for gift-giving within a group, from the data Sahlins (1965) presents and from the Auyana data, it appears that members of the same group do give gifts to one another. One way is the daily loaning of implements, raw materials, etc. Another is the public distributions of food, such as the individual pig distribution in Auyana (cf. Sahlins 1965: 170 ff). There is another response to this objection: donating to a common pooling which is then used as a gift to others is itself a form of gift-giving. There are two reasons for suggesting this was the case in Auyana. One is that as each pooling had a major sponsor, each pooling could be viewed as a series of donations given to aid the major sponsor, and members of Auyana some-times discussed it in this manner. Further, this aid was not given with any specified return in mind when the donor was a member of the same pooling unit. Rather, it was only demanded that the major sponsor donate at the events at which others were major sponsors. This meant that, depending on how many times someone acted as a major sponsor, it was possible for some-one to give more aid than he received, or vice versa, without anyone being angry. The second reason for considering donations to a pooling as a form of gift-giving is that the members of a pooling unit were also those who divided among themselves the gifts given them by others. If we consider this divi-sion to be a sort of mutual gift-giving, and if gifts received were to some extent dependent on gifts given, then each pooling was a delayed mutual gift-giving.

I agree with Sahlins that pooling with redistribution to the poolers does not occur in coordinate control populations. Unfortunately, Sahlins sees pooling and redistribution as synonymous (Sahlins 1965: 141-42) and does not discuss pooling *without* redistribution; that is, the pooled material wealth is given to someone other than the poolers. Let us assume that the degree of friendliness created by gift-giving is directly related to the size and frequency of the gifts. This would mean that if several social units united to form a larger social unit utilizing only gifts and no pooling, each member would have to give proportionately more gifts to those within a social unit than to those outside and each would have to give about the same amount to those outside. This condition would obtain at all levels within the largest social unit, generating a gradient of gifts. While such a coordination of indi-vidual gift-giving might be possible, I propose that pooling accomplishes the same end considerably more efficiently. Hence, I hypothesize that no more than two to three social units can be united to form a larger social unit only through giving gifts to each other. Why social units occur at all, and what the nature of their subdivisions is in coordinate control populations, are ques-tions which I will not attempt to answer here. Rather, I am only suggesting that if they do occur, and if more then two to three of them are united to form a larger social unit, then pooling is necessary to maintain the lower level units.

Before continuing, I would like to refer to the data from Auyana, which I think offer some confirmation for the above propositions. Transfers of material wealth that were most clearly gifts in Auyana were those of individual pig distribution, individual pig gifts, dances, *usi*, and life-crisis events. Trade and *aso'* were specified exchanges of wealth. The distribution of wealth at illness and fighting can be interpreted as being in return for services. As was shown in Table 37, the majority of pigs, at least, were used in the transfers which were most clearly gifts. In line with Heider's argument, the bulk of the items in any gift were those which were rewards outside the context of gifts. Gifts almost always involved at least pig and vegetables. Further, the valued items given were mostly tools or raw materials for tools. At the same time, items like shells seem to have had no utility except as gifts. That is, they appear to have acquired a reward value through their being used in this manner.

The hypothesized relationship between pooling and social units clearly obtained in Auyana. However, the hypothesis that the degree of generalized friendliness was directly related to the size and frequency of gifts was not as clearly confirmed. Although a rough correlation existed between friendliness and both the percentage of gifts and the percentage of donors to a pooling, there were enough discrepancies to indicate that other variables should be considered as interacting with friendliness in order to produce the patterns observed. Unfortunately, the variables that seem most likely to be operative, size and distance, do not seem to account for the discrepancies. A consideration which I have not developed is that of the nature of the prior alliances of *all* the sovereignties with whom Auyana transacted. To pursue this would require knowing the total "social field" of which any given sovereignty was a part. It might then be possible to determine whether the discrepancy was a result of one or both of the sovereignties' being in a process of rapidly changing their relationship to other sovereignties.

I would now like to consider some hypotheses about the distribution of gifts which apply only to coordinate control populations where the sovereignties were small and the fighting severe (see page 182 for a definition of "small" and "severe"). I assume that the mortality rate from illness usually found in these populations, plus the mortality from severe fighting, operated within small sovereignties to produce a situation in which the demise of social units, including whole sovereignties, was probable enough that individuals perceived it to be a contingency for which they must continually be prepared. I hypothesize that this contingency was coped with primarily by the development of alternative relationships, that is, relationships that might one day be converted to replace those which might be lost. I assume that this was done by making small gifts. In addition, let us assume that such gifts were made in as many contexts as possible. If so, then at every event one should find that the various types of transactions were not restricted to only a few individuals or groups, but were extended to a number of individuals and groups (the exact ratio is a question that can be answered only with further quantitative data).

For almost every sort of transfer in Auyana, personal relationships were developed with strangers which converted them into family friends; and donors to poolings, especially those making small donations, were drawn from several pooling units other than the one responsible for the pooling. This aspect of the development of alternatives is one which I believe has resulted in the characterization of the social organizations of such populations as being "loose." This proposition has many ramifications which I am unable to examine here, and I offer it merely as something worth further consideration.

The greatest number of alternatives could be developed by giving a single gift to everyone. However, this would result only in alternatives and no allies. Conversely, if gifts were narrowly restricted to only a few people, then one might have excellent allies but no alternatives. The simplest compromise would be to generate a gradient, dispersing gifts to a wide number and variety of people, while at the same time concentrating on those who were friends. This was, of course, roughly the situation found in Auyana. However, as I am unable to make a quantitative statement about the gradient, the only test of the argument I can offer is to examine relative concentrations of goods. If the argument is correct, then one should find that in the post-contract period the cessation of warfare would result in less impetus to develop alternatives, and hence a relatively greater concentration of gifts and donations to poolings in fewer groups. Tables 41, 42, and 43 demonstrate that those in class I and Auyana received a greater concentration in the post-contract period. However, none of these differences is significant at less than the .10 level in the Chi Square test of significance. Nonetheless, both are in the direction predicted, as were marriages in the post-contact period, and this suggests that the hypothesis is worth further examination.

I think the lack of statistically significant difference can be attributed to the relatively short time since the cessation of warfare (twelve years), the control of material wealth being still in the hands of those who were raised and who lived under pre-contact conditions, and the continued presence of soul assassination. Further work—particularly cross-cultural testing—might contradict this *ad hoc* attempt to save the hypothesis.

I further hypothesize that alternatives were developed not only by groups but by individuals as well, that individuals made gifts as individuals to those in other sovereignties. It may be that organizing poolings in terms of major sponsors who could then distribute some of the pooled wealth individually was another concomitant. If it is true that individuals were each developing alternatives for themselves, then the perceived threat of a social unit's collapse must have been even greater than would be the case if there was only severe fighting. Individual loyalty and a willingness to remain when things were tough must have been perceived as being less secure when individuals gave wealth outside the sovereignty. Hence, one of the alternatives employed to cope with the problem might in turn exacerbate it.

This brings me to the question of whether the above propositions apply to the distribution of marriages; that is, was it the case that women were used much like material wealth? The Auyana data give some confirmation to this notion but, as discussed earlier, there are marked discrepancies. In particular, the correlation between degree of friendliness and percentage of marriages is very weak. Perhaps, as the Auyana maintained, marriages were used to generate alliances only when there was no alliance or only a very weak one. Otherwise, various other factors may have been operating, e.g., the pressure from women to marry close to home, sometimes causing there to be a low percentage of marriages with allies. In any case, the Auyana data confirm that one did not marry one's enemies if one intended them to remain enemies.[1] The hypothesis of the generation of alternatives is confirmed by the data on marriages in the post-contact period, which were more concentrated in fewer sovereignties than in the pre-contact period (cf. Tables 35 and 36). However, this evidence is weak, because the difference was not significant at the .05 level in the Chi Square test of significance.[2] But I believe here, as in the above discussion of goods, that this may be explained by several other factors. At least the data lean again in the direction predicted by the hypothesis.

This approach can be summarized by saying that in coordinate control populations with small sovereignties and intense warfare, material wealth, and perhaps women, are distributed so as to generate the most friends. On the one hand this means a direct correlation between friendliness and gifts and marriages; on the other it means spreading wealth and women over a wide number of sovereignties in order to generate alternatives. The effect of both these techniques is to bring some degree of security to a situation of considerable instability.

[1] Perhaps those who "marry their enemies" have only enemies to marry, or perhaps they are expansionists who have merged with all their prior friends.
[2] $X^2 = 2.46$ df $= 1$ p $= .20$

# 8. Conclusion

I have attempted to demonstrate by the use of covariation within a population over time that intensive warfare between small sovereignties affects the sovereignties' mode of recruitment (Chapter 4) and certain aspects of the distribution of marriages and wealth (Chapter 7). Although my predictions were to some extent confirmed, much of the data consisted of only rough estimates and there were numerous exceptions. Still, I feel that it would be worthwhile to further consider warfare as an independent variable.

What variables in addition to warfare may have been operating to produce the observed phenomena? I briefly discussed and rejected relative size and proximity as relevant variables. But, as I indicated, these variables may be relevant when the entire "social field" is considered.

Other possibilities to be explored are the mutual effects of marriages, distribution of wealth, and mode of recruitment on one another. For example, if distributions of wealth are largely contingent on life-crisis events (especially of children), the pattern of marriages will heavily influence the pattern of distribution. Marriage rates can be relatively easily and rapidly adjusted to changes in degrees of enmity or amity. But to the extent that distributions of wealth are based on events centering on children, the distributions are tied to *past* marriage rates and therefore *past* amity relationships. Perhaps in Auyana and other similar populations, there was always a lag in the distribution of wealth relative to current amity or enmity, because of the connection of *present* distributions of wealth to past marriages. Alternatively, there may have existed a willingness to drop past obligations and negate new ones, thereby giving the appearance of "loose structure."

Another avenue to examine in explaining the divergences between my predictions and my observations is to look more carefully at the various motivations for the behaviors analyzed. I implicitly assumed a high degree of homogeneity in motivations and consequently used summed rates in my descriptions and testing. This assumption may be wrong. Obviously, not all people are equally interested in security, no matter how unstable the situation is. Some may prefer to give wealth for other reasons (e.g., getting a large return), and this may result in altering the distribution pattern from one based primarily on the motive of establishing security from attack.

If the above suggestions were pursued, they might provide further understanding of the relationship between warfare, mode of recruitment, marriages, and distribution of wealth. And there are many other possible effects or causes of warfare, such as leadership (Watson 1967) and male dominance, which should be explored. But it is doubtful that such exploration can be made before the spread of industrialization will render it impossible to obtain the data necessary to test the possibilities.

If this exposition makes such an exploration more likely, then it will have accomplished one of my major aims in writing it.

# Appendix

Of course the demography of Auyana depends upon exactly who is taken to be a member of Auyana. In 1962 there were 99 males and 114 females living at Auyana who claimed to be and acted as members of Auyana. Of the 99 males, 49 were married men, 2 were older men whose wives had died and who had not remarried, 11 were initiated adolescents, and 37 were preadolescents. Of the 114 females living there, 61 were wives of the 49 married men, 11 were older widows who had been married to someone in Auyana and who were now living with their sons, 11 were adolescent girls, and 31 were preadolescents.

In addition, there were two initiated but unmarried adolescent males at the coast, and four married men and their families who had moved into neighboring sovereignties but were still said to be members of Auyana.

Living in Auyana in 1962 were five married men and their families who were said not to be members of Auyana. Two of these men were evangelists. The other three were men who had moved to Auyana from neighboring sovereignties.

# Bibliography

Barnes, J.
    1962    "African Models in the New Guinea Highlands." *Man* 62:5-9.

Barth, F.
    1967    "On the Study of Social Change." *American Anthropologist* 69:661-69.

Berndt, R.
    1962    *Excess and Restraint.* Chicago: University of Chicago Press.

Bohannon, P.
    1955    "Some Principles of Exchange and Investment among the Tiv." *American Anthropologist* 57:60-70.

Brown, P., and H. Brookfield
    1959    "Chimbu Land and Society." *Oceania* 30:1-75.
    1963    *Struggle for Land.* London: Oxford University Press.

Carneiro, R.
    1956    "Slash-and-Burn Agriculture: A Closer Look at Its Implications for Settlement Patterns." In *Men and Cultures*, edited by A. F. C. Wallace. Philadelphia: University of Pennsylvania Press.

Castanada, C.
    1968    *The Teachings of Don Juan.* Berkeley: University of California Press.

Chagnon, N.
    1968    *Yanamamo.* New York: Holt, Rinehart and Winston.

Cook, E.
    1969    "Marriage among the Manga." In *Pigs, Pearlshells and Women,* edited by R. Glasse and M. Meggitt. Englewood Cliffs, N.J.: Prentice-Hall.

Cook, S.
    1966    "The Obsolete 'Anti-Market' Mentality: A Critique of the Substantive Approach to Economic Anthropology." *American Anthropologist* 68:323-45.

Coser, L.
    1956    *The Functions of Social Conflict.* Glencoe, Ill.: Free Press.

Du Toit, B.
    1964    "Filiation and Affiliation among the Gadsup." *Oceania* 35:85-95.

Easton, D.
    1959    "Political Anthropology." In *Biennial Review of Anthropology,* edited by B. Siegel. Stanford: Stanford University Press.

Eggan, Fred
    1954    "Social Anthropology and the Method of Controlled Comparison," *American Anthropologist* 56: 743-63.

Epstein, T. W.
   1962    *Economic Development and Social Change in South India.* Manches-
           ter: Manchester University Press.
Fried, M., et al.
   1968    *The Anthropology of Armed Conflict and Aggression.* Garden City,
           N.Y.: Doubleday.
Gearing, F.
   1962    *Priests and Warriors.* American Anthropologist Memoirs 93, Menasha,
           Wisconsin.
Glasse, R.
   1969    "Marriage in South Fore." In *Pigs, Pearlshells and Women,* edited by R.
           Glasse and M. Meggitt. Englewood Cliffs, N.J.: Prentice-Hall.
Glasse, R., and M. Meggitt, eds.
   1969    *Pigs, Pearlshells and Women,* Englewood Cliffs, N.J.: Prentice-Hall.
Goodenough, W.
   1955    "A Problem in Malayo-Polynesian Social Organization." *American An-
           thropologist* 57:135-57.
Gouldner, A.
   1960    "The Norm of Reciprocity: A Preliminary Statement." *American Socio-
           logical Review* 25:161-78.
Harris, M.
   1968    *The Rise of Anthropological Theory.* New York: Crowell and Co.
Hayden, T.
   1967    *Rebellion in Newark.* New York: Random House.
Heider, F.
   1958    *The Psychology of Interpersonal Relations.* New York: John Wiley and
           Sons.
Hogbin, H., and C. Wedgwood
   1953    "Local Grouping in Melanesia." *Oceania* 23:241-76, 24:58-76.
Homans, G.
   1967    *The Nature of Social Science.* New York: Harbinger.
Keesing, R.
   1967    "Statistical Models and Decision Models of Social Structure: A Kwaio
           Case." *Ethnology* 6:1-16.
Langness, L.
   1964a   "BenaBena Social Structure." Ph.D. dissertation, University of Wash-
           ington, Seattle.
   1964b   "Some Problems in the Conceptualization of Highlands Social Struc-
           ture." *American Anthropologist* 66:162-82.
LeClair, E.
   1968    "Economic Theory and Economic Anthropology." In *Economic Anthro-
           pology,* edited by E. LeClair and H. Schneider. New York: Holt, Rine-
           hart and Winston.
Lepervanche, M.
   1967    "Descent, Residence, and Leadership in the New Guinea Highlands."
           *Oceania* 38:134-58 and 38:163-89 (1968).
LeVine, R., and D. Campbell
   1961    "A Proposal for Cooperative Cross-cultural Research on Ethnocentri-
           cism." *Journal of Conflict Resolution.* 5:82-108.
Littlewood, R. A.
   1972    *Physical Anthropology of the Eastern Highlands of New Guinea.* An-
           thropological Studies in the Eastern Highlands of New Guinea, vol. 2.
           Seattle and London: University of Washington Press.

McKaughan, H., ed.
  1973  *The Languages of the Eastern Family of the East New Guinea Highland Stock.* Anthropological Studies in the Eastern Highlands of New Guinea, vol. 1. Seattle and London: University of Washington Press.
Mauss, M.
  1935  *The Gift.* Translated by Ian Cunnison. Glencoe, Ill.: Free Press.
Meggitt, M.
  1965  *The Lineage System of the Mae Enga.* New York: Barnes and Noble.
Mosca, G.
  1939  *The Ruling Class.* New York: McGraw Hill.
Murdock, G., et al.
  1950  *Outline of Cultural Materials.* 4th rev. ed. Behavioral Science Outlines, 1. New Haven: Human Relations Area Files.
Murphy, R.
  1957  "Intergroup Hostility and Social Cohesion." *American Anthropologist* 59:1018-35.
Pataki-Schweizer, K. J.
  1966  Comments delivered at the New Guinea Micro-Evolution Studies Project Conference, University of Washington, Seattle.
  1980  *A New Guinea Landscape: Community, Space, and Time in the Eastern Highlands.* Anthropological Studies in the Eastern Highlands of New Guinea, vol. 4. Seattle and London, University of Washington Press.
Pospisil, L.
  1963  *The Kapauku Papuans of New Guinea.* New York: Holt, Rinehart and Winston.
Pouwer, J.
  1961  "New Guinea as a Field for Ethnological Study." *Bijdragen* 117:1-24.
Rappaport, R.
  1968  *Pigs for the Ancestors.* New Haven: Yale University Press.
Read, K. E.
  1954  "Cultures of the Central Highlands, New Guinea." *Southwestern Journal of Anthropology* 10:1-43.
Redfield, R.
  1953  *The Primitive World and Its Transformation.* Ithaca: Cornell University Press.
Robbins, R.
  1962  "The Anthropogenic Grasslands of Papua and New Guinea." Paper presented at the Symposium on the Impact of Man on Humid Tropics Vegetation, Canberra, Australia.
Robbins, S.
  1970  "Warfare, Marriage and the Distribution of Goods in Auyana." Ph.D. dissertation, University of Washington, Seattle.
Ryan, D.
  1959  "Clan Formation in the Mendi Valley." *Oceania* 29:257-89.
Sahlins, M.
  1965  "On the Sociology of Primitive Exchange." In *The Relevance of Models for Social Anthropology,* edited by M. Gluckman. New York: Praeger.
Shibutani, T.
  1961  *Society and Personality.* Englewood Cliffs, N.J.: Prentice-Hall.
Simmel, G.
  1955  *Conflict and the Web of Group Affiliations.* Translated by Kurt Wolff. Glencoe, Ill.: Free Press.

Strathern, A. and M.
  1969    "Marriage in Melpa." In *Pigs, Pearlshells and Women,* edited by R.
          Glasse and M. Meggitt. Englewood Cliffs, N.J.: Prentice-Hall.
Turney-High, H. H.
  1949    *Primitive War.* Chapel Hill: University of North Carolina Press.
Valentine, C.
  1965    "The Lakalai of New Britain." In *Gods, Ghosts and Men in Melanesia,*
          edited by P. Lawrence and M. Meggitt. London: Oxford University
          Press.
Vayda, A.
  1961    "Expansion and Warfare among Swidden Agriculturalists." *American
          Anthropologist* 63:346-58.
Wagner, R.
  1967    *The Curse of Souw: Principles of Daribi Clan Definition and Alliance.*
          Chicago: University of Chicago Press.
  1974    "Are There Social Groups in the New Guinea Highlands?" In *Anthropo-
          logical Frontiers,* edited by M. Lecif. New York: D. Van Nostrand Co.
Watson, J.
  1963    "A Micro-evolution Study in New Guinea." *Journal of the Polynesian So-
          ciety* 72:188-92.
  1965a   "Loose Structure Loosely Construed: Groupless Groupings in Gad-
          sup?" *Oceania* 35:267-71.
  1965b   "The Significance of a Recent Ecological Change in the Central High-
          lands of New Guinea." *Journal of the Polynesian Society* 74:438-50.
  1965c   "From Hunting to Horticulture in the New Guinea Highlands." *Ethnology*
          4:295-309.
  1967    "Tairora: The Politics of Despotism in a Small Society." *Anthropological
          Forum* 2:53-104.
Watson, V., and J. D. Cole
  1977    *Prehistory of the Eastern Highlands of New Guinea.* Anthropological
          Studies in the Eastern Highlands of New Guinea, vol. 3. Seattle and
          London: University of Washington Press.
Whiting, B.
  1950    *Paiute Sorcery.* Viking Fund Publications in Anthropology, no. 15.
Wright, Q.
  1942    *A Study of War.* Vol. 1. Chicago: University of Chicago Press.
Znaniecki, F.
  1945    *Social Organizations and Institutions in Twentieth Century Sociology,*
          edited by G. Gurvitch and W. Moore. New York: The Philosophical Li-
          brary.

# Index

Accidents: concept of, 29

Adultery: defined, 77

Age: as criterion in social units, 80, 83, 97, 102; and marriage, 89; and kinship, 163

Agnation: and land ownership, 56-57; summarized, 157

Auyana: territory of, 12, 156; hamlets in, 12; European contact with, 14-15; groups surrounding, 16-21; origins of, 154-56

Birth: and pregnancy, 93; ceremonies, 93

Clothing, 68

Collective soul: and collectivities, 41-43, 71; versus individual souls, 47

Collectivity: defined, 8; in Auyana, 8; and territorial boundaries, 46

Curer: defined, 27; use of, 30-35

Dances, 226

Death: Auyana conception of, 24, 37; ceremonies, 96-97

Demand: defined, 5

Diet: analysis of, 47-49; and preparation of food, 49-50

Domestic animals, 61, 62, 65

Dreams: Auyana conception of, 24; interpretations of, 25

European contact, 14-15

Families: as social units, 102-3

Fights: types of, 72, 77, 184-93; and sovereignties, 72-73; and pooling units, 84; causes of, 214-18

Forest: uses of, 66-67; and masculinity, 67; and sovereignties, 72

Gardens: preparation of, 52-54, 57; and sexual division of labor, 53-54, 59-60; types of, 55-56, 61; and agnation, 56-57; and pigs, 58-59

Ghosts: Auyana conception of, 37; encounters with, 38-39; attacks by, 40-41

Groups: defined, 6

Homicide: and sovereignties, 72, 73, 138, 190; revenge of, 74; and pooling units, 99, 191; and residence, 131; rates, 211

Houses: construction of, 62-68; and masculinity, 67

Hunting: techniques, 65-66